MW01482324

The Sheepshooters

Martel Scroggin

— A Maverick Publication —

ISBN 0-89288-266-2

Library of Congress Catalog Card Number: 97-72134

Published and printed by Maverick Publications, Inc.
P.O. Box 5007   Bend, Oregon 97708

FOREWORD

Mark Twain once said the next best thing to a good lie is a true story no one will believe. This could apply to *The Sheepshooters,* which, although written as fiction, is a true story based on historical fact. The events, dates and sequences are, for the most part, in the order they occurred during the years 1896 through 1906. A few sheep-shooters are mentioned by their real names as these have been published and are a matter of record. No documents exist to verify the identity of other members of the sheepshooter organizations, so fictitious names have been used. These names are not meant to represent any particular individuals or families, living or dead. The State of Oregon and the Attorney General of Crook County, armed with the sworn testimony of secret service agents who had infiltrated the four major central Oregon sheepshooting organizations, held a hearing at the county courthouse in Prineville, Oregon. The recorded transcripts of these proceedings were left in the hall to be transferred to the courthouse safe the next morning. During the night they mysteriously disappeared. As a result, no trial ever took place and additional names were never made public.

Tom Pickett is a fictitious character as he was in *Wasco* and *The Moonlighters,* the two novels that preceded *The Sheepshooters.* So is Rachel Williams.

AUTHOR'S NOTE: For those who may stumble over the word Ochoco, it is an Indian word meaning "willows" and is pronounced Oh-chuh-ko.

CHAPTER 1

May, 1896

Isolated patches of frozen snow still dotted the ground, but spring was working its magic. Tender green shoots of bunchgrass, touched by a just risen sun, spread down finger-like draws that led to a willow-lined basin called Big Spring. A meadowlark sang out, signalling the beginning of a new day. Its cheerful fluted whistles and melodic musical notes were answered by a series of hoarse croaks from a circling raven. The silence that followed was broken by a muffled cough from the throat of one of five men who were watching a ramshackle wood cabin nestled near a spring-fed stream. The five had tethered their horses in a draw an hour earlier, and had crept into position to await dawn's light. The cough was followed by a stifled curse as another of the prone figures scraped his arm on a sharp rock when he shifted position to ease a cramped muscle.

Smoke from a rusted stovepipe on the roof of the shack that held their attention rose straight into a clear, windless sky. Soon the noises of someone preparing breakfast drifted out to them. Twenty minutes later the door opened and a small, suspendered figure stepped out. Breathing in the crisp morning air, he lazily scratched a mop of uncombed red hair before he looked down at the black and white sheep dog that stood by his side. The dog watched its master's face, whining with impatience, ready to get on with the day's work.

"Sure now, Charlie," the spare man spoke. "Be gittin' about your chores while I have meself a smoke." This was all the instruction the dog needed. He raced away as the man pulled a chipped clay pipe from a ragged vest pocket. Holding it firmly between two fingers, he tamped in a pinch of rough tobacco from a pouch he had pulled from the back pocket of his canvas pants. After replacing the pouch, he searched in his shirt pocket for a wooden

1

match. At that moment, a slight movement caught his attention. His pipe dropped to the ground as he stood, open-mouthed, watching five armed figures rise to their feet.

"What the divil . . . ," the herder exclaimed. But before his brain could register and warn him of the danger he faced, a volley of bullets tore into his body, throwing him violently backward into the house.

The shots stirred a band of sheep that were gathered around the perimeter of a man-made pond of water adjacent to the spring. The dog, who had been working to keep the flock bunched, barked furiously as he tore around the herd in an effort to keep them together. Two old bellwether rams tried to bolt, but were turned back as the dog nipped at their heels. They spun and faced the dog, their heads down with front feet spread, ready to try again. The dog paused for a moment, then slowly lowered himself until he was stretched out flat on the ground facing them. His tongue hung out of his mouth as he panted heavily. His eyes never left those of the rams. Finally, the sheep turned and rejoined the herd, all resistance drawn out of them by the sheer willpower of the smaller animal.

The sheepdog rose to his feet and trotted behind the two wethers until he was sure they would cause no further problems. Then he resumed his patrol around the flock. As the herder had occasionally fired at targets or a coyote, he was accustomed to the sound of gunfire.

There being no more need for caution, the tallest of the five men barked out an order. "Kill the sheep. Every last one." He turned to the rider next to him. "Having that dog keep them bunched together like he did is sure going to make our job a lot easier."

For the next hour, the grim-faced men methodically went about their job, firing furiously into the woolly mass of bodies with their rifles, then, when their rifle bullets were gone, with their side-arms. They paused only long enough to reload with cartridges kept in flour sacks tied to their belts. Gunpowder smoke formed thick, choking clouds that hung low on the ground. From time to time a sheepkiller would draw back to avoid the biting fumes and fill his lungs with fresh air. The bleats and screams of dying and wounded animals echoed from the canyon walls that surrounded the spring.

When their ammunition ran out, the killers broke off juniper branches and began clubbing the sheep to death.

The dog, confused by what was happening, suddenly realized these men were predators to his charges. He stood on the bank over the spring, watching a human form that was working its way toward him. The dog snarled a warning and crouched to leap but the throaty growl alerted the man who swung his pistol and fired. The impact of the bullet tumbled the dog into the spring. The blood lust in the man ceased for a moment as he looked regretfully at the carcass of the faithful animal, now floating in a widening circle of blood. He respected the fact the dog was only doing his job.

"Dammit, mutt," the man muttered softly, "now look what you made me do. I didn't intend you no hurt."

When the slaughter ended, the five men gathered in front of the herder's shack. They were exhausted, but adrenalin still pumped through their bodies and they were jumpy and ill at ease.

"Anyone check the herder?" their leader asked, nodding at the prone figure inside the door. This question brought an affirmative response from a raspy-voiced rider. "Yep, Amos and I did. He's deader'n a door nail. There's one Mick who won't be running any more sheep on land meant for cattle." He nudged the body with a boot caked thick with blood and viscera, then he spat at it contemptuously. "You know what they say about Irish sheepherders. They eventually go insane trying to figure out the long side of a square blanket. Guess we did him a favor by shooting him. "

"Maybe we ought to do the same thing to Ed Showns," the man named Amos remarked angrily. "He's the one owned the sheep."

"You know the rules," snapped the lanky man who led them. "We kill the sheep and the herders, but we leave the owners alone. No one much cares what happens to an ignorant sheepherder, but there will be hell to pay at the state capitol if we start shooting tax-paying citizens.

"Another thing we agreed on," he added, "is that we leave no bodies lying around." He gestured at the two grimy, blood-splattered men nearest him. "Chet, Jake, this lice trap has a dirt floor. Dig a hole deep enough to keep the coyotes out and dump his carcass in it. Then fill it back up and

3

stomp it good so's no one can tell there has been any digging. We'll burn this place down on top of him." His gaze turned skyward, taking in the position of the sun, then he glanced back. "The morning is pretty well shot. I'll get the horses. We can clean up when we get back to the ranch. I don't hanker to wash up in water that has a dead dog and a bunch of mangy sheep floating around in it." He started to leave, then turned back as a thought struck him. "Tell you what, boys. Let's give Big Spring a new name. Pass the word along. From now on it'll be Dead Dog Spring. That will help remind sheepmen what to expect when they run woolies on IZ grazing land."

CHAPTER 2

More than seven months had passed since Tom Pickett last visited Prineville. After the death of his fiancée, Tom had thrown all of his energy into building his ranch, the Triple C, and avoided all social occasions and only the most necessary business contacts. Today, he was in town to sign some papers that would give him a parcel of land in Canyon Creek, land that ran adjacent to pasture he owned on Duncan Creek. Tom intended to complete this transaction as quickly as possible, get a haircut and then return home before nightfall.

As he rode west, down Second Street, he shook his head in amazement at how much the small cattle town had grown since his last visit. Construction was going on at a furious pace. The sounds of sawing and hammering filled the cool spring air and mingled with the shouts and high-pitched yells of those doing the work. Where Second met Main he turned right, passing Prineville's first brick building, built nineteen years earlier, after the Bannock Indian uprising. The brick came from central Oregon's first kiln, which was just blocks away on the east bank of Ochoco Creek near Seventh and Fremont. The original owner still operated a general store there, and faded lettering, worn away by countless dust storms, proclaimed "General Merchandise, John Powell, Prop". A host of other brick and stone structures, some new, some old, intermingled with false-fronted wooden ones that lined both sides of the wagon-rutted street.

As he rode north up Main, Tom mentally counted off the new businesses that hadn't been there last year. Next to Glaze Hall, whose portico was supported by four stout, whitewashed wood beams, was a squat, plank shack. Over the door was a sign showing the picture of a tooth and an anvil, followed by the designation, "C.A. Cline, dentist and blacksmith." Directly facing Cline's place of business, on the other side of the street, was a recently built saloon named The Reception.

A new stone structure stood at the corner of Third Street. Chiseled letters over the door read, "The First National Bank". Across the street from the bank was an imposing two-story wooden building whose length was draped with a colorful red and white striped awning. Bright red letters, outlined in black, proudly stated "Wurzweiler & Thompson Mercantile". Below this, in smaller print, was the slogan, "The Cattleman's Friend."

Next to Wurzweiler's was a millinery shop, where Senders' General Merchandise store had been. Memories washed over Tom like a black wave. This was where Mary Kay, his fiancée, had lived and worked with her foster parents, Lou and Martha Senders. He stopped and leaned on the saddle horn, silently studying the building. The old screen door and spring bell were still there, and lace curtains fluttered from open upstairs windows where the living quarters were, just as they had a dozen years ago.

Tom shook his head. It didn't seem possible. Although time had lessened the hurt, he would never be able to forget the day Mary Kay died. They had been picnicking on Mill Creek by Stein's Pillar when she was attacked by a rabid coyote. Tom had driven her back to Prineville's only doctor at a pace that almost killed two carriage horses, but by the time he reached town she was dead.

The Senders were no longer in the area. Shortly after the death of the young woman they had taken into their home as a child, they sold their business and moved to Eugene City in the Willamette Valley. Tom still wrote to them, but over the years their correspondence had dwindled to short notes at Christmas time.

Making a conscious effort to brush away the memories that still haunted him, Tom touched the heels of his boots to the flanks of his horse and continued slowly up the street. When he arrived at the combination office and home of his attorney, he dismounted and slipped the reins through the iron ring of a worn juniper hitching post. He stepped onto the plank walk that began and stopped at the two front corners of the modest building and reached for the glass doorknob on which was hung an "Open For Business" sign.

The door opened to a foyer and long hall. To his left was a carpeted staircase, in a pattern of roses, that led to the second floor. On his right a living room that also served as an office. The sliding doors that offered the room some privacy were open. Tom removed his hat as he entered. A musty, not unpleasant smell from shelves of law books filled his nostrils. Slanted beams of light from two open windows stretched across the room to touch the top of a large walnut table whose leg ends were carved into giant eagle claws that gripped four chipped and scratched blue glass balls. The table rested on a threadbare oriental throw rug. Stacks of papers and several volumes of books—some open, some closed with torn scraps of paper protruding from marked pages—were littered over the table top. Wooden slats covered the mud-filled cracks of hand-hewn log walls. All in all, it was an unpretentious room and, Tom thought to himself, echoed the personality of the lawyer he had come to see.

A portly, red-cheeked man was seated at a roll top desk reading a copy of *Blackstone's Law*. Wisps of grey hair clung to a head that was almost bald. George Watkins reminded Tom of a plump prairie grouse, and had from the first day Tom met him.

"Tom," Watkins exclaimed, getting to his feet to shake hands. After spending a few minutes to inquire about Tom's health and the Triple C Ranch, Watkins got right to the point. "It was good of you to make the trip to town. Sorry for the inconvenience, but the papers you need to sign have to be notarized at the courthouse, and to make it all legal you've got to be there in person." He pulled a cracked, black leather chair closer to the desk, patted it and picked up a sheaf of papers. "Have a seat and look these over," he said, as he handed the documents to his client.

Tom scanned them quickly, then glanced up. "George, this looks fine, but for the life of me I don't know why you lawyers don't use plain English. All of these whereases, wherefores and parties of the first and second part are downright confusing."

Watkins laughed heartily as he removed a pair of wire-rimmed spectacles and put them on his cluttered desk. "Tom, if we were to do that, nobody would need us. That's the secret of our success." He reached for a pen and dipped its point in a stained inkwell. "I assure you everything is in order.

It's just as we discussed." Separating three sheets, he spread them out . "You need to write your name on each of these. Put your John Henry here, here and here." He marked each spot with a tiny check and handed the pen to Tom.

After signing, Tom looked at the bill which was clipped to the top sheet. "I guess I should have taken up the law. $120 for writing a few pieces of paper seems like an easier way to make a living than punching a bunch of contrary-minded herefords."

George Watkins roared in delight. "Maybe you should have, Tom. But if you had, you wouldn't be the most successful rancher east of the Cascades."

Tom grinned back. He knew how much work Watkins had done. The original deeds to the land at Canyon Creek had been a mess. Originally, they had been recorded by different owners under both the Pre-emptive Law Act and the General Pre-emption Act, two similar laws enacted by the government to encourage settlement. The problem with the two laws was that they not only were confusing, they contradicted each other. The Pre-emptive Law Act gave settlers the right to purchase land for $1.25 an acre. The General Pre-emption Act allowed squatters to use either surveyed or non-surveyed land, and often squatters and settlers would file for the same piece of land, or land that overlapped, one filing under Pre-emptive rights and the other using the Pre-emption Act. Watkins had made several trips to The Dalles, where the deeds were originally filed, to straighten out the mistakes that had been made in the courthouse records.

"Don't let Peter French hear you say I'm the most successful," Tom said, referring to the feisty owner of the P Ranch in southeastern Oregon. "He's shot men for less than that."

"That he has," Watkins responded truthfully. "So if you don't mind," his eyes sparkled with this exchange of humor, "we'll keep it between the two of us. I would like to live to a ripe old age." He stood and reached for a battered felt hat that hung on a scarred and rickety three-legged coat rack. "Now, let's trot down to the county clerk's office, then I'll buy you a cup of coffee at The Antler. That comes with the fee, of course," he added with a laugh.

8

As they entered the popular small cafe, the genial lawyer waved to the owner, pointed at the coffee pot and held up two fingers. While they waited, they talked about the Columbia Southern Railway's plans to extend its line from The Dalles through Antelope and Cow Canyon to Shaniko, some 45 miles north of Prineville. "The railroad people are saying Shaniko is going to be the largest wool shipping center in the country," Watkins said earnestly. "And I believe they're probably right. That area is getting to be real sheep country. So much so the Warm Springs Indians have even started calling the big hill east of them Mutton Mountain."

When their coffee arrived, Watkins took a sip and brought up the subject of the baseball team that had just been organized in Prineville, and to Saturday's scheduled game with the newly-formed team from The Dalles. After agreeing The Dalles players would probably win, Tom carefully steered the conversation back to sheep and the new ranches being home-steaded on upper Crooked River, several miles south of town. Watkins had been in Prineville only four years—eight years after Major Duncan and his corrupt gang of vigilantes had been run out of the county by a group of honest citizens who called themselves the Moonlighters. Even so, Tom chose his words carefully as he posed a question. "George, what do you know about the problem Sid Stearney is having with his partners?"

Watkins gave Tom a sharp look. His jaw set and his lips tightened. "A little," he replied tersely. "Why do you ask?"

Tom toyed with his cup. His mind drifted back to the time when Stearney owned a hardscrabble homestead on Paulina Prairie and ran a few head of bone-thin shorthorns. Stearney, a member of the Cattleman's Protective Association, a group the vigilantes had controlled, was at Steve Staats place the day Staats was killed by the vigilantes. Stearney had sworn Staats, a member of the Moonlighters, had committed suicide, but when the body was brought to town for burial the coroner's death certificate stated Staats had been killed by a shotgun blast in the back of his head.

"Just curious," Tom replied.

Watkins' brow furrowed as he looked at Tom. "I'll tell you what I know, and it's not much, if you'll answer a question for me."

"Agreed. If I can."

9

"It's said Stearney and his partners Baldwin and Howard have had a falling out and that he's buying their shares. It's only hearsay, but I was told they wanted to run some sheep and Stearney said it would be over his dead body. That's pretty much the tall of it."

He searched for any sign of expression on Tom's face and found none. "Now, let me ask my question."

"Fire away," said Tom.

"That episode at Dead Dog Spring has caused a lot of comment. Ed Showns claims the man watching his sheep was killed but he can't prove it because he can't find a body. His herder seems to have vanished into thin air."

Encouraged by Tom's sober nod, Watkins leaned closer. "Word is the IZ ranch has gotten together with some other spreads to form a group called the Izee Sheepshooters. Word also has it," his voice lowered, "they were the ones killed the sheep and dog at Big Spring."

Tom sighed and slumped back in his chair. He knew for a fact everything the lawyer said was true. One of the participants had told a 3C rider, who told Tom. The hand also passed along the information there was going to be another killing soon, but he didn't know when or where it would be.

"I guess you're right, George," Tom answered. "Was that your question?"

"No, it wasn't." The attorney fidgeted nervously and his face took on a serious look as he thought through his next words. Taking out a pocket handkerchief, he dabbed at some beads of sweat that had formed on his forehead. "Tom, I don't want this to affect our relationship. I was wondering if any ranchers this side of Crooked River are involved in..."

The look that crossed Tom's face stopped him in mid-sentence. "I wasn't implying that you . . ." he started again.

Tom held up a hand, stopping Watkins before he could finish. "I said I would answer your question if I could, and my answer is I can't because I honestly don't know." He continued, biting off each word. "I do know there have been attempts by the Izee Sheepshooters to spread their poison, just as I know there are some cattlemen in Paulina and around Crooked River who agree with what they are doing." His face softened as he looked at his friend. "I want you to know I'm not one of them. For the first time in the last thirty years there has been some semblance of order here. And it was bought at a heavy price—the lives of decent honorable people. Now a few hot-heads want to start the pot boiling again."

Tom placed both hands on the table, palms down. His body stiffened. "I'm a cattle man through and through. I don't have much use for sheep, and I make no bones about it. Sheep tear up this country's fragile soil with their sharp hooves; they skin the land bare by eating the grass, roots and all, and they're so blind dumb they foul up their own drinking water. Not only that, they leave their diseases behind for the cattle. But slaughtering helpless animals and killing sheepherders who are just trying to make an honest living plain goes against my grain."

He slammed a fist on the table, rattling both cups. "Mark my words, if this senseless killing doesn't stop now, it's going to pit neighbor against neighbor just like the Civil War did. And there will come a time when a man has to choose sides,whether he wants to or not. I guess you know that, just as I guess this is the reason you asked your question. You want to know where I stand." He looked down at his hands and muttered, as if to himself, "It seems I've spent most of my adult life choosing sides." His head swung back and he locked eyes with his companion. "I side with law and order. I always have and I always will."

"Thanks, Tom, " the pudgy attorney said, "I figured this would be how you felt." He got to his feet and extended his hand. "I feel the same way. If push comes to shove, you can count on me to stand with you."

Lynn Wood put down the paper he had been reading and rose from the single barber's chair that was positioned in the center of his small, untidy shop. Hair of all shades and colors from a dozen previous haircuts littered the floor. He hitched up his pants and greeted the arrival of his customer.

"Howdy, Tom. Been awhile since you've been around. How are things at the Triple C?"

"Can't complain, Lynn. The price of beef has been holding up, and we have a lot of fat doggies just about ready for market. I guess we'll do fine."

"Hear you got the papers signed and sealed for Canyon Creek. That's a piece of land a lot of cattlemen have been drooling over for as long as I can remember."

Tom had to smile. There was little gossip that Lynn Wood missed. "That's old news, Lynn," he responded. "At least thirty minutes old. You're slipping."

Wood slapped a bony thigh in glee. "You weren't here twenty-five minutes ago, Tom. I could have told you then. Five minutes after your papers were filed, Bob Henry was in to have his ears lowered."

Tom's grin grew wider. Then he chuckled aloud. Henry was the notary public who had witnessed the deed papers. "Tell me, Lynn. Did he really need a haircut, or did he stop by just to tell you the news?"

"Might have been a little of both," Lynn agreed, waving Tom to the chair he had just vacated.

"Anything of note in the Portland paper?" Tom asked, nodding at the one Wood had been reading when he came in.

"Not much. It's a month old, anyway. One of the stage passengers left it. The church folks are still putting the heat on the governor to do something about all the moonshining going on in the state. He's making all the right noises, but the way I hear it he likes a snootfull like the rest of us, so if I was runnin' a still I wouldn't lose too much sleep."

Wood raised part of Tom's hair with an oversized comb and began clipping. A long moment passed before he voiced a cautious comment. "This sheepkilling reminds me of the way the Cattleman's Protective Association acted when it was started by the vigilantes back in '82." Getting no response from Tom, he continued. "That slaughter of Showns' sheep at Dead Dog Spring sure takes the cake. Nobody's calling it Big Spring anymore." He put down the scissors and sprinkled some powder on a long-bristled brush which he used to dust the back of Tom's neck. This done, he pumped the chair backward until Tom was flat on his back.

Avoiding the subject because he knew anything he said would be passed along to the customers who followed him, Tom just grunted and said, "I'll tell you one thing, Lynn, this new chair of yours is a big improvement over that old straight-back chair you used to have."

"Yep, have to keep up with the times," Wood answered proudly.

Tom started to comment about Paul Orebaugh, the new barber in town who was now offering baths, but decided to hold his tongue as he knew it was a touchy subject with Wood, who, up until last year, was the only barber in Prineville.

After lathering Tom's face, Wood wiped the foam from Tom's lips with a gnarled finger, then lazily stropped his ancient pearl-handled straight razor. "Too bad about W.R. Mascall's sheep, wasn't it?"

Tom rose to his elbows. A frown covered his face as he looked at the barber. "What about Mascall's sheep?"

"Thought you probably hadn't heard," Wood said slyly, secretly pleased to have gotten this reaction from Tom. "It happened early yesterday morning, on the bluff between Beaver Dam and Rager Creek. A group of masked men killed over 200 head and scattered another 150 for the coyotes. Someone slipped a note under the front door of the *Prineville Review* last night giving the details and saying the paper should now refer to the spot as Battle Ridge. Jerry O'Neal, the editor, says it's the same handwriting as the note he got after Showns' sheep were killed saying Big Spring should be renamed Dead Dog Spring."

"What happened to the herder?"

"He's alive, but his feet are all tore up. The sheepkillers took his boots, pointed him toward Dayville and told him to start walkin'. Mascall's riders found him a few hours later as they were bringing in more ewes."

Wood gently pushed Tom back down and pinched his nose with two fingers as he began scraping away at the whiskers on Tom's upper lip. "What's your reading on this?" He asked curiously, releasing his grip so Tom could answer.

Tom's jaw set as he replied, "I'm afraid we might have the makings of a full-blown range war on our hands unless these killings can be stopped. How do you read it, Lynn?"

"Same as you do. Only I figure the fat's already in the fire. I doubt if there's any way on God's green earth anyone can stop it now."

Tom rode the twenty miles home deep in thought. He failed to notice the two red-tailed hawks that floated gracefully in the sky above him, calling to each other as they searched for food. Nor did he stop to watch the herd of mule deer he passed, whose fawns cavorted playfully, like young goats, in the meadow he was riding through. He was too preoccupied with what Wood had said. If true, a cattle-sheep war could set fire to the whole territory, and its violence might well pass along its legacy of hatred to future generations.

After an hour's ride, Tom Pickett made a decision and a promise to himself. "This madness has to be stopped, even if it means losing what I have spent a lifetime building." Unconsciously, he straightened in the saddle and squared his shoulders. The years melted away. He was no longer 52, he was the young man of 26 who gambled everything when he crossed the Cascade Mountains with a few head of cattle, fighting Indians and rustlers and suffering hardships that would have broken an ordinary man.

CHAPTER 3

Shortly after his trip to Prineville, Tom was riding the fence line on his newly acquired property. Satisfied that it would only take a few days work to put it in shape, he urged the bay he was riding down the shoulder of a rim-rocked canyon and dropped into the narrow valley that met the Mitchell stage road. There, he turned east and rode until he passed under the gated arch that announced the entrance to his ranch.

Thirty yards farther, he paused to watch a beaver who was hard at work constructing a dam on Ochoco Creek. The beaver, by now accustomed to curious stares, busily went about his job, showing no concern whatsoever at Tom's presence. He swam the length of the pond he had created with determined strokes, a severed willow gripped firmly behind his yellowed front teeth. The current helped carry him toward the jumble of sticks he had already arranged to slow the flow of water. Two mallard ducks, a colorful green-headed drake and a more conservatively feathered hen, slowly paddled out of his way. The beaver's larger V-wake floated out to meet their two smaller ones, causing both birds to bob gently on the surface. The female quacked softly to her mate, as if complaining about this minor annoyance. The male responded with a reedy-voiced "rah-rah-rah".

Tom watched as the beaver released its burden, letting it ride free. Then the industrious mammal deftly grasped the branch by one end and worked it into the tangle of willow shafts that would soon impede the flow of the creek and form his pond.

Gently, Tom spoke to him. "You and the ant must be related. With the both of you it's always work, work, work."

15

As if to give credence to Tom's comment, the aquatic rodent swam to the bank, slid ashore and hurriedly returned to the patch of willows he had been cutting. His flat tail left a slick trail in the mud behind him.

"It's too bad the human race can't take a lesson from you," Tom voiced his thoughts. "If we all worked as hard at our own jobs and left our neighbors alone, we wouldn't have the time or the inclination to be causing problems for each other."

Before proceeding on, Tom glanced up at the sky—a rancher's habit in country where a summer squall could spring up at a moment's notice. His attention was caught by a golden eagle that hung gracefully in the still air. The eagle spread the tips of its wing feathers to maintain an almost motionless position, then plummeted earthward, causing a stir of dust where it hit the ground. It rose empty-handed, leaving a frantic rabbit that just managed to scurry into its burrow and safety. The eagle, seemingly unconcerned over its loss, flapped lazily in widening circles until it regained its altitude. Then it drifted downwind to seek another unsuspecting small animal or exposed snake.

When Tom reached the corral that faced his own living quarters, he waved to a familiar figure waiting for him. It was Reub Hassler, his foreman. Reub had been with Tom since he first came to central Oregon from Portland in the spring of 1869. They had seen good times and hard times together; working and fighting side by side through severe winters, summer drought, Indian wars and battles with rustlers. Reub was close to seventy and Tom didn't know what he would do when it came time for Reub to turn in his saddle. In fact, he didn't want to think about it. He would face that problem when the time came. Meanwhile, despite Reub's protests, he had his friend and companion doing less arduous ranching chores.

Tom dismounted and looked into a wrinkled and leathered face. Alert grey eyes, framed by grizzled white hair and whiskers, returned Tom's gaze, while an arthritic hand gently reached up to pat his mare's neck.

"Did you happen to cross trails with two waddies on the way in?" Reub asked, turning sideways to unleash a stream of brown tobacco juice at the ground. "They left here 'bout an hour ago."

"Nope. Guess I missed them," Tom replied. "Anyone we know?"

"Yep. One of M.N. Bonham's IZ riders and a Bar S hand. They were visiting ranches in the Blues." Reub waved in the general direction of the Blue Mountains to the northeast. "The IZ 'poke did most of the talking. Said they wanted to get a reading on how people in that part of the country felt about sheep."

Tom grabbed the stirrup of his Denver saddle, hung it on the horn and loosened the cinch. "More likely looking for recruits than opinions, would be my guess."

"Mine, too. Said they were headed back home, so I figured they might have bumped into you."

"Didn't see hide nor hair of them," Tom grunted as he lifted the saddle from his horse's back and carried it into the shed they used as a tack room.

Reub followed him in. "Might be they spotted you first and decided to change their route, knowing how you feel about things."

"That's likely," Tom answered, placing the saddle over a wooden rack. "If one of Stearney's riders was tagging along, I guess that takes any doubt out of which side of the fence the Bar S is on."

It was Reub's long silence that made Tom glance back over his shoulder. "Something else you're not telling me?"

"There's been more killin'."

Tom sucked in his breath. "Sheep?" he asked.

"Wish it had of been. This time it was humans." Reub frowned, then continued. "Although there are some folks who still don't think Indians belong to the human race." He spat again, directing the tobacco juice toward a spot of soiled hay.

Hassler now had Tom's full attention. "Tell me everything you heard," he said. "Everything. And start from the beginning."

"It has to do with John Hyde."

Tom's eyes narrowed as he nodded. Hyde's spread adjoined that of the IZ ranch, and Hyde had a reputation for being short-tempered.

Reub continued. "Chief Albert and a handful of his Columbia braves were passing through Izee land on their way back to the Columbia River Basin after spending a few weeks hunting at Bear Valley. They camped for a spell at Deer Creek. One night, their horses were run off. Next morning,

17

mad as hornets, they followed the tracks and bumped smack into Hyde, who claimed he found them wandering loose.

"Not being in very good humor, they bunched around him and tried to pull him off his horse. He managed to get away and rode to the IZ ranch. They sent riders out that night and by next morning had gathered fourteen men who decided to teach the Indians a lesson. By this time the Columbia's had packed up and were travelling north, down Deer Creek. The ranchers caught them in a coulee and killed them to a man. The two riders who stopped by told me this." Hassler grimaced, then continued.

"Just for cussedness, each of them fired a round into Chief Albert's body. Then they shot all the horses. But they didn't get away scot-free. One of the Indians had been playing possum, and while they were all ceremoniously putting bullets in the Chief, he rose up and shot George Cutting dead. Needless to say, they worked him over pretty good before he went to the happy hunting ground."

Hassler spat again. "The IZ man also said they were spreading the word that Deer Creek had a new name now: Dead Indian Creek.

"They also said to tell you that some of the ranchers around Paulina are forming a sheepshooters organization of their own. They intend to have a meeting soon, and if you're interested in joining you should contact Stearney for the time and place.

"He was sneering when he said this, and the Bar S man plumb laughed aloud, so I don't reckon they expected you would accept." Hassler scratched at a week's growth of whiskers. "I wouldn't even have mentioned this, 'cept you asked me to tell you everything they said." His eyes hardened. "When men get their bloodlust up like these sheepkillers have, they plain don't know when to stop. And to them everything is black or white. There are no shades of grey. You're either with them or against them." Concern showed on his face as he added, "For sure, if I was you Tom, I'd be watching my back and not go riding off alone. Even on 3C land."

CHAPTER 4

Shadowy forms materialized out of the night, drawn to a massive bonfire that lit up the sky, like moths to an open flame. Their number grew steadily as they rode in from all points of the compass. Singly, in pairs and in small groups. First a handful, then a dozen. Finally, thirty-nine solemn figures were gathered together. They mumbled hushed greetings to one another as they waited for the man they had come to hear speak.

Without preamble, a tall, lank figure stepped out of the shadows. The light from the crackling fire played over his thin body, emphasizing the gauntness of his face. He stood before them, narrow-shouldered and stooped. His loosely hung frame was topped by an unusually small head and a mane of uncontrolled silver-flecked hair that blew over his face as a gust of wind caught it. He reached up and brushed it back, then placed both hands in his hip pockets, leaning forward as he did so. Strange though his looks were, it was his piercing eyes that caught, and held, their attention. The flickering firelight danced from coal black irises that missed nothing as they darted from face to face, like a crane observing a pond of frogs. Apparently satisfied with what he saw, he spread his thin legs and crossed his arms over a sunken chest.

It was a few minutes past midnight and the lone yellow pine near which they stood filtered out the weak reflection of a quarter moon. The spell under which he held them was finally broken by a nervous cough. As if this were the signal to start, the form before them began to speak, his hollow voice fading, deathlike, into the vast open space that surrounded them.

"For those of you who don't know me, the name is Snodgrass. Henry Snodgrass. I'm a rancher, like you, and as most of you are aware I was responsible for organizing the Izee Sheepshooters."

Silence greeted his statement. In the distance a coyote howled mournfully and was immediately answered by a series of doglike barks and cries from the surrounding hills.

Snodgrass continued. "I make no bones about it, I hate sheep lovers. And worse than that, I hate sheep. But that's why you asked me here, isn't it? We know the sheep are taking over our grazing land, ruining it in the process, and crowding out our cattle. They're even eating the grass at our very doorsteps."

This brought a murmur of agreement from his audience. His reference was readily understood by all as it was only last week that a Paulina rancher opened his front door to find a herd of sheep grazing in his yard.

"That's why the Izee Sheepshooters were formed, and that's why you ranchers are here tonight. From Paulina Valley, Beaver Creek and Crooked River." His voice rose an octave. "Here to decide whether to form your own sheepkillers association. And why?" His voice, pitched with emotion, rose even higher. "Because for the sake of a few votes the gutless politicians in Salem have turned their backs on us to kowtow to the settlers, sheepmen and riffraff who have invaded our grazing land. Land that, up until now, was meant for cattle and has been used by cattle."

At that moment, a dead juniper trunk settled into the heart of the fire, sending up a shower of sparks that backlit the speaker. The effect was startling, and brought a murmur from the crowd. Taking advantage of this, Snodgrass dramatically pointed a skeletal finger at each man facing him. His hand moved slowly, first left, then right.

"Why is it," he continued, "we have to meet in the middle of the night, in the flats of the desert so no one can sneak up on us, to talk secretly about a problem that plagues us all?" He answered his own question with a shout. "I'll tell you why. Because we're surrounded by fools and sycophants who have turned against us." Anger torched his distorted face. "Who was here first? Who settled this country? Who carved civilization out of what was once a savage wilderness?" His voice became a piercing shriek. "The government? The military? Where were they when we were asking for help? You all know the answer. They were sitting on their behinds, floundering in their own bureaucracy. The law? The law's a joke. Where's the marshall

20

or sheriff when someone runs off a dozen head of your beef? Or horses? Sitting on their cans, that's where. We're our own law and always have been.

"And how about the homesteaders?" His voice suddenly lowered, filled with contempt. "They're too busy fencing in land with wire that tears the hide off our cattle.

"And don't let me forget to mention our good friends the bankers and merchants. Our pillars of society who sell themselves to the highest bidder. If you offer them a nickel and someone else offers a dime they roll over on their backs like the whores at Nikki Hyde's cathouse."

Snodgrass raised a clenched fist defiantly. His eyes blazed with fever from the hate that fed him. "There's only one group you can count on and that's the one gathered here tonight. We have a God-given right to this land. We built it. We take care of it, and by damn we own it!"

A chorus of cheers greeted this fiery statement. Finally, after several attempts to be recognized, a voice made itself heard above the din. It was Billie Congleton, a rancher from the north fork of Crooked River.

"Henry, I've got to hand it to you. You talk up a storm, but all I've heard so far is a preacher giving a sermon. Let's have it straight."

"Billie," Snodgrass responded, his voice grew quiet and cold, "in 1880 a few sheep were introduced to the Camp Watson area, no more than a day's ride from here. Around fifty or so. They came by way of the pass from the Willamette Valley and none of us paid much attention. Three years ago there were only five or six bands of sheep this side of the Cascades and they kept to summer graze between Big Summit Prairie and Spanish Peak: country not suitable for cattle. Again, none of us really cared, or paid much attention. Then the Mormons started bringing in migratory sheep from as far away as Idaho and Utah. By the thousands. Next came the herds from Shaniko and Antelope. Then they started pouring in from the John Day Valley. More thousands because the land there couldn't hold them all. Now they're crowding our range, trampling our grass and fouling our water holes."

Snodgrass, whose long arms dangled out of his sleeves, shook a finger at Congleton and continued his lecture. "Do we push our cattle on their land, destroy their grass and leave them with no pasture? Of course we don't. And if we did, we would damn well deserve to have our cattle killed and our riders run off."

Snodgrass threw his shoulders back and stood as straight as his bent back would allow. "I can tell you this. We either fight back or we get out of the cattle business. It's as simple as that."

A voice called out. "How do we start, Henry?"

"We start by organizing," Snodgrass shot back. "Tonight. And any of you who are not of a mind to do so should leave now and go home to bed."

"Seems like each of us should make up his own mind, according to his own conscience," Congleton responded. "I'm not one for buying a pig in a poke. Let's hear what you propose first."

Snodgrass wiped his snipe-like nose with the back of his hand and gave a curt nod of agreement. "Before I tell you what the Izee sheepshooters have sworn to, I want a show of hands from every man here that what I tell you will be kept secret. And don't take this promise lightly. Each of you has to agree that any who violates their pledge will be hunted down and killed without mercy."

"Fair enough," said Congleton raising his hand, which was quickly followed by all of the others.

"First, we establish a boundary, a dead line. Any sheep who cross it get killed. The reason for this is plain simple. The only thing a sheepman understands is losing his livelihood. Second, we scare off the herders. Or kill them and bury their bodies where they can't be found. This includes camp tenders as well.

"Third, we ride with our faces covered." Holding up both hands to still the protests he knew would follow, he hurried on. "I know some of you may not like the idea of masks, but consider this: to survive as an organization we can't afford to be seen and identified. Secrecy is the key to our safety as well as our success."

"What about the brands on our horses, Henry?" John Lawrence, a rancher from Camp Creek asked. "We can't hide those."

Snodgrass's answer brought forth a ripple of laughter. "No, we can't. But have you ever heard of a horse testifying in court? The burden of proof is on the law to prove who pulls the trigger. Horses can't talk, and without sworn testimony from a live witness there is no case."

His next comment stilled any hint of humor that might have remained. "Fourth, if one of us is killed in a raid, we bring the body back for burial and say nothing. If one of us gets shot we tend our own wounds, no matter how bad."

A protest was voiced. "But Henry, sometimes you got to have a doctor or you'll plain die."

Henry Snodgrass singled out the speaker. "I know it's a tough choice. I didn't say you couldn't have a doc. You can if you're willing to kill him after you're patched up. Just keep in mind though, we only have two sawbones and they're both in Prineville. The supply might not last too long.

"Here's something else might stick in your craw. Every man who takes the oath must agree that if any of our crowd is arrested or brought to trial for sheep or herder killing, he will go to the witness stand and swear to lies in order to obtain an acquittal."

A blazing limb rolled out of the fire and landed by Snodgrass's foot. He turned and kicked it back into the embers. For several seconds he stared at the flames, then looked back at the men standing and seated around him. He knew there was nothing more that he could say, just as he knew questions would serve no purpose. Shifting position, he acknowledged Dick DeWitte, the rancher from Beaver Creek, who had asked him to come and speak.

"That's the long and short of it, Dick. I can't vote, so I'm saying no more. I suggest a show of hands on forming the Paulina Sheepshooters. The decision is yours." He moved back into the shadows.

DeWitte stepped forward, removed his hat and self-consciously ran a hand through his wiry hair. Looking down, he scuffed at the sandy soil with the toe of a work-worn boot. When he raised his head, it was clear a decision had been made in his own mind. "I guess we all have things we might want to say. Or ask. But Henry has pretty much covered the sum of it. I know sheep are crowding my Beaver Creek range. I've had to move cattle to Wolf Mountain because of it. This means an extra day's ride for my crew. So, unless there is an objection, I'm going to call for a vote."

DeWitte walked from man to man, getting an affirmative vocal answer or nod. When he got to Billie Congleton he stopped, then asked, "Well Billie, what will it be?"

Congleton spoke without hesitation, in a voice loud enough for everyone to hear. "Sorry, Dick. The terms are too harsh. I'm out. You all know my word is good and that I won't repeat what I heard here tonight. You have no worry on that score. But killing and lying is just not my style." He turned on his heels and walked away. Two others, Sam Courtney and Fred Powell, silently rose from where they had been sitting on the ground and followed him. The 36 men who stayed turned their backs on the three men as they left.

CHAPTER 5

The weekly edition of the *Ochoco Review* carried a full report on the formation of the Paulina Sheepshooters. No names were mentioned, only the fact that a midnight meeting was held by a group of concerned cattlemen near the Roba Ranch on Wolf Creek, five miles northeast of the town of Paulina.

The paper got its information from a scrawled letter that was slipped under the door the night after the meeting. With it was a hand-painted cloth poster that contained the following message:

WARNING TO ALL SHEEPMEN!

You are hereby ordered to keep your sheep on the north side of this plainly marked line or you will suffer the consequences

Signed
The Paulina Sheepshooters Association

The letter explained that a boundary dead line had been established and sheepmen were not to cross this line. The dead line would be plainly marked in open country by notices like the one enclosed with the letter, or with plain pieces of tin. In heavy timber, a saddle blanket blaze would be cut on both sides of those trees that straddled the line. The portion of the letter that pointed out, "The spacing of these marks would be close enough and visible enough to avoid any confusion or misunderstanding, even by the dumbest and most illiterate herders," was heavily underlined.

The newspaper prominently printed this notice on its front page, along with the designated boundary, which was shown in bold type. It read:

Beginning on the summit of Wolf Mountain following the main dividing ridge between the waters of Beaver Creek on the south and Rock Creek and Little Summit Creek on the north to the top of Roba Butte (also known as Paulina Butte) thence in a northerly direction to Dead Dog Spring (previously known as Big Spring), thence from Dead Dog Spring to Deep Creek, thence down Deep Creek to Crooked River, and down Crooked River to the ranches located there.

A statement had been added below the boundary geography: "Let all sheep owners, herders and tenders be advised that this dead line has been established and is well marked. Enforcement goes into effect immediately. Anyone violating this line will be dealt with in the harshest manner. YOU HAVE BEEN WARNED. In the spirit of fairness, we serve notice to all owners of sheep that are now camped inside this boundary that they will be given ten days to remove said sheep. Any found within the boundary after this period of time will be killed."

Eleven days from the publication date of the *Ochoco Review,* the sheepshooters made good on their promise. A burly, red-whiskered Tennessean boasted one night in a Canyon City saloon that he had sheep over the line, intended to keep them there, and "the Paulina Sheepshooters be damned!" He told a group of whiskey soaked listeners that he had two friends who were going to help him. When asked who they were, he patted a holstered .45 Colt revolver and lifted high a 45-60 Winchester rifle that rested beside him against the bar. "These, " he said defiantly.

Despite a boast that he always slept with one eye open, the Tennessean was awakened one sultry afternoon while tending his sheep. He had been taking a nap under the shade of a giant pine when the sound of a rifle hammer being cocked brought him wide awake. He was quickly trussed up by one of six masked men. His shoes were removed and he was tied, face down, over the back of his mule which was then led to the dead line and whipped until it disappeared, in a bone-jarring trot, over the nearest ridge.

Several hours later, after managing to work himself free, he limped back to his camp. There he found his boots and a note:

"You will find your guns in the big hollow tree at the upper end of the meadow. When you count your sheep, you will find all five hundred dead. Cross the line again and you will be joining them."
It was signed, "The Paulina Sheepshooters."

Four days later, the sheepshooters struck again. This time six miles west of Beaver Creek.

A boy in charge of 200 sheep found himself in a box canyon too late in the afternoon to cross back over the boundary. Afraid to build a fire that might attract attention, he sought safety and warmth by bedding down in the midst of the herd. In the darkness of a cloudy night, he awoke to the sounds of gunfire which stampeded his charges. They raced out of the canyon and around the bottom of the butte facing it into several hundred longhorns that were waiting to be driven to pasture. The cursing cowhands didn't dare fire at the sheep for fear of hitting their own cattle. In the confusion, most of the sheep made their escape through a sage filled valley with the boy high-tailing it right behind them.

This story was later told and retold throughout central and eastern Oregon. It took two days for three cowhands to talk the boy out of a lava cave where he had taken shelter, threatening to shoot anyone who entered. The half-starved youth finally came out when one of the punchers got the idea of starting a fire and cooking some bacon and beans where the smell would drift in to him. After wolfing down a hasty meal, he was given an honor guard across the dead line and turned loose. Shortly after the incident, he was seen heading toward the Rockies on an ancient sway-back mule they had provided.

The biggest joke of all, they felt, was that he had no weapon of any kind. "A gutsy young'un. He talked us into believing he had a Winchester and we fell for it," one of the participants joked. "With a gift of gab like that, I guess he'll do all right. Probably end up as a congressman or senator. Maybe even President."

There was no humor in the incident that followed six days later. In fact the killing of sheep and four herders was so violent the dead line became known, from then on, as the death line.

It started when more than a thousand head of sheep crossed the Blue Mountains from the Mormon settlements in Idaho and began their graze inside the boundary line.

By this time, the Paulina Sheepshooters had adopted the technique used by their Izee counterparts. They did away with the time-consuming meetings that required the attendance of all of its members and began operating as smaller individual units in their own immediate areas. This gave them the flexibility to move faster, and make decisions on the spot. It also had a detrimental side affect in that it encouraged younger cowhands, bored with the monotony of ranch life, to react impetuously when they got together—like domestic dogs that are docile by themselves, but can turn vicious when they run in packs.

The sheep were spotted the day they crossed the line by an outrider looking for strays. He spurred his cow pony back to the main herd and sought out the foreman, Clarence Phelps. Phelps listened stoically, then turned to the rider with him. "Better ride back to the ranch, Billie, and tell your daddy the news."

The youngest son of the herd's owner gave the foreman a contemptuous look. Pig-like eyes, set in an oversized head, glistened with excitement. "Ain't no need to waste pa's time." He raised his chin in the direction of Art Kemp, who brought in the news. "Art says he only saw four herders. There's a dozen of us. Enough to take care of the job ourselves."

By now, most of the cowhands who had been attending the cattle and whose attention had been caught by the fast riding Kemp, had gathered in a circle and were listening intently to the conversation between the boss's foreman and the son of Walter Grandberg, owner of the Flying G. Only one of them was above the age of eighteen; a man called Stumpy Remelard, who had lost the lower half of his left arm when it was caught between a rope wound around his saddle horn and a wild steer.

"Billie, your pa said we was to get these cattle to south pasture today, and as long as I'm in charge, that's what we'll do. The sheep can wait unless he says otherwise."

Billie Grandberg's cheeks flushed with anger. He was being faced down in front of the crew and he didn't like it . "Well, old man, maybe I'll just put you out of charge," he said belligerently.

"Now Billie, don't go off half-cocked," the foreman replied soothingly. He realized young Grandberg had put himself in a spot he couldn't back down from unless he was given an out. "I don't mind taking your orders, so long as Walt would agree. He's only an hour's ride from here. I'll send somebody else to ask him what we should do."

For a moment Clarence Phelps thought he had won the hand. The younger man hesitated, then turned his bulky body to peer at the riders watching them. To a man they were looking at him, waiting for his reply. Gaining confidence from the support he saw there, he made his decision. With a cruel, thin-lipped grin he leaned over his saddle to get closer to Phelps, as if to whisper. But his voice, strong and confident, rang out so all could hear. "That's a good idea, Clarence. Why don't you send yourself."

"By dog," the foreman snapped back, "maybe I'll do that. Provided you tend the cattle. I don't want to face your daddy knowing the herd isn't being taken care of."

"As far as I'm concerned, they can take care of themselves." Grandberg reined his gelding back and addressed nine expectant faces. "I'm for a little sheep killing, and those who want to join me are welcome to follow." Kicking his horse into a gallop, he rode away.

With shrill cries, the drovers raced after him.

"Well, that cuts it," Phelps remarked to Remelard, the only rider who had remained behind. "Neither of us can ride in because we're going to have our hands full keeping these cows on the move and in one bunch." He sighed wearily. "That durned young whippersnapper has a streak of meanness in him. He's the only one in the whole outfit who uses Spanish spurs. You'd think that daddy of his would chew his hide good when he brings his horses back all tore up from being rowelled.

29

"But then at forty dollars a month, Stumpy, I guess we aren't supposed to think. We're expected to follow orders. And as our orders were to take care of this herd and move it to south pasture, that's what I intend to do."

"We'd best get to it, then. Them cows have already started to wander. And as for keeping our hands full, you're right about that," Stumpy said dryly as he scratched an itch on the stub of his arm.

By noon, Billie and his riders crossed the trail of the sheep. An hour later they found them. The sheep were contentedly grazing on grass that covered the surface of a rimrock mesa.

"Blackfaces," Billie muttered as he and Art Kemp watched from a vantage point that gave them an unobstructed view of the milling animals below. "They're the worst. Won't be no grass left when they get through." He cursed loudly. "At least two dozen steers could graze that patch of land all summer for what that bunch will clean up in a day."

"I don't recognize their brand, Billie. They must be from out of state," Kemp remarked. "Maybe we should just give them a warning and run them off."

Billie glared at the man sprawled in the dust beside him. "In a pig's eye we'll warn them. They're on Flying G property and they need to be taught a lesson. If they don't know about the boundary line, they will when we finish with them. Let's get back to where we left the others."

They scurried backward on their bellies until they were sure they couldn't be seen, then stood and quickly followed a deer path that led to the bottom of the draw where their eight companions waited.

Billie Grandberg walked over to one of them. "Ned, I'm trading you my carbine for that coyote scatter gun you're carrying." Holding up his 30-30, he took the short-barreled Greener that was handed down. "And that saddle-bag of double aught shells you're packing." After checking the loads, he stuffed as many in his pockets as they would hold and tied the bag to his saddle.

"When we reach the top of the bluff, spread out," he instructed. "We'll hit them straight on."

"Don't you think we should warn the herders first?" a nervous voice asked.

"They'll be warned as soon as the first shot is fired. It's up to trespassers to look out for their own skins, not us. Art," Grandberg addressed Kemp, the rider who brought them the news of the sheep, "were they carrying any weapons?"

"None that I could see. Just those long poles they snag sheep with."

"Good. Let's ride!"

Only one of the herders noticed the group of horsemen coming out of the east. He shaded his eyes to see better. He had noticed the strange blazes on the timber they had passed through, but neither he nor the other three tenders had seen a posted notice. And it wouldn't have mattered if they had. They were French Basque, from the Pyrenees, and none of them could read, speak or understand English.

The herder's passive gaze turned to a frown as he saw the riders had their guns drawn, then to an expression of alarm as the line of men began firing into the sheep.

"Mon Dieu," he swore, as his eyes frantically searched for his comrades. At first the sheep began to mill, then they swirled madly around him, eyes bulging and faces distorted with fear. The herder was knocked to the ground and lost his hook. Groping, he found it and rose to his knees. A rider appeared above him out of the alkali dust, shooting point-blank at the animals that surrounded him. Splattered with blood and deafened by the roar of the shots, the herder panicked. Stark fear caused him to involuntarily void his bowels as the distorted face of a madman stared down at him, then swung a shotgun toward his chest. Instinctively, the shepherd swung his crook, catching the gun and throwing it up just as it fired. Then, he screamed in terror as both horse and rider fell on him.

The killing went on for two hours, until there were no more than a handful of sheep left. One by one, the sheepkillers gathered around three herders being guarded by a lone Flying G hand. They dismounted and slumped to the ground in exhaustion.

"That's a day's work," one rider volunteered as he undid his neck bandanna and wiped sweat and fresh blood from his face.

"You can say that again," another tired voice answered. "A day's work and then some. There are going to be a lot of fat coyotes around here for a long time to come."

"Too bad it isn't calving season," another said. "If it was, we wouldn't have to worry about the newborns being carried off to feed some mama coyote's brood."

The conversation ran on as they gathered their strength.

"Anybody have any ammunition left?"

"Are you crazy? I used mine up an hour ago. My arms are so sore from clubbing heads I can hardly lift them."

Finally, one of them asked. "Where's Billie?"

They looked at each other, faces blank.

"He must have fallen off his horse," Art Kemp said, getting up stiffly. "He wouldn't have left without letting us know, so he must be hurt."

Groggily, the rest of the punchers rose and pulled themselves into their saddles.

Forming a picket line, they carefully worked their way through the carnage they had created. The once placid mesa was now a field of dead and dying animals. A gagging odor of feces and escaping gas from the sun-bloated corpses caused one of the killers to lean over his saddle and vomit. The others covered their faces with kerchiefs. Two smarter ones stuffed snuff in their noses to kill the smell. As they searched, swarms of green blow-flies and yellow jackets surrounded them, their angry buzzing filled the air as they rose to challenge the presence of those who were disturbing their bloody feast.

"Over here," a voice, cracked with emotion, cried out.

A second rider joined him and hastily crossed himself as he removed his sombrero . "Madre de Dios," he exclaimed softly.

The others arrived and stared, speechless, at a head, shoulder and left arm completely blown away from a body that was pinned under a horse lying on its side. The right hand of the mutilated body still gripped a short-barreled shotgun. A broken shank bone protruded from the skin of the suffering horse, who lifted its head and rumbled a throaty moan.

Beneath the mare's rump was a crushed figure whose neck had snapped and whose body was resting grotesquely on a shepherd's staff.

"By the looks of it, I'd say Billie shot himself by accident when he ran down the herder," a hoarse voice croaked, adding, "I don't envy the man who tells his daddy about this."

"It sure ain't going to be me," Art Kemp replied. Searching out two men he said, "Tom, shoot the horse, then you and Tim wrap what's left of Billie up in a saddle tarp. The rest of you come with me. The least we can do for his pa is to hang those other herders for bringing this all about."

"Clarence, they're back," Stumpy Remelard shouted over the backs of the slow moving steers they were pushing as he gestured with a handless arm.

Phelps rose in his saddle to get a better look, then worked his way to Remelard's side. "Can't see for all this dust, but by my count there seems to be one missing. Let's ride up the side of that butte yonder where we can get a better look."

As the herd milled about below them, the rangy foreman dismounted and squinted off in the distance. "Stumpy, my eyes ain't what they used to be, but I only count nine horses, and one of them is riderless."

"There are nine of them all right, and one is carrying two men. Something's tied to the back of the riderless horse. I don't see Billie's horse, either." Licking dried and cracked lips, he added nervously, "I don't like the looks of this, Clarence. Not one bit."

They sat motionless as the group labored up the hill and stopped before them. For a long time, no one spoke. Phelps examined each face then asked, "Is that Billie?" gesturing toward the bloody tarp. A silent nod gave the foreman his answer. Art Kemp told him what had happened, leaving nothing out.

Clarence Phelps' shoulders sagged and all life seemed to go out of his body. He slowly turned his horse and started to ride away.

Stumpy pulled up by his side. "Where are you going, Clarence? Back to the ranch to tell Walt?"

"Nope. Not me. I've no taste for cold-blooded and senseless killing, and I 'specially don't want to be around when Grandberg sees his baby." His voice turned bitter. "I'll leave the telling to those brave lads who left the herd against my orders to show how tough they could be against a bunch of defenseless sheep."

He stared long and hard at the skyline of the Blue Mountains, then swiveled in his saddle to face the crippled, middle-aged man he had ridden with for the past fourteen years. "Stumpy, you take care of yourself. Come morning, I intend to be just as far from this part of the country as I can get."

CHAPTER 6

They came to Shaniko by the thousands, pushing out of crowded holding pens and spilling into the dusty main street. Others waited, as far as the eye could see, on the gentle slopes outside of town.

It was shearing time. Open-sided sheds were filled to capacity with bleating, wool bearing sheep as dozens of grime-covered shearers bent to their task. Like the pendulums of grandfather clocks, they stooped, clipped then rose in steady rhythm. When one animal was finished, they reached for the next in line, pulling each struggling beast between legs and knees to hold them firmly in place. Occasionally, a weary worker would pause to stretch or reach for a drink from a bucket of water that hung nearby. Hands so coated with the lanolin grease that lay under the thick coats of fleece made gripping the dipper handle a slippery, if not impossible task. Most didn't even bother with the dipper, but would grab the rough wooden pails and pour water down their throats and over sweaty, naked upper bodies. Many of the shearers had sons, daughters or wives standing by to wipe the sweat and dust from their faces, knowing the lanolin grease—or scam as they called it—could burn or permanently damage their eyes. To add to their discomfort, a permanent cloud of choking powder-fine alkali dust, mixed with the acrid smell of lime, sulphur and creosote from the dipping pits, hung in the air.

Most of the cutters were professionals. Some came from as far away as Australia and Spain, following the seasons like migrant fruit pickers. To all of them time was money. They worked methodically and steadily, seldom pausing to rest. The best shearers and those most sought after, could clip as many as 200 sheep a day, earning the princely sum of seven cents per head.

35

Once the sheep went through the humiliating process of being stripped of their wool and dipped, an identifying mark was painted on their sides. Confused and anxious, they gathered in groups to seek solace from one another. Once a band was finished, they were quickly led away by a bellwether and the herder responsible for them to make a rush for the mountain ranges, each hoping to be among the first to find the best camps.

Hour after hour the shearers toiled, as sheep of all types were led to the special sheds that kept the wool from being mixed: Lincolns, Rambouillets, Blackfaces, DeLaines, Shropshires and Merinos.

At each shed, a procession of wagons stood end to end waiting for huge, fleece-filled sacks. Once loaded, they would drive away, their place at the loading bin filled by the next dray in line.

Two men watched this chaotic scene from the second-story veranda of the Shaniko Hotel. One was portly and well dressed. He wore a black frock coat and a brocade vest that was decorated with a heavy gold watch chain on which dangled a hammered gold Masonic fob. His face, partially hidden by full sideburns and a large handlebar mustache, was openly congenial. Long hair, peppered with grey, hung below a flat-brimmed white Stetson hat. In one hand he held a copy of the *Northwest Livestock and Wool Growers Journal.* The *Journal,* published in Pendleton,Oregon, was considered the bible of all serious Oregon sheepmen.

His companion, shorter by a good eight inches, was leaning on the veranda's rail, surveying the scene below. He was wiry and lean and dressed in working ranch clothes. A battered and sweat-stained hat covered a head of unruly blond hair. Crowlines led to bright blue eyes, a heritage of Swedish ancestors. He held a pad of paper and was totalling a line of figures with the stub of a well-chewed pencil, which he occasionally licked as he wrote.

The larger of the two men was Dr. David W. Baldwin, owner of the Baldwin Sheep and Land Company. The other was Allie Jones, a sheepman who had a ranch east of Prineville, between Mill and Marks Creeks. Jones, a stubborn and contentious man, was known for his mood swings and recourse to violence when he didn't get his way.

"Well, Allie," Baldwin chuckled. "I can see from that gleam in your eye that it's going to be a good year."

"Best yet, Doc. If my addition is correct, and the price of ten and a half cents holds up, my take this year, after costs, should be in the neighborhood of twenty-five hundred dollars. And that's not counting the yearling ewes and wethers I plan on selling." Jones thrust his chin at the paper in Baldwin's hand. "What price is the *Journal* quoting?"

"Two dollars for ewes and a buck seventy-five for wethers."

"That's the same as what the *Shepherd's Bulletin* lists, so I guess that's what it most likely will be, give or take a penny or two. I should do right well. Unless my sheep come down with the scabies," he added soberly.

"Allie, if the good Lord wills the sheep to have scabies, then that's what they'll have. That's just the way it is. Nothing in this life is guaranteed, we both know that. Besides, it seems like I remember you worrying about the same thing last year." Dr. Baldwin gave a sharp laugh. "With the price of wool what it is, we should be celebrating, not mourning. If you're buying, that is," he added with a twinkle in his eyes.

"Well, I guess I could buy the first one, anyway," Jones answered in good humor. "And maybe even a second if these prices don't fall before we get there. Where would you like to have this celebratory snort?"

"How about The Ramshead. It's the only bar in this God-forsaken town that serves decent whiskey."

Allie Jones pondered Baldwin's remark, then asked a question. "Tell me, Doc, Shaniko has 600 permanent residents, yet there are fifteen saloons and four brothels but no churches. How do you figure that?"

"That's easy, Allie," Baldwin replied, a mock serious expression on his face. "There are precious few women here, and there's not a preacher this side of Portland who can't find a more lucrative practice somewhere else. Sinners we have plenty of, but you wait, times will change and churches will come. Until then," he grinned, "we can enjoy our drinking without some righteous female and her followers shaking a tambourine in our face and blocking the doors of our favorite watering holes."

The two men pushed their way through the crowded street and entered The Ramshead, which was overflowing with fleece buyers and salesmen conducting business or passing the time of day with sheep owners and dust-caked drovers. The sour smell of the bar was a welcome relief from the choking dust and obnoxious odors of the dip pits.

"Allie! Doc!" A voice hailed them over the din. A tall, stocky figure by a large table at the rear of the smoke-filled saloon stood, motioning them over.

They elbowed their way through a mass of bodies lined three deep at the bar to reach him.

"Howdy, Jack," Allie Jones said, sticking out a hand as he spoke. Jack Edwards, owner of the Hay Creek Ranch, gripped it firmly and pulled Jones closer to the table. Jones waved at two other men seated there. "Afternoon, Will. Joe," he said, nodding to Will Lord, president of the Shaniko Warehouse Company and Joe Bannon, a sheepman from Antelope Valley.

Dr. Baldwin's voice boomed over Jones' shoulder. "Business looks good, gents." He focused on Lord. "What are you doing here in the middle of the day, Will?"

"Doc," Lord replied, "there's no room left in my warehouse. When they started stacking bales in my office, I decided it was time to leave. I'm conducting my affairs here." He slapped a hand down. "Right at this table."

"Sensible solution," the affable doctor replied, slapping Bannon on the back in way of a greeting as he passed behind him to take a seat. "Allie was going to buy, but with you making four cents a pound on this year's clip, Will, you'll probably want to do the honors." Baldwin eyed the bottle of Cyrus Noble on the table.

Will Lord placed a clean glass over the neck of the bourbon bottle and slid it to him. "Help yourself, my Scottish friend." He pushed another glass to Jones. "You, too, Allie. I was just telling Joe and Jack how much cleaner this year's wool is. Not as much sand in the fleece as last year. That means a better price by three cents than what's been quoted in *The Bulletin* and *Journal*, which should be good news for all of you." He stroked a full growth of beard. "Guess it's because we had a milder winter and grazing was done in the foothills and not the wetter bottom lands. Big crop of ticks, though. We were talking about that, too, when you came in."

Jack Edwards spoke up. "You know, it always amazes me how few shearers get Rocky Mountain spotted fever. You'd think they would be the first to go down, what with those little devils crawling all over them."

"Doc Belknap in Prineville is working on a serum right now," Baldwin remarked. "He figures the shearers have been bitten so many times by the little beasties that they have built up an immunity to them. If he's right, and what he says makes a lot of sense, a simple inoculation could do away with the fever once and for all."

"If he can pull that off, he should get a medal," Jones said. "There's hardly a family in central Oregon that hasn't had at least one case."

"Yep. And most who get it die from it," Joe Bannon added, lips drawn tight.

A period of silence followed. Everyone at the table knew Bannon had lost both a son and a father to the fever.

To break the mood, Will Lord turned to Edwards. "Jack, you must be real proud of yourself, crossing those DeLaines and Rambouillets from France with them Spanish Merinos. Thickest wool I've ever seen. Rumor has it your new breed is yielding as much as 150 pounds of fleece a head."

"It's no rumor, Will," Edwards answered proudly. "A few have even weighed in at 200. They're giving more wool and mutton than any known breed in the world. As a matter of fact, a feller from South Africa says he'll take as many as I can ship him."

"You better send along a saddle with those weighing in at 200 pounds, Jack," Joe Bannon chided Edwards. "Then when one of those African herders sees a hungry lion he can jump aboard, aim his spear and charge. Any self respecting lion would lose his appetite fast if he saw a sight like that coming at him."

"With leather saddles running $16.00 each that wouldn't leave me with much profit, Joe," Jack Edwards chuckled, going along with the good-natured ribbing.

"There's a simple solution, Jack," Allie Jones chimed in. "Go into the saddle-making business and charge extra. That way you can make a profit on both saddles and sheep. Why," he exclaimed, his face lighting up, "a little more breeding and you might get one the size of a horse. You could even put the horse breeders out of business. Think of it! A horse you could ride, eat and shear all in one. Only thing is, it would need a name."

"How about shorse," Baldwin volunteered. "That has a good ring to it, and it fits in with the natural evolution of things."

The combination of liquor and good fellowship began working its spell. Joe Bannon raised his glass. "A toast then, to the Jack Edwards' shorse."

When they had drained their glasses, Edwards picked up the bottle and refilled each one. "Did I tell you Bill Brown and one of his brothers came all the way from Fife just to check out my crossbreeds?"

Baldwin burst out laughing. "Did he offer you a check?"

It was a well known fact that Brown wrote checks on almost anything, much to the frustration of his banker: The back of wallpaper, tin can labels, butcher paper, envelopes and once, when he was on the range branding cattle, he even burned a check on a piece of wood with a branding rod.

"Nope," said Edwards. "He decided they probably would eat too much grass. But before he made his decision, he kept eyeing the rump of my horse while cleaning his nails with that big jackknife he carries. For a minute, I thought he might decide to buy one and scratch out a check on the rear end of my mare before I could stop him."

Dr. Baldwin rose, left for the bar, and returned with another bottle which he placed on the table. "My compliments," he said, adding, "as long as we're telling stories about our fellow citizens, did you hear what happened to George Green, who lives on the John Day River near Charlie Clarno?"

"No, but I think we're about to," said Will Lord, reaching for the whiskey.

"Well," Baldwin started, "seems like George was waiting for his cows to come to the barn at milking time. When they didn't show up, he went looking for them. After traipsing all over, he found them in a neighbor's field of spring clover. They were all swelled up from eating too much and belching gas from an overload on their stomachs. He finally got them headed home, but by the time he caught up with them they were lined up at the trough, guzzling water and swelling up even more. With all the pressure built up in their innards, they started passing wind. George got out his corncob pipe, not knowing it was methane gas they were letting out, and when he struck a match to light up, he wound up in a ball of flame that burned off his eyebrows and most of his beard. Not knowing what had happened, he fell to his knees and cried out, 'Lord, if you'll deliver me from these flames of hell I promise to give up hard liquor and never beat my wife again'." Tears filled Baldwin's eyes as he struggled to control himself. "Last I heard he hasn't missed a Sunday sermon since. And his wife goes around looking like a cat that's been fed a saucer of cream."

After the laughter died down Will Lord asked, "You mentioned Charlie Clarno. What's this I hear about him buying a steamboat?".

"He bought one, all right," said Joe Bannon. "I saw it. Charlie calls it the *John Day Queen*. He intended to run stock upriver to the Columbia and downstream to the gold miners at Canyon City. The only problem was he forgot how low the John Day can get in hot weather. After spending most of the summer hauling it off sandbars, he finally gave up and is using it for birthdays, grange outings and such. I imagine if anyone was interested in a sidewheeler they could get one pretty cheap now that the novelty has worn off."

"Joe, wasn't Charlie Clarno at the Idle Hour Saloon in Antelope when Frank Forrester killed Phillip Brogram?" Jack Edwards interjected.

"He sure was. He and twenty others saw Brogram stabbed to death right in front of their eyes. Charlie said Brogram and Forrester were arguing about wages Forrester claimed he was owed for tending some of Brogram's sheep, and both pulled out their knives. After the killing, Forrester lit out. The sheriff tracked him to Winnemuca, then took him to the courthouse at The Dalles for trial. After the jury heard his story, it only took them five minutes to reach a verdict of not guilty."

"I guess the moral of the story is that a man should pay his honest debts," Lord commented soberly.

"What's this about honest debts?" one of two men who had just arrived at the table asked.

"Andy," Dr. Baldwin exclaimed as he looked up. "And Jim. When did you two hit town?"

"Just got here," Andrew Morrow said, waving a hand in greeting to the others. "Along with two thousand Shropshires that need a haircut. We've

41

been looking for Will, but his office is full of wool bags. One of his clerks said we might find him here."

"Well, that you did, boys. Grab a chair and take a load off your feet," Will Lord said. "Today the Shaniko Warehouse Company is holding court at The Ramshead." Lord caught the eye of a bartender, circled his finger around the table, pointed at one of the empty bottles, then he turned to the newcomers. "So, how are things at the Morrow-Keenan ranch?"

"Wish I could say it was peaceful, but, like most sheepmen around Willow Creek, we're a little edgy," Jim Keenan replied. "That dead line the sheepshooters set up is going to affect us. If we recognize it, that is," he said hotly.

"We've been discussing what we should do," Andy Morrow added somberly, as he draped an arm around his partner's shoulder. "We'd like to sit down with the sheepshooters and talk this out, but they don't seem to be in the mood to palaver."

"If you find anyone that'll listen, let me know," Allie Jones said. "I don't intend to violate their boundary because I'm running my sheep in the hills this side of Mitchell. But talk is running high among cattlemen in Crook County that maybe they should form a sheepshooters organization of their own. If they do, that will affect most of the free graze in the county."

"Has anyone talked to Tom Pickett?" Dr. Baldwin asked. "He's a level headed cowman."

Jim Keenan snorted. "When it comes to sheep, he's about the only cattleman in Crook County who is. He makes no secret of the fact that he has no love for sheep, but that doesn't color his thinking about someone else's right to run sheep."

Silence followed as the waiter arrived with another bottle. When he left, Allie Jones leaned forward. "As you know, his Triple C spread is not far from my place. He's always played square with me, and you can take his word to the bank."

"There's your answer then," said Jack Edwards . "Why not set up a meeting with Tom. He has a lot of clout, and if I know him like I think I do, he'll listen and give you some straight talk. But I ..."

Edwards was interrupted by shouts from the front of the saloon. These were followed by a babble of excited voices. Looking toward the door, they spotted Morrow and Keenan's Irish foreman working his way to them.

"It's the Izee Sheepshooters," the foreman gasped when he reached their table. "They just killed Chief Fighting Horse for crossing the boundary line below the Blue Mountains. Shot him out of the saddle, then pumped his body full of lead."

"But Fighting Horse doesn't have any sheep," Edwards exclaimed. "He's a nomad."

"Mebbe so, but that didn't stop them from killing him," the foreman responded.

"Was he alone?" Morrow asked.

"No, he was with two young braves and his old squaw. They killed the squaw, too, but the bucks got away. Otherwise, we might never have got the news." The Irishman stopped to catch his breath, then went on. "The killers have been passing the word that Indians as well as sheep aren't welcome inside the boundary."

"That's damned outrageous," Dr. Baldwin sputtered. "The Indians have hunted that land long before any of us were born, and Fighting Horse has ridden through there every year for as long as I can remember. Besides, he's as peaceable an Indian as they come."

"Was as peaceable," Joe Bannon corrected him.

Will Lord studied the faces of his friends. He took a deep breath and squared his shoulders. "Level heads and sane voices are what's needed now. I suggest we get hold of Tom Pickett and let him know we'd like to talk to him. All of us have too much at stake to let these killings continue. But," his voice grew hard, "if the cattlemen who are behind all of this won't listen to reason, we have to be prepared to do whatever has to be done to stop them."

CHAPTER 7

When Tom Pickett acquired the remote and rugged section of Canyon Creek, he also inherited its lone squatter, a character by the name of David Leviticus Lonergan, who, for some reason known only to himself, went by the name of Finnegan.

Rumor had it that Finnegan was distantly related to Barney Prine, after whom the town of Prineville was named. The relationship was said to have been through Prine's great uncle, William Randle, who ran a freight wagon between Shaniko and Prineville before he was killed by sheepshooters while tending a band of sheep for a sick friend. When asked one night in Burmeisters Saloon if this was the case, Finnegan just grunted, shrugged his shoulders and replied in a raspy voice, "Anything's possible, I guess."

No one knew Finnegan's age, but most people suspected he was somewhere in his seventies. He had worked for the Hudson's Bay Company when they trapped for beaver on Crooked River, liked the country he saw and decided to stay. But there was one thing he didn't like and that was the inroads of a civilization he felt too confining. So he withdrew into the ruggedest section of land he could find—a remote canyon in the upper reaches of Canyon Creek. Finnegan's first shelter was an abandoned wolf's cave. As he grew older, winter's chill and the aches and pains of advancing age led him to construct a more sensible sod and timber shack. He lived mainly on venison and elk meat, or trout he speared in nearby Wolf Creek. Occasionally, porcupine or bear supplemented his diet, as did camas roots and potatoes from a small patch he watered and nurtured during the summer months. He also kept a scrawny nanny goat that provided him with milk and cheese.

Finnegan had also worked in the hay fields during the summer to pay for staples such as salt, coffee, beans and other necessities. When he got too old and bent to handle such hard labor, he searched the mountains for unbranded stray cattle that he would corral, fatten and bring to town to sell. He subsisted on this income until he became too crippled with arthritis to handle these wild steers. It was at this point he turned to raising sheep, usually no more than five or six head at a time. In spring, he did his own shearing and traded the wool for whatever store-bought supplies he needed at the time. His clothes and shoes were made from the hides of the animals he killed for food, the exception being a black cap with a white stripe that ran down the center, the hide of a skunk that had made the mistake of choosing a home under Finnegan's woodpile. They lived together peaceably until the skunk gave Finnegan a full squirt of highly toxic oily liquid one moonlit night as the old trapper was gathering firewood. Finnegan dropped an armload of wood, picked up the stoutest piece, and ended their relationship then and there.

Even though Finnegan was a recluse, he was sociable when he made one of his rare trips to Prineville. Particularly when he came in, as he put it, for a "two dollar toot." His stories and recollections were both hilarious and legendary. John Tibbett, the postmaster, recalled that Finnegan had received only one piece of mail in the forty odd years he lived in the Ochocos. It was addressed to David Leviticus Lonergan and Tibbett figured it would still be gathering dust if he hadn't mentioned it in Burmeisters Saloon one day when Finnegan was there. The old trapper said, "That's me," and that's how they came to know his true name. When he was handed the letter, Finnegan indifferently stuffed it into a shirt pocket, as if he could care less about where it came from or who sent it.

One fall in Kelley's bar, when Finnegan announced he had given up cattle and was raising sheep, he became the target of some good-natured ribbing. Most of the remarks were along the same vein. Like, "It's about time you found someone and settled down", or even cruder ones such as, "The best way to hold those ewes, Finnegan, is to put a hind foot in each boot" or "Push 'em up to a cliff and get 'em when they back up".

"Joke all you want," Finnegan had replied. "I should have gotten some sheep years ago. They're like a production machine. A lamb each spring and a sack of wool every summer. Easiest way to make a dollar that I know of."

When asked how the sheep ever found anything to eat on the rocky terrain where he lived, he would purse his lips, look thoughtful as if he had never thought about that, then reply, "They can't. They have to bring their own grass."

A favorite story of his, one all of his bar friends knew but encouraged him to tell when someone new was in town, was about a supposed neighbor who lived on an alkali flat several miles west of his cabin. "His land is so hardscrabble," Finnegan would say, "that I asked him one day how far he had to go for water. 'Three miles,' he answered. Then I asked him why he didn't dig a well." Finnegan would always stop at this point and gaze off into the distance, or sip his drink until the victim would impatiently ask, "Well, what did he say?" or, "Why didn't he?" At this point Finnegan would look at the questioner with a straight face and reply, "He said it was just as far thataway."

When, in the course of a conversation, someone might comment, "I see we're all here," Finnegan could always be counted on to reply, "Yep. We're all here because we ain't someplace else."

Finnegan had a constant companion, a black and white sheep dog that someone had dumped along the stage route and left to die. He found the animal and carried it home in his arms. For ten days he fed the stray with a rag soaked in goat's milk until the animal was strong enough to keep solid food down. It was barely more than a puppy when it had been abandoned, but with Finnegan's tender care it regained its health. A bond developed between the two of them and they became inseparable. If you saw one, you always knew the other was nearby. Finnegan's friends quickly became aware that it was a one-man dog. Although "Hiner" had never bitten anyone, if someone other than Finnegan tried to pet or talk to the dog, their kindness was rewarded with a snarl or a low growl.

Finnegan named the dog "Hiner" after his old friend, Cincinnatus Hiner Miller, who had lived in Prineville for a short time with his wife Minnie, their three children and Miller's brother, Jim. Miller later moved to Canyon City where he became the county judge. He abandoned his wife and family to tour Europe under the name and title, Joaquin Miller, The California poet. Finnegan admitted to being confused as to why Miller had changed his first name to Joaquin. "Probably the effect of his stay in California where there was a kissing bandit by that name," he guessed when asked. "He always was a romantic-type cuss. Loved the women, too," he added with a wicked grin, "when he wasn't scattering flowers in their paths he was bowing to them or kissing their hands. Guess that's why he got married so may times."

Finnegan loved Miller's poems, and could quote "Through the Alkali on the Oregon Trail", "Mountains of Oregon" or his favorite, "Indian Mortality", by heart. He closely followed the exploits of his friend and would gleefully recount the joke Miller told on himself after he had a toe freeze off when he was a newspaper correspondent in the Klondike: "I'm the most famous no-toe-rious poet in America."

In his own independent way, Finnegan was a compassionate person. He wasn't a church going man, but he was among the first to volunteer when the Union Church sought help to re-roof their building. And it wasn't an unfamiliar sight to see him and Hiner trudging along the Mitchell stage route in the dead of winter with a haunch of game over his shoulder for a widow who had lost her husband or an elderly couple who had run short on food. He neither asked, or expected, any return for his kindnesses.

As far as anyone knew, Finnegan didn't have an enemy in the world. That's why a letter, crudely addressed to "sheep lovr Finnigun", which was left in the post office in-coming mail barrel, came as such a shock to Prineville's postmaster John Tibbett.

Unable to overcome his curiosity, Tibbett slipped the letter out of its unsealed envelope, read it and blanched. He quickly reached for his frock coat, hung a "Back in 10 minutes" sign in the door window and left. Tibbett had seen one of Tom Pickett's men in town earlier and hurried to find him.

As the postmaster crossed the dusty, summer-baked street, he saw the 3C hand he was looking for in front of Smith's leather goods loading a saddle onto a buckboard. Waving to catch his attention, Tibbett quickened his pace.

"Headed back to the Triple C?"

"Yep."

"Would you mind giving this to Tom?" He held out the letter.

"Nope," the puncher answered.

"Soon as you see Tom, tell him who gave it to you. You won't forget, will you?"

The cowpoke frowned, then lifted himself to the spring seat and picked up the reins. Before he gave them a flick, he looked down and laconically replied, "I guess not."

The bespectacled postmaster stood in the street, watching as the wagon pulled away. "You did the right thing," he told himself. "Finnegan lives on Tom's land, so he should know about this. Besides," he rationalized passing along another man's mail, "Finnegan may not be in town for months."

Tom Pickett was crossing the yard when the buckboard returned. He stopped and waited as it swung his way. "Have a good trip, Sven?" he inquired.

"Yep. Postmaster said to give you this," his rider handed down the letter that had been given to him, clicked his tongue at the horses and pulled away.

Tom smiled at the taciturn reply. Sven Ohlson was a good trail hand, but he wasn't much on conversation.

Noting the envelope was addressed to Finnegan, he frowned as he slipped the letter out and began to read. When he had finished, he muttered a curse.Then he reread the message again. His jaw set as he trotted toward the stable. Reub Hassler stuck his head through the door as Tom was slipping a halter over the ears of a spotted appaloosa.

"That pony is built for hard riding," Hassler observed. "I thought you were planning on doing some paperwork this afternoon."

"Plans have changed, Reub. Take a look at this." Tom Pickett held out the letter. Reub read it, then looked up. "I know you like that old coot. That where you're heading?"

Tom nodded affirmatively, his lips drawn into a hard line.

"Want me to tag along?"

"Thanks, Reub, but I can travel faster alone."

"Maybe there's no rush. Finnegan isn't known for being in a hurry to pick up his mail." Tom glanced at his foreman, anger in his voice. "Reub, that letter wasn't meant for Finnegan. It was meant for me. That's why the envelope wasn't sealed. Whoever wrote this figured Tibbett would read it and pass it along to me."

"But Finnegan is on 3C land, Tom. They wouldn't dare..."

Pickett cut him off. "Reub, you know as well as I do that the piece of land Finnegan lives on lies next to the sheepkillers' boundary, just as you know that rock-strewn ground where he grazes his sheep is on the other side of it."

"But he only has five sheep this year," Reub Hassler said. "And that land he's using isn't worth spit. Nobody's going to do anything over a handful of sheep."

"Read the letter again, Reub, and tell me if you really believe that," Tom snapped as he swung into the saddle.

As the Indian pony raced away, Hassler read the message one more time:

Finigun
yu hav vilated owr bowndry fer the last tim jist becuz yu liv on pikets
land wont sav yur hyde

The illiterate writing wasn't a warning from the Izee or the Paulina Sheepshooters because it didn't carry their name. It was just signed,

a sheepshutr

Tom carefully studied the sod and plank shanty in the draw below. It was nestled in a grove of jack pine, which was surrounded by a grove of taller, more majestic Douglas fir. A small brook idled lazily a few steps from the shack's front door. Cured and oiled deer hide covered its two windows. The skins had been rubbed until they were translucent; letting the light in but offering the occupant more privacy than glass panes. A stack of wood was neatly piled by the front door, within easy reach of the stone fireplace inside, or the open fire pit outside. An overturned coffee pot rested on its side by the cooking fire which, like the chimney, showed no sign of smoke although it was supper time. By the creek, a wash basin rested on a round of fir that had been cut for firewood. About ten yards uphill, a worn path led to a dirt-covered cold cellar.

Tom peered intently at each and every feature. The place looked deserted. Even so, he cautiously urged his horse forward and slowly descended the steep slope, following a winding game trail that zig-zagged to water. Closer now, he stopped to shout out a "Haloo". In remote country it was dangerous, and sometimes even fatal, to come upon a man unannounced.

While he waited for an answer, Tom's eyes fell on a small patch of potatoes that had been planted where it would catch most of the day's sun. His heartbeat quickened as he noticed the fragile green plants had been trampled into the soil. Even at this distance he could tell the damage had been done by a single rider. The tracks continued and passed over the coffee pot, which Tom now could see was bent and misshapen.

Tom called out again, his cry falling flat as it was absorbed by the dense timber. He tensed as a slight movement caught his eye. Something on the door fluttered, lay still, then moved again as it was stirred by a late afternoon breeze.

The scream of a raucous jay split the silence as two of the crowned birds landed in the ash of the cooking pit, poking and scratching as they strutted about searching for remnants of food.

"There's been no fire for the last day or so or it would be too hot for the birds," Tom muttered, half aloud, half to himself. "Finnegan should have his sheep gathered in by now, too." Earlier he had noticed the empty pole corral. "And where's Hiner? Normally he would have heard me a half mile back and should be raising a racket with his barking."

He eased slowly across the clearing, his eyes in constant motion as they searched the ground and studied each shadow in the forest. Satisfied that there was no visible threat, he dismounted and removed a note that had been pinned to the door with a skinning knife he recognized as Finnegan's. Tracing the uneven printing with one finger, he mouthed the words as he read:

Let ths b a lesen to al sheepluvrs
hu cros the ded line.

Tom sucked in his breath. Afraid of what he might find, but knowing he had to look, he nudged the door open with the toe of his boot. His fingers touched the butt of his revolver. "Finnegan?" he called, in a voice not more than a hoarse croak.

Cautiously, he entered, letting his eyes adjust to the dim interior. Diffused light from one of the windows fell on an unmade bed built against the wall. Below the other window was a rough wood table and a three-legged stool. A single shelf held a can of baking soda, an almost empty bottle of One-Minute Cough Syrup, a tin of coffee beans and what looked like a jar of black molasses.

The room was surprisingly neat. A well-tamped and watered dirt floor had recently been swept clean, but now showed two sets of footprints; those of moccasined feet and some boot imprints. They indicated the sign of a struggle.

Tom knelt to examine the prints. The moccasin tracks were surely Finnegan's. The boot tracks were large and bore the weight of a heavy man. The right heel was marked by a deep v-shaped cut in the leather.

Tom was so deep in thought that he missed the creak of one of the thong bound rafters, but a gentle nudge against his back brought him to his feet, his hand tugging at his six-gun.

Bile rose in his throat as he stared up at Finnegan's body, which hung from one of the ceiling beams. Finnegan's neck had been stretched to twice its length, and both hands had a death grip on the hemp rope strung tight above his head. A blackened tongue protruded from his mouth and dry, congealed blood ran out of sockets that held bulging eyes. A cold fury tore at Tom as he saw a common bowline knot behind and below Finnegan's head. "The bastard!" Tom shouted his anger. Finnegan had been hung without the benefit of a hangman's knot and had slowly and painfully strangled to death. The position of his hands showed he had died trying to keep his weight off the rope.

51

Tom took out his pocket knife and cut the thick strands of hemp, catching the stiff corpse as it fell. As he was easing it to the floor, a muted, barely noticeable scratching sound reached his ears. Unceremoniously, he dropped Finnegan's body, whirled and drew. Crawling toward him was a bloody black and white form. A series of low growls came from a torn throat that leaked blood.

"Easy, Hiner. Easy, fella. I'm a friend." Tom holstered his Colt and dropped to his knees. "It's all right," he crooned softly. "I'm not here to hurt you." He held out the back of his hand for Hiner to smell, then carefully stroked the wounded animal's head and back. The dog responded with a low whine.

Tom struck a match to better assess the damage. Seeing little but blood-matted hair, he went outside, took off his canvas jacket and laid it on the ground. Returning, he kneeled and, as gently as possible, took the dog in his arms and out to better light, placing him on the coat. Next, he filled the wash basin with water from the creek and gently began to probe with his fingers, washing away the blood with a bandanna as he went. He found a hole in the flesh of the neck where a bullet had entered and exited without damaging either the windpipe or spine. There was also an open scalp wound between the dog's ears and a deep furrow in the dog's left hip. As far as Tom could tell, Hiner had been shot three times.

"Just lie still Hiner and we'll get you bandaged up. If you haven't lost too much blood, you just might make it. Once you're taken care of we'll see that your master gets a proper burial."

As if he understood every word, the dog lifted his head and licked Tom's hand.

CHAPTER 8

It was the following spring before six of the seven sheepmen who had gathered at The Ramshead bar in Shaniko the previous summer, met with Tom Pickett. They were: Dr. David Baldwin, of the Baldwin Sheep and Land Company; Allie Jones, whose ranch was near Pickett's, between Marks and Mill Creeks; Jack Edwards of the Hay Creek Ranch near Grizzly Mountain; Will Lord, president of the Shaniko Warehouse Company; and Andy Morrow and Jim Keenan, partners of the Morrow-Keenan ranch on Willow Creek.

Fall roundup and the time-consuming job of moving their animals to winter pasture had kept them all busy from dawn to dusk until late October. Then the county was struck by one of the most severe winters since the disastrous years of 1886 and 1887.

Heavy snowfall started early in November and fell continuously through mid-April. Snowdrifts, some reaching heights of fifteen feet, made travel impossible. For weeks on end, the stage roads from The Dalles, Mitchell and Dayville were closed. People ventured out only when they had an emergency, and babies were often delivered without the help of a mid-wife or doctor. The bodies of those who died had to be left in the snow until a space over frozen ground could be cleared and a fire started to thaw the earth for digging. Those who wanted their loved ones buried, with Christian services in a cemetery or family plot, were forced to wait for the spring thaw.

Time has a way of taking the fever out of hot tempers, so the sense of urgency that prompted a call for this meeting months ago had eased considerably. The main preoccupation of the sheepmen who were now gathered at the Triple C was on repairing the damage the past season had

53

wrought on their outbuildings, fences and livestock. This was the frame of mind they were in when they gathered in Tom Pickett's ranch house.

Tom asked Reub Hassler to join them because he felt Reub had a good feel for how most of the ranch hands in the area felt about the sheep situation. This, and because he valued Reub's opinion.

Tom had planned the evening with care. His cook had worked for two days to prepare a sumptuous supper that was accompanied with wine from San Francisco. Following the meal, the group gathered around a roaring fire in the living room to enjoy Havana cigars and imported brandy.

After virtual isolation for almost six months, they were eager to hear all about their friends, neighbors and the community, and the topics of their conversation ranged from C.A. Cline's decision to give up his job as a part time blacksmith and become a full time dentist, to Prineville's acquisition of its first piece of fire fighting equipment—a ladder truck and pumper. Other subjects they discussed were the new race track that was being built outside of town, Prineville's scheduled baseball game with The Dalles on the Fourth of July and the recently formed six-man town band, started by Til Glaze, that consisted of five horn instruments and a bass drum.

When Jack Edwards, owner of the Hay Creek Ranch, brought up the subject of the Christmas eve fire at Silver Lake, a small desert town in south central Oregon, a pall fell over the room. The fire had started in the community's social hall, which was located on the second floor of F.M. Chrisman's general merchandise store. Close to two hundred people had jammed into a space no larger than 25 by 50 feet to watch a festive Christmas program that would later include gifts for the children. In an effort to get a better view of the show being presented, one of the spectators climbed onto a table. His head hit a hanging kerosene lamp and knocked it to the floor. The spilled kerosene caught fire and spread to a Christmas tree, then to the pitch-laden pine boughs that decorated the walls. The crowd panicked and rushed for the single exit door that led to an outside staircase. Under the weight of too many bodies, the stairs collapsed as the dry wooden building burst into flame. Forty-three people, a third of the town's population, were killed. As it was impossible to identify any of the charred bodies, they were buried in a common grave.

After a moment of awkward silence, Dr. David Baldwin cleared his throat and said, "A tragedy. A true tragedy. But that hasn't killed the town, and it won't. Adversity often brings out the best in people. We've all lived through fires in our own communities, and had our own share of grief, but I can't think of one person, not one, who hasn't rolled up his sleeves and gotten on with his life."

Realizing that his mention of the Silver Lake fire had put a damper on the evening, Edwards cleared his throat. "I guess we could go on gabbing all night. Lord knows we're all starved for news, but that's not why we're here. Doc," Edwards addressed Baldwin, owner of the Baldwin Sheep and Land Company, "while you were in the outhouse, the rest of us decided that rather than talk in all directions we needed a spokesman. And because you're so good at words, we felt it should be you."

Baldwin's nod indicated he would accept. "On one condition," he stated. "That anyone here speak up anytime he feels like it." Immediately, he caught himself and turned to the only person in the room who had taken neither a cigar or brandy. "My apologies. Or she, too, of course."

All eyes turned to Rachel Williams, who smiled graciously. "No apologies are necessary, Dr. Baldwin. It is a pleasure and an honor to be included. Please allow me no deference because of my gender. I would like to be treated as you treat one another. And," she added, "if you feel the urge to use a strong word now and then, don't be embarrassed or afraid of offending me. I've heard them all. In fact," a deep laugh filled her throat, "I've been known to use one or two myself."

Andy Morrow had alerted Tom that they had asked Rachel to join them. "She thinks like a man, but she has something else in her favor. Where men can get carried away with their tempers, particularly if they feel their manhood is in question, she stays calm and collected, analyzes the problem, and usually has a good solution to offer." Morrow had carefully watched for Tom's reaction to having a woman attend the meeting, and before Tom had a chance to answer, he hurriedly added, "She has a darned good business head, too. There's not a one of us who hasn't been bested by her at one time or another." Then he added with a dry chuckle, "Although I reckon those who were don't want to admit it."

55

Tom Pickett knew this to be true. Rachel Williams and her husband Paul came from the French settlement at Tualatin in the Willamette Valley. They moved to central Oregon to start a ranch at Ashwood, near Trout Creek, where Howard Maupin shot and killed Chief Paulina. A year after their arrival, Rachel's husband was bitten by a rattlesnake and died. Childless, she had the choice of moving in with her parents, who owned a section of farmland in the Willamette Valley, or running the ranch she and her husband had started. She chose the ranch.

Just ten months after her husband was buried, she sold all their cattle and invested in sheep and additional land. Her property now spread over several thousand acres, and was considered to be some of the best grazing land between The Dalles and Prineville. Tom knew this was true, because it was property he would have chosen for himself. The company she formed and ran, Williams Enterprises, had the reputation of being tough to deal with, but fair and honest. She didn't suffer fools gladly, much to the chagrin of many businessmen who felt they could slip one over in their dealings with a "mere woman".

Tom had not met Rachel Williams before, and his eyes kept drifting across the room to study her. Short, auburn hair that was turning grey, complimented her violet eyes. Her skin was fair and her posture straight and self assured. Tom guessed her age to be in the early fifties. She was dressed casually but neatly in a white silk blouse, soft leather vest and a denim riding skirt which was accented by a beaded and hammered silver Indian belt. Tom was impressed with her attire. She neither dressed above or below the men assembled around her. Nor did she accentuate her femininity. She was dressed exactly right for the occasion.

Rachel Williams caught Tom's glance and held it. A pink flush shaded his cheeks at being caught staring at her. The corners of her lips lifted in a soft smile, then she looked away.

Tom made an effort to compose himself, for her directness had unsettled him. To cover his embarrassment he turned to the men in the room who had now gathered in small conversational groups. "Let's all have a seat and be comfortable. Coffee's on the table. Help yourselves."

Andrew Morrow and his partner James Keenan poured themselves a cup, as did Allie Jones. They seated themselves on one of three leather sofas that faced the open fireplace. Baldwin, Pickett and Williams joined them.

Will Lord of the Shaniko Warehouse Company also helped himself to a cup of coffee, but remained standing. "Before I sit down," he said, "Joe Bannon asked me to extend his apologies for not being here. He came down with a case of the grippe last week that he hasn't been able to shake. I'll fill him in on what we talked about on my way home tomorrow." Holding his saucer in one hand, he raised his cup to Tom with the other. "I'll also tell him he missed a mighty fine meal, some excellent wine and brandy and one of the best cigars I've had since my last visit to Portland. Many thanks for your hospitality, Tom. And for the night's lodging you are offering a bunch of disreputable sheepmen." He directed his cup at Rachel Williams. "And one not so disreputable sheepwoman."

As Lord was talking, Hiner limped into the room and headed directly for Tom. Pausing just long enough to rub the length of his body against Tom's leg, he hobbled to Rachel William's chair. As she leaned down to pet the crippled dog, Tom leaped to his feet. "Don't touch. . ." he cried out, but before he could finish his warning, Rachel had leaned over and was gently scratching Hiner behind the ears. The dog responded with a sigh heard throughout the room as he slumped over her small, booted feet. His knob of a tail thumped happily against the braided rug he was lying on.

The eight men watched in open-mouthed astonishment as the dog rolled on his back to have his stomach rubbed.

Reub Hassler, who hadn't said one word until that moment exclaimed in wonderment, "Well I'll be damned! Er, I mean gol durned." He looked apologetically at Rachel Williams. "I'm sorry ma'am, but that's the first time I've ever seen Hiner wag his tail before, or take to someone other than Tom or old man Finnegan."

"I guess you've all heard what happened to his master?" Tom said. There was a hard edge to his voice.

Baldwin responded for them all. "We have, which brings us to why we're here tonight—to try and find some way to put a stop to all this senseless killing."

"I'm more than willing to hear you out," Tom replied. "And help if I can. Seeing Finnegan hanging there wasn't a pleasant sight. Nor was the goat out back, whose throat had been cut, or the dead sheep that had been clubbed to death, then mutilated for no good reason. Only a sick mind would do something like that. One of these days I'll find out who did it, then I'll settle the score."

He missed the fleeting expression of concern that crossed Rachel's face when she heard the bitterness of his words.

Baldwin rose, pushed his coat back with this hands and hooked both thumbs behind a pair of bright red suspenders. He took a deep breath. "Tom, that's why we felt this meeting was important. This is not meant as flattery, but right now you're the only cowman we know who will listen to our side of the story. We're not violent people, sought on revenge. Nor do we believe in an eye for an eye and a tooth for a tooth, in spite of what the Bible says. Just the opposite. We'd like to find a peaceable solution that both sides can live with. And we're plain stumped as to how to go about it. We're hoping you can tell us what to do."

Tom took a deep breath before he replied. "If I'm not able to stop the hanging of someone living on my own land, how can I possibly advise you?"

William Lord spoke up. "No one's blaming you for Finnegan's death, Tom. If anything, it just points out what Doc just said about stopping all the killing before it gets worse. There must be other cattlemen who feel like you do. Couldn't we enlist their help?"

"I doubt it, Will. Cattlemen are a pretty tight-knit group. Even when we don't approve of what our neighbor is doing, we'll back his right to do it."

A moment of silence followed, then Jim Keenan volunteered a thought. "Maybe the sheepkillers got the violence out of their system last year."

"Wishful thinking," Tom replied. "This past winter did a lot of damage to everyone. The hay sheds are empty and so are the stomachs of the cattle and sheep. With both sides looking for the best grass, this could be a more violent year than last."

"Well then, maybe we should quit trying to look for a peaceful out and form our own cattle killing association," Allie Jones shouted as he slammed a fist on the coffee table in front of him, rattling the cups that were there.

Tom replied calmly. "I don't blame you for feeling the way you do, Allie, but that would be like pouring oil on an open flame. Believe it or not, the majority of cattlemen don't like what the sheepkillers have been doing, but with all of the migratory herds from out of state invading our grazing land, they can't agree on any other way to stop them."

"They're right about the migratory sheep," Keenan said bitterly, nodding toward his partner. "Andy and I are as frustrated about them as you cattlemen are. They destroy our pasture as much as they do land your cattle graze on. They pass through, like locusts, and leave nothing behind but destruction. We respect the land because we live here and make our living off it. Besides," he added hotly, "we pay taxes in Oregon and they don't. We buy our supplies locally and they don't. Yet we suffer because of the damage they do." His voice rose in anger. "It's not fair. There ought to be a law to keep them in their own state and out of ours."

Fueled by frustration and Keenan's emotional remarks, the room exploded in talk as Jones, Edwards, Lord and Morrow loudly vented their feelings, all at the same time.

Dr. David Baldwin rose from his seat, held out his arms, palms down, and made a patting motion. "Hold on now. All this yammering is getting us nowhere. We can gab all night, but it won't do much good unless we come up with an idea or two. Rachel, we haven't heard from you yet. Would you like to venture an opinion?"

Rachel Williams stood, one hand resting in the palm of the other. "Yes, I would. Contrary to how you seem to feel, several good ideas have been expressed here tonight. And they were tied together when Jim Keenan said there should be a law. In so many words, Tom indicated most cattlemen would like to see an end to the killing and might be appeased if the migratory sheep problem was eliminated. And you, Dr. Baldwin, said what we needed most right now was a good dose of common sense. I'm sure all of us realize that violence begets more violence, just as I'm sure Allie wasn't really serious when he suggested forming a cattle killers organization." She paused until Allie Jones mumbled in sullen agreement.

"So, the answer seems obvious. This is a land of justice, founded on a set of laws. We should be spending our time, energy and money to make our influence felt in the state capitol as well as the Department of Agriculture and their Division of Forestry, who manage the land we use. With the right legislation, several things could be accomplished: Cattlemen would have the excuse they need not to join, or side with, the sheepshooters; land in Oregon could not be used by migratory herds from out of state; and grazing rights could be put under an allotment system for both cattle and sheep."

Andy Morrow nudged Tom with an elbow, winked and whispered, "What did I tell you. We were so hog-tied over the problem that we couldn't see the forest for the trees."

William Lord responded. "Rachel, your ideas are good, but we all know how slow politicians work. It could take months, even years, to accomplish such a goal."

Both Morrow and Edwards voiced their agreement.

"That's why we have to get started. And right away," Rachel Williams replied passionately. "Think it over gentlemen. If you have a better plan, I will abide by whatever you agree to." Her tone softened. "Right now, it's late. It has been a full day and I have to get an early start in the morning, so I'll say goodnight." She turned and left the room, Hiner tagging along at her heels.

Reub Hassler issued a low whistle. "If that don't beat all," he said.

Tom wasn't sure whether his comment referred to her stand on what should be done, or the fact that Hiner had added Rachel Williams to the very short list of people he liked.

The next morning, Tom stood on the sheltered porch that faced Lookout Mountain and the meadow that spread to the foothills of the Ochoco range. It was his favorite time of day. The sun had just broken over the mesa-topped mountain and its warmth was drawing the chill from the land. Wisps of mist, caught by rising cold air from Ochoco Creek, hung in veiled layers close to the earth. The ranch as yet had not started to stir and antelope grazed peacefully by the willow-lined stream. Yesterday morning, the same spot fed a herd of Roosevelt elk.

One old buck deer, with a magnificent set of horns, stood proudly on a nearby ridge, guarding his charges: four doe and six brown and white splotched fawns who chased and butted one another in bursts of child-like energy. They were shy and graceful animals, yet quick to be startled by any movement that caught their attention. Tom had given strict orders that the old buck was not to be shot, knowing his matched set of antlers made him a tempting target. Tom had seen the grey in his coat and knew that soon enough his place would be taken by a younger and stronger male who would challenge him in battle and win. So, Tom felt, let him play king for the short time he has left.

A dusting of snow still capped the peaks of the higher mountains, indicating winter had not fully given over to spring. Dancing crystals of light from frost-laden meadow grass sparkled brightly as the sun dissolved the dark shadows of the mountain range. Soon, this enchanted moment would be lost. Already he could hear the familiar sounds of men awakening in the bunkhouse; a hacking cough, a cleared throat and the mumble of voices. Soon the cook would beat on the iron triangle he used to call the men to breakfast and the peace that signalled a new day would be shattered.

He was about to go inside when he felt a light touch on his arm.

"Good morning, Tom" a soft voice greeted him.

He turned. "Morning, Rachel. Sleep well?"

"Like a log, thank you. And you?"

"Like another log."

They both laughed easily, enjoying the moment.

"The flowers in the room were a nice touch."

"Spring daffodils. But I can't take the credit. It was Reub's way of making you feel welcome. I suspect beneath that gruff exterior of his lies the soul of a poet."

"It was very thoughtful. I'll be sure to thank him."

"How long have you been standing behind me?" Tom asked.

"Just long enough to see how much you love this land and the spot you have chosen for your home," she said seriously, then in a lighter vein added, "I'm starved. How about escorting me in to breakfast?"

"It would be my pleasure," he said, offering his arm.

As they entered the dining room, Tom's other guests were conversing around a large oak table laden with food. Dr. Baldwin made a show of pulling out Rachel's chair, and when she was comfortably seated the rest of the men took their seats. Little was said as they attacked their meal. Each of them considered eating a necessity, not a ritual. If conversation were necessary, it would be after the last person had finished. Normal procedure was to eat, then leave to do the day's chores. But today was different. The cook brought in a fresh pot of coffee, then cleared the table. Tom opened, then passed around, a box of fresh cigars. The mood was relaxed, although expectant eyes drifted to Dr. Baldwin.

"Rachel," Baldwin cleared his throat. "After you left last night, we discussed your ideas in great detail." He paused to dab at his mouth with a linen napkin. "Some of us agree with you. Others don't think we have the time to wait until the legislators take it in their heads to act. As Will said last night, getting their help could drag on for months. Maybe years. Then we have to consider the possibility that, like all politicians, they will do nothing at all if they think it might lose them a few votes."

The men at the table shifted their attention to Rachel, whose expression never changed. She reached for the pot of coffee, refilled her cup, took a sip and looked blankly at Baldwin. Then she spoke. "If you don't like my idea, what did you arrive at?" There wasn't a trace of emotion in her voice.

Baldwin nervously glanced around the table seeking support. Seeing that he would get none, he examined his hands and exhaled deeply. "That's the problem. We don't have anything better to offer. The decision was to wait and see if the violence starts up again. If it doesn't, our problem has solved itself. If it does, we'll have to hold another meeting and go from there."

Rachel Williams rose, her back straight and rigid. A flush of anger crossed her face, then passed quickly as she gained control of her emotions. "I said last night I would abide by what all of you agreed to, but as I see it, you have agreed to do nothing at all. If we can't decide here and now what course of action to take, it's my opinion that another meeting will fare no better. As far as I'm concerned, we are just wasting each other's time." Her voice carried an intensity they hadn't heard before. "I for one am not willing to wait. I intend to go to the state capitol and will stay there until I can find someone who will listen and act." She paused for a moment as if undecided what to do next, then whirled and left the room.

An embarrassed silence followed. Tom got to his feet. "If you'll excuse me, I'll see my guest out."

He caught up with Rachel as she reached the stable. She faced him, eyes blazing, rigid with anger. "If I were a man they would listen to me," she said fiercely. "Nothing will change and they know it. The killing will start again and they'll still be wondering what to do." Her tone softened and she searched his eyes. Then she stepped to him, her arms circling his body, holding him tight as she placed her head on his chest. "Oh, Tom. Tell me I'm right. I have to be right."

His arms enfolded her. Awkwardly at first, then more tenderly as he bent his head and pressed a cheek against her hair. Her woman's scent filled his nostrils. He wanted to reassure her, to tell her she was right, but it was not his call to make. He did realize one thing, however, and that was he very much wanted to see Rachel Williams again.

CHAPTER 9

Tom woke with a start. His heart was pounding as if it were trying to burst out of his chest and sweat had soaked through his nightshirt into the muslin sheets of his bed.

Relief flooded over him in a wave when he realized the nightmare was over. The horror of it had been so real it violently jolted him out of a troubled sleep. The feeling of relief was soon replaced, however, by a feeling of depression. For what he relived in his sleep had actually happened and he knew the dream would be repeated again and again by a mind playing its hallucinatory tricks.

The year was 1869. He was twenty-six then and on a trail drive from the Willamette Valley to central Oregon with his new partner, Todd Howard. Everything they owned was tied up in the small herd that carried their 3C brand.

As they were crossing the Santiam Pass, their stock was stolen from them by a group of outlaws who worked for Frank Allen, an influential but dishonest rancher from southern Oregon. Allen was a member of the Oregon Steamship Company's board of directors, a company determined to maintain its monopoly in the state and keep all cattle but their own out of the vast country that lay east of the Cascade mountain range.

When Allen's men took the cattle, they also killed Darrel Vaughn, the Triple C's trail boss. It took several days for them to track and find the rustlers, but Tom and Todd did. And when they did, Tom, in a rage over the loss of their cattle and Vaughn's death, ordered the rustlers hanged. Months later, in a face-to-face showdown, he killed Frank Allen.

Tom's dream had haunted him for twenty-eight years, and it was always the same. The eight riders would come back to life, sitting motionless on their horses before him. Their bulging eyes stared, unseeing, from faces with lips peeled back in a snarl that showed huge, glistening teeth. Tom never failed to wonder, even in his dreams, how the killers' rotten, broken and stained teeth could become so dazzling straight and white. Bloody ropes hung from necks stretched to twice their normal length, and, as Tom faced them, unable to move and barely able to breathe, each man's neck began to grow, then turned into the writhing body of a huge snake. Their bulging eyes narrowed and white pupils became triangular and black, like those of a poisonous reptile. Forked tongues darted in and out of now toothless mouths.

As Tom watched the silent riders, their brands began to glow, then smoke, as if they were being touched by a hot iron. He could even smell the odor of burning flesh. Frank Allen's FA mark slowly dissolved and reformed into a grinning death's head, the signature used by the Crook County vigilantes Tom rode against twelve years ago. But, this night, for the first time, there had been a change. The silent men were draped in bloody sheepskins, and from the mouths of their horses came the plaintive cries of frightened sheep.

Tom dropped back onto his pillow and pulled the covers up to his chin to ward off the night's chill. He tried to relax, but each time he closed his eyes the ghostly images would return. Knowing that sleep was impossible, he slipped out of bed, reached for the box of wooden matches he always kept on his bedside stand and lit a kerosene lamp. Then he turned the wick up to dispel the distorted shadows that filled the room. A quick glance at his pocket watch, which rested by the lamp, showed the time to be 3:00 a.m.

Tom pulled on a wool robe and felt for his fleece slippers. Then he went to the stone fireplace in his bedroom, crumpled up some old newspapers, added kindling and wood, and built a fire. As the blaze caught, he moved an easy chair into the fire's perimeter of warmth, threw a blanket from the bed over his shoulders, and settled back, lost in thought. His mind drifted to Portland when it was a growing community, surrounded by so many cut trees that it was referred to as Stumptown. It was there he first met Todd Howard, who was to become his best friend and partner, along with Phil Geyer, a river boat captain. The three of them had challenged the powerful Oregon Steamship Company and had won: both on their cattle drive over the Cascades and by ship up the Columbia River. Frank Allen had been directed by the OSC—the initials by which the steamship company was known—to stop passage of cattle through the passes from the Willamette Valley to the lush grasslands east of the Cascades. The OSC plot had been foiled by Tom and Todd's persistence in tracking Allen's rustlers and regaining their herd. Jack Bartels, another lackey of the OSC, had been ordered to stop Geyer's steamship which was taking a separate load of 3C cattle up the Columbia. Bartels failed when Geyer destroyed the five OSC vessels that opposed him before safely landing his cargo at The Dalles portage.

Tom's partner, Todd Howard, had been adopted in San Francisco after the death of his mother. It was only after his arrival in central Oregon that Todd, for the first time, met his maternal grandparents, Clay and Ellie Howard. The Howards, who had lost contact with their daughter, were unaware they had a grandson. As soon as they found out who Todd was, they welcomed him with open arms.

When Todd got word that his foster father, Jamie Fields, was ill, he returned to San Francisco to take charge of the family's many business enterprises. Todd had planned on returning in a few months, but Fields was in such poor health he stayed on.

Later, Todd married the Fields' daughter Ann. They had three children, and Tom Pickett was named their godfather. Throughout the years Tom and Todd kept in touch, but Tom never visited them in San Francisco, although Clay and Ellie Howard had. Their great-grandchildren had been the joy of the Howard's lives.

Tom lost his own family when he was four years old. They were slaughtered by Cayuse Indians. So, with no living relatives of his own, he told those close to him that he had "adopted" Todd's kin, which included the Howards. "Or maybe it was the other way around," he always added. In any case, when Clay died from influenza in 1890, and Ellie died six months later—probably from a broken heart as those who knew her felt—Tom grieved as if they were his real parents.

Tom deeply missed the Howards. Not only for the love they offered him, but for their advice and support. Clay was someone he could always turn to when he had a problem. When the town of Prineville was being torn apart, Clay was the driving force that rallied a frightened community into action and drove out a group of vigilantes who had terrorized the county for two years. Tom knew Clay would have known what to tell the sheepowners who had been Tom's guests two night's ago, because Clay would have known what action to take.

Tom rose, stirred the fire and added another log, but his mind never lost its train of thought. When Clay was alive he had explained the reason for Tom's nightmares. That was when they were so frequent Tom thought he might be losing his mind. Unable to keep them to himself any longer, he had blurted out his anxiety one evening at Clay's home on Deer Street in Prineville.

Clay had taken both of Tom's hands in his own. He could still remember the gentle man's words: "Tom, we all have our crosses to bear. Mine was the loss of a daughter. After forty years, I still wake up in the middle of the night, choking on a scream I can't get out. I wish I could tell you that your bad dreams will go away, but I can't. I can tell you this, though. If you can accept them, and learn to live with them, they will grow farther and farther apart. Keep in mind you did what had to be done. There was no other choice. The curse we carry, and one that is a burden to all Christian-minded people, is that we have a conscience. And troubled sleep is one of the prices we pay for this conscience."

Years later, when Tom had asked Clay why he didn't have nightmares about the violent death of his fiancee, Clay's answer had been short and simple. "You loved her, and did not cause her death. There was no anger in your actions to save her, only anger and confusion as to why she died. Time healed this wound because you came to grips with the fact that this is the way life is. In the case of the hangings, your anger caused the deaths of eight men. That's the difference."

Tom pulled the blanket tighter around his shoulders and mused to the coals of a dying fire. "Clay, you have given me something far more precious than friendship or advice. You have given me a set of standards which guide my life. I bless you for it, just as I will always cherish the memory of our friendship."

The insistent clang of an iron rod against the cook's metal triangle snapped Tom out of his reverie. He rose, hurriedly shaved and dressed, then left for the breakfast he always shared with his crew.

"Well, boss, what are the marching orders for today?" Reub Hassler asked as he slipped into the vacant seat next to Tom. He briefly glanced at his employer's drawn face as he reached for a handful of hot biscuits. "Didn't sleep very well last night," he added, rubbing an elbow. "This rheumatiz got me up early, so I poked around outside for awhile." He broke the biscuits in two, then poured a generous helping of hot gravy over the pieces. "Saw a light in your window. This sheep thing keeping you awake?"

"Not last night, Reub," Tom replied. "Just a bad dream that crops up now and then."

"Well," said Hassler philosophically, "when you're young, it's bad dreams that interrupt your sleep. When you get old, it's aches and pains."

Tom chuckled as he turned sideways and placed a hand on Reub's shoulder. Hassler had been with Tom when he had ordered the outlaws hanged, and knew the memory still haunted Tom. This was Reub's way of letting him know he cared. "Reub, I can always count on you to put things in their proper perspective." He released his grip and turned back to his plate. "To answer your question, I would like you and the boys to fix those fences the elk knocked down in the south pasture. As for me, I think I'll check things out on upper Canyon Creek."

Hassler's eyes narrowed. "I suppose you'll be riding along the boundary line, too," he said, referring to the one the sheepshooters had established. "And I also expect you'll be pokin' around Finnegan's place to see if you might have missed something." He pushed his empty plate away. "I'll keep you company."

Tom answered softly. "Reub, you're acting like a mother hen with one of her chicks. I appreciate your offer, but it's more important to get the fence fixed before we lose some cows than it is to tag along with me."

"At least take a couple of the boys along with you to watch your backside." There was genuine concern in Reub's voice.

"I'll be fine. Hiner will be with me, and he can smell trouble a mile away." Tom rose and hitched up his pants. "Besides, I guess I'm old enough to take care of myself."

He didn't catch Reub's mumbled reply as he left.

The beauty of the day more than made up for Tom's sleepless night. The early morning sky was such a deep blue it almost seemed purple, and the air was tangy with spring smells. Grey and blue hues of fragrant sage blended with patches of yellow bells, lavender-colored mariposa lilies and the deep red tones of wild peony to create the effect of vivid splashes of paint on an artist's palette.

Tom looked down. "Guess you can't see all this beauty from down there, Hiner." On hearing his name the dog, who had been limping alongside, looked up and cocked his head. Tom reined in his horse and patted his leg. Knowing what the signal meant, Hiner crouched, then leaped into the air. Tom caught him easily. "Friend, you've put on a little weight, but your limp is not as bad as it has been, so we'll just make this a short rest. Then you can start running off some of that winter fat." The dog nuzzled the hand that held the reins, and, with a comfortable grunt settled in Tom's lap.

When they came to the spot where Canyon Creek emptied into Ochoco Creek, Tom stopped. "That's it, Hiner. The free ride is over." The dog looked up, checking Tom's face to see if he was really serious, then, deciding he was, gave a small groan of protest and jumped down.

Tom swung left and followed the creek into the deep recesses of the canyon until he reached Finnegan's abandoned cabin. Hiner whined nervously until they had passed and were well beyond his old home. After half-an-hour's ride, Tom stopped. He stood in the stirrups and turned to check his back trail. Then he carefully studied the forested ridges that surrounded him. For some reason he felt uneasy. No more than twenty yards to his left were the blazes and pieces of tin that marked the dead line established by the sheepkillers. The last time he had crossed this line was the day Finnegan had been murdered, and he went to check on the dead man's sheep.

Tom wasn't sure why he had returned, but something seemed to draw him to this spot. For sure, there wouldn't be any sign left. The winter storms would have erased any that he might have missed on his first search. Still, he felt there was some reason to be here.

With a click of his tongue, he urged his mount to a slow walk, following the line of markers. Then he stopped. "Devil's wire!" He spit the words out with a curse. "And brand new."

Invented in France in 1860 to protect shrubs, and consisting only of twisted strands of sheet metal, it wasn't until 1867, when barbs were added, that barbed wire became known in the United States. And not until 1876, in Texas, was it used for fencing cattle. Until 1894, because of its high cost, not many ranchers in central Oregon even considered using "bobbed", or "bob" wire as many called it. But in 1895, so many manufacturers were producing this type of wire that the price fell from $12.00 to $1.80 per hundred-weight, making it affordable for even the smallest landowner. It became so popular in Crook County that Wurzweiler & Thompson Mercantile in Prineville carried over two dozen different manufactured brands. Ray Thompson, a clerk at Wurzweiler's, had told Tom there were over five hundred types to choose from, if a man were so inclined. He also said the wire had earned its sobriquet "devil's wire" in Texas during the severe winters of '85-'86 and '86-'87, when thousands of cattle, moving south to escape the bitterly cold north winds, were trapped against the hide-tearing wire and froze to death.

Tom had fenced some of his land with barbed wire, but he used the less cruel Glidden type, not the vicious inch-long double barbs he now saw. Why would anyone use that type of hide-tearing wire here? And whose is it? The land inside the cattleman's boundary was government, not private, land.

Puzzled to find it here, and curious to know where it went, he followed the glistening strands down the draw. When the fence turned north, a frown creased his forehead. He looked down at the dog. "Hiner, if that doesn't stop this side of the next ridge, it's going to cross over onto our land." He rode on.

The wire crossed over a mound of rocks and continued. Anger flushed Tom's face. The rocks marked the corner of the northwest section of Triple C land, and the fence was now on his property and well away from the dead line. He jerked his horse to a stop, but his eyes continued to follow the wire as it circled a field of Idaho fescue and disappeared into the woods. If it continued beyond the hill, it would cross Wolf Creek, which was also on Triple C land.

Tom spurred his horse. When he crested the hill, he swore aloud. The wire did cross the creek. Not only that, there were cattle grazing on the hillside and they were on Triple C land. Somewhere between forty or fifty of them. Tom strained his eyes to make out the brand, but they were facing away from him. They were Durham's, like his own, and fat and sleek. "Hiner..." He had started to say whoever owned the cattle had good taste in breeds and they were well taken care of, but the words stuck in his throat as a cow turned and he saw whose brand it was. His body grew rigid and a band of tightness gripped his chest. They were 3C cattle, grazing on pasture he had not intended to use until fall when his herd would be pulled out of summer graze in the Ochoco Mountains.

Anger turned to fury. Whoever it was that had rustled his cattle, fenced in his land and was using his grass must have known no one from the 3C would likely check this remote section of Canyon Creek until late summer.

Tom threw himself out of the saddle and fumbled with the buckle on his left saddlebag. Reaching inside, he withdrew a pair of wire clippers and in three steps was at the fence, cutting the twisted strands. He didn't have time to return to the ranch for help as it would be dark by the time he got there and back. But with Hiner, who had become a good cattle dog, he should be able to get his cows home before the light gave out. Then, tomorrow, he would come back to see if he could find out who was behind all of this.

Just as Tom was lifting the saddlebag cover to return the cutters, Hiner began to growl. He glanced at the dog, who was crouched and trembling. The hair at the back of Hiner's neck bristled straight up, and a series of deep guttural sounds rolled from his throat. Tom glanced in the direction of the animal's gaze, which was toward a heavy stand of pine on a knoll to the left of the peacefully grazing cattle. Had he been a second late, he would have missed the slight movement that caught his eye. It could have been caused by a sage hen, a skulking coyote or even a nervous rabbit, but Hiner was not likely to react as he was for any of these. Slowly and carefully, without taking his eyes from the spot, Tom removed his Winchester from its saddle scabbard, jacked a shell in the chamber and gathered the reins in his left hand. Keeping the horse positioned between himself and the dense timber, he moved forward. As he did he whispered the word "follow" to Hiner, whose growls had turned to high-pitched whines.

Sweat drenched Tom's shirt as he crossed open land. He crouched still lower behind his horse's shoulder. The .30 -.30 rifle was cocked and gripped firmly in his right hand, supported by the seat of the saddle. He had place his hat over the saddle horn to give his face further concealment, and was peering beneath its brim and over the horse's mane at the spot he had seen something move.

He proceeded in this manner until he reached the shaded cover of timber. Only then did he stop to listen. Hearing nothing, he glanced at Hiner who was intently watching his face for a word or gesture of instruction. Tom knelt below the horse's flank and gave a slight nod and jerk of the head. At this signal, Hiner began a series of widening semi-circles. He was twenty yards in front of Tom when he stopped, dropped to the ground and froze. Knowing he had spotted something, Tom left the cover of his horse and ran in a crouch to where Hiner was waiting. It took him only a second to see what the dog had found—a low depression in the soil where a body had lain, and tracks running away. As Tom knelt to examine the fresh prints, his breath caught. They were identical to the ones he had seen the day he found Finnegan's body. The imprints were large, and the indentations in the dirt showed they had been made by a man of great weight. There was also a wedge-shaped mark in the right boot heel.

As Tom started to rise, a shadow passed over him. He jerked his head up in time to see an ox-like figure hurtling toward him. Light glistened from a wicked foot-long blade that was pointed at his belly. Instinctively, Tom threw up an arm to protect himself, but he was off balance and as he stumbled backward the knife entered his body. As he fell, he caught a flash of fur and heard Hiner's enraged cry as the animal leaped up at the mountain of a man who was drawing his arm back for a final thrust. Tom struggled to his knees, feeling for the open wound. Finding it, he tried to staunch the gush of warm blood with both hands, realizing that if he lost consciousness he would either bleed to death or be at the mercy of his assailant. But shouts, the yelp of a dog, shots and a piercing scream all blended together as he pitched forward and fell into the darkness of a swirling, black void.

CHAPTER 10

The eight apparitions were back. Silently, they faced him, then in unison, raised their reins and guided their horses until he was completely surrounded. Their movements were slow and deliberate, and when they had completed their circle they stopped. Slowly, Tom reached for the gun in his holster. Sweat poured down his face, drenching his collar and shirt as he felt emptiness where his Colt should have been. The dead riders' faces distorted into hideous grins, then a strange laughter pealed from their throats. One brayed like a donkey. Another howled like a coyote announcing his kill. Suddenly, as if on signal, the laughing stopped and the faces turned sullen.

Two of the riders parted and a white-haired figure was pushed to his knees in front of Tom. A hangman's noose hung from the man's neck. None of the riders looked at him. It was as if he didn't exist. Instead, they stared at Tom, and with such intensity he became dizzy and confused. The loose end of the rope was thrown over the branch of a stunted pine tree whose top had been split and blackened by lightning. The shadowy form holding the rope's end pulled out the slack, forcing the kneeling man's head up. Tom gasped and fought for breath. It was Clay Howard, and the rider who held the rope was Frank Allen. With an evil grin, Allen wrapped the rope around his saddlehorn and backed his horse until Clay Howard was pulled to his feet. Howard's arms stretched toward Tom.

Tom tried to rush forward to help, but his legs wouldn't move. He strained to lift one foot, then the other, but they were locked in place as if bolted to the ground. In a frenzy, he fought to raise his arms, but they, too, wouldn't respond. As Howard was dragged into the air, Tom screamed at Allen to stop but the only cry to escape from his lips was a high-pitched moan. He closed his eyes to shut out the sight of Howard, whose face seemed ready to explode from the pressure of compressed blood. As he did, a giant hand reached for his own face. With a stifled cry, he struggled to break free, but a strong force pinned him to the ground. His eyes flew open. Circling faces swam above him. Then, unexpectedly, the hand that had been choking him turned gentle and the faces that looked down on him came into focus. The hand held a cool cloth and was wiping perspiration from his forehead. He shuddered with relief as he recognized Rachel Williams, and beside her, Reub Hassler.

Rachel and Reub glanced at each other worriedly, then back at Tom. "Guess I can let go of your shoulders now," Reub said apologetically. "You were starting to thrash around and I didn't want you to tear your wound open."

Tom tried to speak, but no words came. Only a slight croak managed to escape from lips that were parched and cracked.

"Don't try to talk now. Take a sip of water if you can," Rachel said as she gently lifted his head and held a glass to his mouth. Tom drank greedily, spilling the cool liquid down his chin and onto his neck. As Rachel set the glass down, he managed to barely whisper, "More." She patted his arm. "Later. The doctor said not too much at one time. You can have another drink soon. Then some hot soup."

Tom tried to nod, but the effort was too great. His eyes closed and he drifted off, this time into a peaceful, dreamless sleep.

Several times during the night he woke and asked for water. Each time Rachel was there. "What's she doing here?" he wondered, but before he could think on it he heard himself softly snoring, and was asleep again.

As dawn's first light entered the room, Tom woke. His fever was gone, and his bedding and nightshirt were dry. But he ached in every joint. His head was propped up with two pillows, so he was able to take stock of the room. It was obvious that he was in his own bed, but he had no idea how he got there. The last thing he remembered was a mountain of a man bearing down on him with a knife in his hand. And blood. There was lots of blood. Tom's fingers gently searched his body until he found the bandages tied around his stomach. He turned cold. He had seen what happened to men with a stomach wound. They couldn't eat or drink and they suffered horribly before they died.

After a brief moment of panic, rational thought returned. He had taken water, apparently with no ill effect, and there was pain but it wasn't excruciating. His tense muscles relaxed, and as they did, one arm fell over the side of the bed. He felt fur, then the fur moved and a tongue licked his hand. Hiner. It must be Hiner. He started to roll on his side to see, but a sharp pain made him gasp and fall back onto his pillows. The happy thump of a tail against the bed and the vibratory shake of a dog that has just gotten up, along with a further nuzzle of his hand, left no doubt in his mind that it was indeed Hiner.

As the light in the room grew, Tom turned his head toward the night stand and saw there was someone else with him. It was Rachel Williams. She was asleep in a chair by his bed. Her hand lay close to his on the quilt cover, and her head rested at an awkward angle against the back of an old rocking chair Ellie Howard had given him. He recalled Ellie's words as he watched Rachel. "Every home should have a rocking chair for the ladies, Tom. Even yours." For a brief moment, his eyes misted as he thought of Clay and Ellie, then they turned to concern as he studied Rachel. The appearance of good health that always radiated from her had been replaced by a look of total exhaustion. She was much thinner than when he had last seen her, and her usually tanned face looked sallow and peaked in the early morning light. Dark circles under her eyes accentuated a face that looked drawn and tired.

How long had she been here? It was obvious that she had been taking care of him. He remembered his first drink of water and the fact she had been there to help him throughout the night. How had she known he was hurt, and again that nagging feeling came over him—how bad was he hurt? These and a dozen other questions flooded his mind as he tried to recall what had happened.

A convulsive jerk of Rachel's body, caused by fitful sleep and a muscle spasm, brought his attention back to her. He didn't know how she came to be here, but he was glad she was. It was comforting to know she had been watching over him. Without thinking, he reached out and took her hand.

Immediately she became fully alert and turned to him. Her deep violet eyes anxiously searched his face, then she let out a long breath. What she saw brought tears of relief. As they ran down her face, she tried to brush them away with the back of her hand. She rose and leaned closer to place her head on his chest. "Oh Tom, if you only knew how I have prayed your fever would break, and that you would get well. I've ..." subdued sobs choked off the rest of her words.

Awkwardly, Tom tried to comfort her. He patted her back and held her as tightly as his wound would allow.

"This won't do," she exclaimed, sitting up and dabbing her eyes with a handkerchief she had pulled from a sleeve. "What would Reub think if he saw us like this."

Tom reached for both of her hands and held them in his own. "I don't care what Reub thinks. Or anyone else for that matter. I only care what we think."

Color rose to her cheeks as she straightened, smoothing out her dress as she did so. Then she bent over and quickly kissed him on the forehead. "Well, the first thing that needs to be done is to get some hot broth in you. And, most definitely, the second thing is to see that you get a shave." She brushed back a lock of hair that had fallen over her face, paused a moment to smile down at him, then left the room.

After Rachel had gone, Tom ran a hand over his chin. She was right about the shave. He had a good growth of bristly whiskers. I must smell like a pig, too, he thought. But, as he examined his bedding, he saw it was fresh and clean. The sheets had been ironed, as had the night shirt he was wearing. The cook never bothered to iron anything, and it was obvious that someone had giving him a bath. His face turned beet red when he realized who it must have been.

A low cough caught his attention. He turned his head to see Reub Hassler standing in the door frame, nervously fiddling with his hat. "Guess you're going to live after all," his foreman said, placing a weather-stained Stetson on the seat of a nearby straight chair. Reub entered and sat on the side of the bed. "How're you feeling?" he asked.

"Sore, and weak as a kitten," Tom replied.

"Doc Belknap said that was to be expected." At Tom's questioning look, Reub continued. "Don't suppose you remember, you being out of your head and all, but he's been here to check on you three times."

"Three times!" Tom exclaimed. "How long have I been lying here?"

"All week. The county marshall was here, too. He wanted full particulars on what happened."

"So do I, Reub. Everything I remember is just a blur: A dark shadow, then a giant of a man coming at me full blast, with what looked like the world's biggest toad sticker in his hand. I tried to stop him," Tom felt at the bandages, "but he caught me off guard. How come he didn't finish the job, and how did I get home?"

Reub shifted uncomfortably. He ran a work-calloused hand over the back of his neck, then glanced around the room. His eyes settled on his fingers, which he examined carefully. "I guess Randy and I brought you home," he said, not looking up.

Randy Baxter was one of the Triple C ranch hands. Tom looked puzzled. "That answers the last half of my question, but it doesn't explain why I'm not pushing up daisies."

Before Reub could respond, Rachel entered the room holding a tray which she handed to Reub. "Hold this while I prop up his pillows, would you please Reuben."

Reub's face flushed crimson at hearing his full Christian name but he kept quiet, guessing he had better get used to it when she was around.

After making Tom comfortable, Rachel placed the tray on his lap and tucked a linen napkin under his chin. The tray contained a bowl of chicken broth, a cup of steaming black coffee and a small vase that held a colorful bouquet of wild desert flowers. Both Tom and Reub looked at the flowers, then at each other, but neither said a word.

The rich smell of the broth made Tom realize how hungry he was. He reached for the spoon, dipped it into the soup, and lifted it to his lips. His hand began to tremble so violently that he spilled its contents on the napkin. Without a word, Rachel took the utensil from his hand and began feeding him.

When the bowl was empty, Tom leaned back. "Thanks," he said gratefully. "I've had to spoon feed calves. Now I know how they must feel." He paused. "I think I can handle the coffee myself if I use both hands." His eyes focused on Reub. "Now then, Mr. Hassler." He emphasized the Mr. "I believe you have deliberately avoided answering my question as to how I got here."

Rachel spoke up. She had heard the question asked when she entered the room from the hall. "Reuben thinks he disobeyed your orders by following you and sending someone else to fix the pasture fence. I for one say it's a good thing he did, and I don't think you should criticize him for it." A spark of anger flashed from her eyes, which Tom immediately recognized as a danger signal. "You tell him the rest, Reuben."

"Mrs. Williams is right, Tom. I figured when you heard what I did, you'd feel I wasn't a man of my word." He brightened somewhat. "But, at the breakfast table when you said you was old enough to take care of yourself and walked away, I guess you didn't hear me say that was probably true but I was going to follow you anyway."

Tom suppressed a grin. "I guess I didn't Reub, in which case you had every right to do what you did."

His actions justified, Reub visibly brightened and squared his shoulders. He didn't see Rachel, who was standing behind him, cover her mouth to hide a smile.

Reub continued. "When you were out of sight, I grabbed Randy and we lit out after you. We was probably as surprised as you to see the barbwire fence. Particularly when it crossed 3C land. We got to where you had cut the fence in time to see you go into the trees, hiding behind your horse, with your saddle gun out." Reub closed his left hand and rubbed his nose several times with the knuckle of his forefinger. He looked thoughtful as he organized his words. "We spent a minute too long thinking on what to do before we decided to ride across open ground and follow you. We got there just as you took the stab. We yelled and got off a couple of shots, hoping to scare your attacker off just as Hiner jumped him." Reub slowly shook his head. "That dog plumb tore the man's throat apart." He glanced respectfully in Hiner's direction. "I'd shore hate to have that mutt get mad at me."

Tom also looked at Hiner, who had heard his name mentioned and was happily wagging his tail, looking from face to face. Tom spoke to the dog, who rolled on its back, tail still thumping. "I guess that evens the score, doesn't it boy?"

"The marshall said the man was a no-good drifter." Reub seemed eager to continue the account of what had happened now that he knew Tom had forgiven him. "His name was Chad Schneller, and he was wanted for cattle rustling. When he was a child he fell off his horse and landed on his head. Never was right after that. About ten years back he joined up with the Roslyn Robbers, but even they couldn't handle him. They ran him off after he started shooting rustled cows for no good reason at all. Know what Schneller told us before he died?" Reub's face squinched up at the memory.

Tom shook his head.

"He could hardly talk on account of what Hiner did to his throat, but he swore at us for being on his land. Gargled through the blood that he had the biggest cattle empire in the country and he was going to hang us for trespassing. When I told Doc Belknap what his last words were, the doc expressed the opinion that he must have been suffering from dee-lusions of grandeur, whatever that is."

After looking at Tom expectantly to see if his boss might tell him what the words meant, but getting no response, Reub continued. "The marshall said as far as he could tell, Schneller had no connection at all with the sheepshooters and that he probably left the note at Finnegan's shack to throw us off track by laying the blame on them."

Tom took a sip of coffee as he thought this over. Then he nodded. A great weariness came over him. "Being touched in the head explains why he put barbwire on our land. No one in his right mind would do that. Or keep rustled cattle in plain sight." He touched his bandages. He had to ask, even though he dreaded what he might hear. "What damage did he do with the knife?"

"He ran that pig-sticker into your side and cut open six inches of hide, but Doc Belknap was able to sew it back up. Your arm and ribs deflected his blow so most of the damage came from loss of blood and infection. We suspect the blade he used on you was the same one he used to skin coyotes.

80

We found fresh hides in a cave he slept in. Nobody figured you would live. Nobody but Rachel, that is. She hasn't left your side since we brought you in."

Reub's voice was beginning to take on a hollow sound, as if he were talking from a well. I must ask Rachel how she came to be here. And thank her. This was Tom's last thought as he drifted back to sleep.

The room was filled with light. Both bedroom windows were opened wide, letting in the smells and sounds of a warm spring day. A gentle afternoon breeze stirred the freshly-starched chintz curtains. They rose and fell in gentle dipping motions.

Tom stretched lazily. The food had done him a world of good. Remembering how Rachel had nursed and watched over him, he spoke her name and turned his head toward the rocking chair to thank her properly. A pang of disappointment hit him when he saw she wasn't there. With a grunt, he rolled on his side and threw back the bedcovers. A week on his back was long enough. It was time to quit lollygagging and get up. As he tried to rise to a sitting position, the room began to spin. He would have fallen forward onto the floor if two massive arms hadn't caught him.

"Whoa, boss. According to Reub, Doc Belknap says you're supposed to stay put for another week."

Tom saw six faces spinning around each other. Then as the vertigo slowly went away he recognized Unk Tanner, one of his riders. "Well, maybe another day then, Unk," he said hoarsely as he fell back onto the pillows.

"Reub posted me outside the door," Tanner explained. "When I heard you call out for Miz Williams, I knew you wuz awake, so came in to see if you needed anything. About that time you were ready to take a belly flop on the floor."

"I would have, too, if you hadn't caught me."

"Yep, that's a fact," Tanner said, adding, "Miz Williams went to get a few hours sleep. She told me to wake her when you came to."

"No need to do that, Unk. Let her sleep. She needs it and she's earned it." He frowned at Tanner. "Don't you have anything better to do than act like a darned nursemaid?"

81

"Nope. Not until Reub tells me different." He shifted a bulging wad of tobacco and searched for the spittoon. Tom usually kept one handy for those who chewed, but it was gone. The eyes of both men looked for it, and it was during this search that Tom became fully aware of the changes in his room A vase of meadow larkspur decorated the table by his over-stuffed chair, and the newly woven Indian rug from the guest bedroom was by his bed on the bare wood floor. Everything was clean and neatly arranged, including the extra quilt from the closet that had been washed and lay folded on the chest at the foot of the bed.

Tanner read his glance and shrugged. He was about to leave the room to find a substitute spittoon when Reub entered.

"He been behaving himself, Unk?"

"You'll have to ask him."

"Not necessary. I can see by his peaked look that he tried to get up." For Tom's benefit he added, "The doc said he'd probably keel over if he did." He peered closely at Tom. "Did you fall out of bed?"

Tom answered sheepishly. "No, Unk caught me as I was about to."

Reub nodded his head in satisfaction. "I don't think he'll try that again, Unk. You missed dinner. Go on down to the kitchen and ask cookie to fix you something. If he gives you a bad time, tell him I said it was all right. Then you can get back to your chores."

As Tanner left, Reub stood at Tom's bedside, his fists planted on his hips. "Give me your word you won't try that again or I'll send somebody else up to baby-sit."

"You have it." Tom knew he had lost the argument, but he had some questions that needed answering.

"Reub, was Rachel here when you brought me in?

"She was."

"And has she been nursing me ever since?"

"She has."

"I see she's done some rearranging." Tom thought this would bring a chuckle of amusement from Reub. Instead, he was taken aback by his foreman's angry response.

"She's done a little tidying up, I reckon, but she's also taken care of you day and night for a week, watching over you and fretting and getting no more than a wink or two of sleep, and then only because she's too exhausted to stay awake. Half sick for worrying whether you would make it or not. Even had the cook kill a chicken every day, so you would have fresh broth when you came to." Reub paused to catch his breath. "She was the only one thought you would get well. Doc Belknap said you had little chance of making it, what with the fever rackin' your body like it was. So to keep her mind busy, she fixed up your room some. Lord knows it needed it, anyway."

Reub stood there, his mouth open, surprised at his own outburst and drained by it.

Tom spoke gently, knowing the pressure his friend had been under. "I know, Reub. I wasn't being critical. I appreciate the care and concern you both have given me."

"Just thought you should know the facts," Reub said gruffly, embarrassed that he had lost control of his emotions.

"I appreciate hearing them." Tom paused, then asked, "Did Rachel tell you how she came to be here when you brought me in?"

"Yep."

"And?"

"It had something to do with the sheepkillers. She wanted to get your thinking before she headed for Salem."

Tom's pulse quickened. "What happened?"

Reub's jaw tightened. "Rather than run it through second hand, I'll let her tell it to you in her own words."

CHAPTER 11

After Reub left, Tom drifted back to sleep. Four hours later, a gentle rap on the door woke him. He stretched lazily, then tested his side for soreness by raising an arm. He moved too quickly and the result was a searing stab of pain which caused him to answer gruffly, "Come on in. There's no need to knock, no one else does." When he saw who entered, he could have bitten his tongue.

"Well, well, we must be getting better. The doctor said when you started to complain that would mean you're on the road to recovery."

It was Rachel. Tom's eyes widened as he stared open-mouthed at her. Sleep had done wonders. The darkness under her eyes and the pallid look on her face had been replaced with a glow of radiant beauty. She had washed and arranged her hair, which was now tied back with a bright red velveteen ribbon, and her clothes rustled with freshness. He stammered an apology, which ended in a mumble. "I, I didn't know who it was. I mean..., what a dumb thing to say. I guess I..."

She laughed at his discomfort and placed the tray of food she was holding on a nearby table. "Sit up and I'll fix your pillows." As she leaned over him, a hint of lavender filled his nostrils. He reached up and held her arms, her face just inches from his. "I know," she said. The tips of her fingers brushed his lips. "I know."

She rose and brought the tray to him. It held a bowl of soup, two slices of heavily buttered fresh bread, four thick slices of lean bacon and a steaming cup of black coffee. He ate like a starved animal. When he had finished, he glanced at his empty plates, then at Rachel. A satisfied smile filled his face, and he sighed happily. "That was pretty good for a start. What's the main course?"

She retrieved the tray with a laugh. "You just finished it." Then, in answer to his mock frown, "But I'm taking orders for breakfast."

"In that case I'll have a platter size steak smothered in onions and potatoes, about a dozen eggs—fried with their eyes open, a pot of coffee and hot apple pie."

Her skirt swirled around her ankles as she left the room. Over her shoulder she said, "You'd be wiser to expect some mush, a couple of poached eggs, perhaps a biscuit or two and maybe, just maybe, a small piece of steak." As she walked down the hall, the echo of her voice came back to him, "Don't go away, I'll be right back." In a few minutes she returned with a basin of steaming hot water in which floated a washcloth. Wrapped in a towel she carried under one arm was a shaving mug and brush, a straight razor and a strop.

Tom watched as she neatly arranged each item, after which, she placed the towel around his neck. Next, she gingerly reached in the basin and pulled the cloth out by one corner with her fingertips. Carefully, she wrung it out, shifting it quickly from hand to hand to dissipate the heat. "Lie flat and brace yourself," she said as she dropped it over his face.

"Yow!" he cried. "That's hot."

"Of course it's hot. Cold water isn't going to soften those barbs."

After a minute she pulled the cloth from his face and dropped it into the basin. "One more time and I'll lather you up."

Tom nervously watched as she picked up the razor. "You're not intending to shave me yourself, are you? Have you ever handled a straight raz..." His words were cut off as the cloth again dropped over his face and mouth.

He couldn't see, but he heard the razor being stropped.

"If you were going to ask if I have ever shaved anyone before, the answer is yes. In the weeks before my husband Paul died, I shaved him every morning. In fact," her face took on a mischievous look that Tom couldn't see, "I only cut his throat twice. Fortunately, I was able to get the bleeding stopped each time."

Tom tore the cloth from his face and stared at her in horror. "You mean you really cut . . ." he stopped when he saw the expression of delight on her face and realized he was being teased.

After Rachel had lathered his face, Tom wiped the soapy foam from his lips with a finger so he could talk. "Reub said you stopped by to tell me something about the sheepkillers, and that's how you came to be here when they brought me back."

Rachel picked up the razor and brought it to his face. Silently, she shaved one side, then the other, occasionally rinsing whisker speckled suds from the blade as she worked. After she had finished his neck, she answered. "The news is not good, Tom. The day before you were hurt, John Alexander shot and killed Lem McCarthy for crossing his land with a band of sheep."

"But McCarthy is a cowman, like Alexander," Tom exclaimed. "How many sheep was he running?"

"That's the tragedy. He just had a small flock, not more than a dozen."

"Where did it happen?"

"On Buck Creek. Where Alexander's property ends."

Tom stared out the window, lost in thought. Then he turned to her. "Nowhere near the dead line, then. There's always been bad blood between those two. If it hadn't of been sheep, I suppose something else would have triggered a confrontation."

Rachel's silence drew his attention back to her face. He sat up, took the razor from her hand and placed it by the basin. Then he took her hand and held it in both of his. "There's more." It was a statement, not a question.

She nodded. "Art Wagner was running a larger band of sheep across the dead line, two miles above Wolf Creek—where it runs into Beaver—and was attacked by nine masked riders. Two of his herders were shot and most of his sheep were either killed or wounded. And there's more. Charlie Winnek..."

"The druggist in Prineville?" Tom interrupted sharply.

"Yes," Rachel's lips set, "he, his wife and eleven-year-old daughter were camping out Sunday before last below Gray's Ridge. He has a timber claim there. They were fishing when they heard shots nearby. Not knowing what was happening, they got in their buckboard and headed back to the cabin Charlie was building. Halfway to it, they saw a group of unmasked riders firing into a band of several hundred sheep. About a quarter of a mile later they passed that half-soddy, half-log dugout that is used as a sheepherder's summer shelter. There were four men there, all holding rifles. One rode out and told Charlie that if either he or any of his family mentioned their names, it would go hard on all of them." Rachel's jaw set. "The man further warned him that if they didn't keep their eyes straight ahead until they reached their cabin, they would be seeing more dead sheep and a dead herder and his dogs. He told them when they got there to pack up and head for home. When they got to town, they were to tell the editor of the paper about the dead herder and sheep, and that in any stories he might write now or in the future, he is to change the name of Gray's Ridge to Dead Sheep Ridge."

"Did Charlie recognize any of the men?"

"He told the sheriff he didn't, but his daughter was with him and when she blurted out one was a teenager who was dating a girlfriend of hers, he turned white and clamped a hand over her mouth."

"I can't say as I blame him," Tom said. "I imagine he's scared stiff."

Rachel squeezed his hand. "Tom, this happened in Crook County. I've heard from sources I trust that there's talk of forming a sheepkillers group here. And one in Lake County, too."

"Have you discussed this with the others?" Tom asked, referring to the sheepmen who were at the Triple C with Rachel when they came to ask his advice.

Rachel's head snapped up. "Oh, yes," she replied sarcastically. "We had another meeting, and the decision was to wait and see how this plays out." Her voice became shriller and rose an octave. "To see how this plays out!" she repeated. "How do they think this will play out? It's obvious to anyone with an ounce of sense that it's only going to get worse."

Tom waited for the moment of anger to pass, then asked what she felt should be done.

"The same thing I said at the meeting. That the best bet we have is to get the state capitol involved." Rachel rose from the bed and paced the room, her hands tightly gripped her elbows. "I was on my way to see you, to find out what you might have heard, and to discuss what I was going to do, when Reub brought you home. When I saw the condition you were in it suddenly didn't seem that important anymore and I put it out of my mind." She

87

stopped, ramrod straight, a decision made. "I'll stay two more days, then I'll return home and pack. John Mitchell, the president of the state senate, is from this area and has been trying to do something about the problem. I'll work through him to get to the governor. It's important to know where he stands." Rachel's voice became more intense. "He'll have to listen. The wool industry is a vital part of this state's growth. There are over two million sheep in Oregon now, compared to 600,000 cattle. He can't ignore those figures. All we're asking is the right to be left alone and go about our business in peace. That's only fair, isn't it?" She looked at Tom, hoping he would confirm how she felt, and what she was going to do.

Tom knew better than to argue with Rachel, considering the mood she was in, but he also knew there would be a lot more cattle if the winter of 1889 and '90 had not been so devastating. Ninety-five percent of all of the cattle in the state had died, leaving those ranchers who managed to survive frightened and angry. This was one reason many cattlemen had taken the stand they did against sheep. They feared the loss of precious grassland and pasture that was necessary to rebuild their herds. He had suffered as well, but instead of making him bitter it had increased his understanding of the woolgrowers' problems. They were only trying to survive and make a living, too. In fact, many of them had been cattlemen whose losses forced them to turn to sheep to feed their families.

"Rachel," he replied softly, "I can't suggest any other course of action. What you say makes sense, and for sure it's better than sitting around moaning and groaning and doing nothing."

True to her word, two days later Rachel was ready to leave. By now, Tom was up and walking, so he accompanied her to the veranda where her horse was tethered and waiting. He didn't want to see her go, and desperately wanted to tell her how he felt before she left. But he had kept his feelings to himself for too many years, so they remained bottled up inside him now. He also knew this is what she felt she had to do and he respected that.

They stood together, each trying to find the right words, then Rachel broke the silence that separated them. "I'll miss you, Tom. Take care of yourself and don't overdo."

Still unable to say what he wanted to say, he awkwardly replied, "I'll miss you, too, Rachel. And all of that good nursing. Good luck at the state capitol."

"Thank you, Tom. I'll keep in touch." She hesitated briefly, then reached up to touch his face. Just as quickly, she turned away, went to her horse and lifted herself into the saddle.

As Rachel rode down the dusty lane that led to the main gate, a mantle of loneliness fell over Tom. His spirits rose, just for a moment, when Rachel reached the wooden bridge that crossed the creek, stopped, and turned to wave.

CHAPTER 12

In the southeastern corner of Crook County, a few miles from the small desert town of Fife, William Walter "Bill" Brown, also known as "Wagontire Brown", was being interviewed by a reporter from *The Portland Oregonian*, the state's largest newspaper. The newsman, who had travelled first by stage, then by horseback to get to this remote spot, was on a special assignment. He had been sent by his publisher to get full particulars on Brown's acquittal for the murder of one Johnny Overstreet. Overstreet had been an employee of Riley and Hardin's giant OO ranch that spread throughout Harney County. Brown lived in the corner of Crook County that lay adjacent to Harney, and much of Brown's grazing land—particularly the area around Wagontire mountain—was in Harney County.

Brown was in his late thirties. He was six feet tall, slender, well built and broad-shouldered. A balding head topped a pleasant, well-proportioned face. His nose was straight and Romanesque, and his blue eyes normally held a glint of hidden humor.

Born in Wisconsin, where he graduated from college, Brown migrated to California, and became a teacher. Later he moved to the high desert country of eastern Oregon to raise horses and sheep. A few years after his arrival, he became the largest and most respected supplier of horses in the country. His Horseshoe Bar brand was known throughout the world. He supplied mounts to the U.S. Cavalry as well as South Africa for use in the Boer War.

Bill Brown was also a religious man. He didn't drink, smoke or swear and the men who worked for him, as well as those who knew him, said the strongest language they had ever heard him use was "shucks" or "confound it," the latter his most favorite expression.

Although he was single, Brown planned to marry. He made these intentions known and said when he decided to settle down he wanted a strong and healthy younger woman who would provide him with a large family. "At least six or seven sons, with children arriving one a year, like the ewes in my flocks." Toward this end, Brown built a large home on Buck Creek, just west of Fife, that was the equal of any of the palatial homes in the more cosmopolitan city of Portland. In the desert area where he lived, it was considered a mansion of great proportion. All of his neighbors got their water either from wells or creeks, but Brown's 14-room house had its own water system that provided for numerous indoor bathrooms as well as the kitchen. In addition to its vast number of private bedrooms, the house had a palatial ballroom, a huge living room and a large dining area. Directly over the spacious kitchen and utility room, he built one large room that was to be used as a nursery when he married and started his "flock of young ones."

In addition to the house, Brown's Buck Creek Ranch included a number of wool sheds, a stable, several storehouses, a blacksmith shop, a number of outbuildings and a mercantile store that offered staples and dry goods to his hired help as well as local homesteaders and ranchers.

The interview was being held in Brown's office, which also served as his bedroom. Paned glass windows stretched the length of one wall, facing northeast, toward the Blue Mountains—a sight Brown never tired of. He had had so much difficulty in trying to decide whether his office should have the view, or if it should be from his bedroom, that he finally told the workers building the house, "Confound it, let's combine my bedroom with an office, so I can see the mountains all day long."

After a hearty ranch breakfast, he and Jim Crowell, the reporter from *The Oregonian,* were seated in heavy leather chairs that faced the view. Brown sipped a cup of black coffee as the reporter arranged his notes on the coffee table that separated the two men. A roaring fire had been built in the natural stone fireplace to take the chill from the room. The fire not only added warmth, it also helped provide an air of relaxed informality.

"Mr. Brown," the reporter started, "before we get to the circumstances that . . ."

"Bill," Brown held up a hand. "Call me Bill. I don't have much truck with that 'Mister' stuff."

"Bill, then," the reporter replied, somewhat uncomfortable to be addressing a man as important as W.W. Brown in such a familiar manner. He hurried on. "I was going to say, before we get to the circumstances that led to the death of Johnny Overstreet, I'm sure our readers would be interested in knowing more about the man who has been called both the 'Horse King of the Northwest' and 'America's Horse King'."

At Brown's nod of agreement, the reporter went on. "You are also called 'Wagontire Brown'. Why is that?"

"I suppose it's because that's where my two brothers, Bob and George, and I got our start. When we first came to Oregon, we put up a cabin on the northern side of Wagontire Mountain, pooled what little money we had, and bought a few head of sheep that we put to graze there."

The reporter glanced up from his note pad, a questioning frown on his face. "Wagontire is an unusual name. Is it because the mountain is shaped like a wagon wheel?"

"No, and that's an interesting story," Brown replied. "Jim Miller, the brother of Joaquin Miller, the poet, had a blacksmith shop in Prineville some years back—before he started running freight from The Dalles. He heard about some immigrants who had camped on the mountain for a spell. Their teams had given out, so they had to abandon their wagons. As Miller needed iron to use in his shop, he hitched up a mule team and headed out of town to see if he could find them. When someone asked him where he was going, he replied, 'To that mountain where the wagontires are.' The name Wagontire stuck and has been used ever since." Brown stroked his face with the slender fingers of his left hand. "I guess because I got my start there, and still run sheep on and around the mountain, is how I came to pick up the nickname 'Wagontire'."

Brown rose and added more juniper wood to the fire, stirring the coals as he did. Then he returned to his chair and comfortably settled back into its oversize cushions. "It might interest you to know how Bear Creek came to get its name. It was because of Miller, too, and happened on the same trip."

Brown took the confused look on Crowell's face as an invitation to continue and went on. "That's the big creek that runs south of the Maury Mountains and empties into Crooked River," he explained, then continued. "On his way back, about thirty miles south of Prineville, Jim stopped to camp overnight. In the early hours of the morning, he felt a tug at his bed covers which woke him up. By the light of the moon, he saw a grizzly bear pawing through his grub box. One of the bear's hind feet was tangled in Jim's bedroll and that was what was doing the pulling. When the bear found the bacon he was after, he wandered off with it and the blanket, too. Jim named the place Bear Creek, and that's what it's been called ever since." A huge smile lit Brown's face. "Some of his friends thought he'd misnamed it, and felt if the truth were known, it really should be called 'wet-his-pants creek.' " He chuckled heartily at his own telling of the story.

Seeing that the reporter had stopped taking notes, and was listening politely, Brown grinned sheepishly. "Shucks, I guess I wandered some."

"No, learning about Bear Creek was very interesting," Crowell said half-heartedly. "Perhaps I can work it into the story somehow. But let's get back to how you got started. What caused you and your brothers to go from sheep to horses?"

"A matter of survival," Brown said solemnly. "We worked on building our herd until we had several thousand head of sheep. Then the winter of '89 hit early and before we could get them to shelter we lost almost all of them. The following spring we were down to a count of less than three hundred scrawny critters, most of them so weak they could barely stand up. Even at that we did better than most folks," he mused sadly, then continued. "Hoping to make a few dollars to get us by, we corralled some wild Spanish mustangs. I guess we hit the market just right. They brought in four times the money we thought we would get, so we just kept adding more. The market held, then got better, and pretty soon we were on our feet again."

"Wasn't there an incident in Prineville with the county assessor about how many horses you have?" the reporter asked, suppressing a grin.

"Yes, confound it," Brown answered. "His name is Tom Green. Stopped me right on the street one day. Said, 'Bill, my assistant has you down for 800 horses.' When I answered that was about right, he said he thought maybe

I had more than that. So I said, all right, let's make it 1,800. When he frowned and gave me a dark look, I told him I would settle for 2,800." Brown scratched his chin and looked thoughtful. "You know, what with all the horses I have, moving from place to place in Crook, Harney and Lake counties, I really didn't know how many I did have in Crook County at that particular time. It's possible there were only 800, but it's just as likely there could have been as many as 2,800. Truth of the matter is I really didn't know and I told Green that."

"Bill, you have the reputation of being an honest man and this certainly is an example of that. However, it's been said that sometimes you're too honest for your own good because you measure people by your own standards and believe everyone is as trustworthy as you are. I have also heard you were excused from jury duty at one time because of this."

A broad smile creased Brown's face and his eyes sparkled with delight as he recalled the incident in question. "It wasn't jury duty," he exclaimed. "I was to testify at a trial."

The reporter flipped a page of his pad, licked the end of his pencil and looked up. "So what happened?"

Brown leaned forward, clasped his hands together and stared into the fire, mentally organizing his thoughts. After a few moments, he settled back. "A fellow by the name of David Klemish was accused of stealing some of his neighbor's horses. He tried to sell them to me, but he didn't have a receipt of sale for the brand they were carrying. I recognized the slash-bar on their rumps as that of his neighbor, so I felt something might be a little fishy." Brown reached down to pick up his cup and took a swallow of coffee. "I was to testify to the fact that Klemish tried to sell them to me, but when I saw who was serving on the jury I told the judge it wouldn't do any good for me to be a witness because most of the jury were horse thieves themselves. The judge got red in the face, pounded his gavel and said I was dismissed for cause, which was fine with me."

"There are two other stories about your honesty, Bill. One has to do with the general store you run here and the other is about two strangers who were passing through, stopped overnight for a couple of free meals, and ended up getting paid for two days work. Could I have your comments, please?"

"Yes, you may. First off, I'm morally certain that everyone is honest. And I trust them as I would expect them to trust me." Brown's deep frown and set lips gave indication that he was not pleased that anyone might consider he was too honest for his own good, and he wanted Crowell to know this. "In my book, there's no such thing as being too honest. As for the general store," Brown rubbed his bald spot with the tips of his fingers, "I feel duty bound to help my neighbors and the homesteaders in this part of the county. Any goods the store carries come from The Dalles—more than two hundred miles away."

"So you're saying you freight in supplies for them when you bring in your own?" the newsman asked softly, realizing he had come close to offending Bill Brown.

"Sort of. I just buy up what I think they might need, then leave it in the store unattended, and they help themselves to whatever they want."

"But, how do you keep track of what they take?"

"They write it down in a book I keep there for that purpose. Sometimes they're able to pay by the end of the month, sometimes it takes a little longer. When they can pay, they scratch their name off the ledger and put the money in a glass jar under the counter. If they can't pay, I don't bother them because I know they'll come up with the money when they're able."

"But," Crowell asked in amazement, "don't you think some people may take advantage of this and pick up merchandise without writing their name in the book or paying for it?"

"Maybe. But if I knew someone took something he needed and he's having hard times, I wouldn't say anything. That would be between him and his conscience."

"Could I ask you one more question about the store before we get to the cowhands who drew two days pay?"

"Shoot," Brown replied, satisfied that he had convinced Crowell there was no such thing as being too honest.

"Rumor has it that you once ordered a wagonload of shoes—all the same size. Is there any truth to that?"

Brown frowned, then pursed his lips. "Unfortunately, there is. I realize now that I made a mistake, but when I bought them the price just seemed to be too good to turn down. All but a few pair are still sitting out there in one of the sheds." Brown waved toward the back of the house where the outbuildings were. "I've been thinking maybe I would give them to the old folks home in Salem. If you'd like to take a few pair back to Portland with you, help yourself." When Crowell didn't accept his offer, he sighed and said, "Well, what's done is done. There's no use crying over spilled milk."

Brown nodded toward Crowell's coffee mug. "Want a refill?" When the reporter shook his head, Brown stood, picked up his own cup and threw the dregs into the fire. He refilled it from a large smoke-stained pot that was resting on the hearth near the coals, took a tentative sip to test how hot the black liquid was, nodded to himself that it was satisfactory, then returned to his chair. "About those two men I paid, I guess you're probably referring to a payday last October. Two punchers were on their way to Montana, looking for work, and stayed overnight." Brown cleared his throat. "It has always been my policy to provide bed and board for any rider passing by, so when they got in the pay line, thinking it was the chow line, I thought they worked for me and asked them how long they had been at the ranch. They said they arrived the day before and spent the night, but flat-out told me they hadn't done any work because they were just passing through and would be gone after breakfast." Brown paused and gave Crowell a hard stare. "They were four-square honest," he drew out the words to make his point, "so I told them I was paying everyone else and as they had been here for two days, I would pay them, too. Which I did."

As the reporter scribbled furiously, Brown leaned back and folded his arms. He waited until the reporter had finished. "I don't see anything wrong with that, do you?" There was a touch of belligerence in his voice, and his eyes took on a hard look.

"Of course not, Bill. It seems to me that was a very Christian thing to do."

This answer seemed to appease Brown, who waved an arm and said, "Enough of this honesty business. Let's get on to your other questions."

Relieved to be off the subject, Crowell said, "Bill, this is a personal question. I'm curious as to why you carry dried prunes and raisins in the same pocket that you carry a bottle of strychnine? This seems somewhat strange to me."

Brown sat erect in his chair, and thrust out his chin. "It's not strange at all," he replied testily. "I'm not much at remembering when it's time to eat, so when I'm out in the hills and get hungry, I have something to nibble on. The strychnine is well corked and I use it on dead sheep and game to kill coyotes. The handiest place to keep both is in my coat pocket where they're easy to get to." Brown glowered at the reporter.

It was obvious to Crowell that his previous questions had offended the lean stockman and he didn't want to irritate him further, but he knew there was one peculiarity Brown had that he was famous for and it couldn't be ignored if his article was going to be complete. He took a deep breath and summoned up his courage. "Bill, it's a well-known fact that you have a habit of writing checks on whatever is handy—the backs of tin can labels, wall paper, old receipt slips, even cowhide. Why not use checks the banks print and supply?"

Brown visibly bristled and eyed the reporter to see if he was being teased. The ticking of the room's grandfather clock and the crackle of the flames in the fireplace, made more noticeable by Brown's prolonged silence, were the only sounds until he curtly replied. "I don't know why people think that's so strange, and laugh about it behind my back." He held up a hand to stop any protest from Crowell. "Oh yes, I know they do." His voice became intense. "Stop and think about it. No law says a check has to be written on paper printed up by a bank for their own convenience. Let me ask you this, and I would like an honest answer. Doesn't it make more sense to use whatever is handy rather than carry a pocketful of checks around with you all of the time; particularly when you never know when you're going to use one?"

Crowell was searching his mind for a diplomatic answer when Brown suddenly jumped to his feet and strode to the center window, his hands clasped behind his back. For several seconds he stared through the wavy, distorted glass then turned to the reporter. "Fiddlesticks," he said. "There's no cause for me to take your questions so personally. You're paid to get a story on me and you're just doing your job. And you are a guest in my home. My apologies, Mr. Crowell. Ask any questions you would like and I will endeavor to answer them honestly and to the best of my ability."

With an inward sigh of relief, the reporter continued. "Thank you, Mr.," he paused and corrected himself, "Bill. You raised sheep first, then horses—for which the Horseshoe Bar is well-known. Now you are back to raising sheep again." Crowell stopped and thumbed through some notes. "County records show you have 12,000 horses and somewhere in the neighborhood of 40,000 sheep. Also claim to at least 34,000 water holes and over one hundred thousand acres of land."

Bill Brown offered a compliment. "I would say you have done your homework well. That sounds about right to me." He turned back to the window and gazed at the shimmering leaves of some poplar trees that lined a nearby creek. His face became serene. "I guess I just like sheep better than horses." He turned again to face Crowell. "They are mentioned often in the Bible, you know. Abel was a keeper of sheep. They are God's own creatures, a gift to us all, watched over by Him." His voice grew softer. "One of my favorite passages from the Good Book is, 'To a close shorn sheep, God gives wind by measure'." Seeing the newsman's blank expression, he explained, "God regulates the cold to a shorn lamb. Jim," he said, his voice rising with emotion, "sheep are the innocents that provide us with food to fill our stomachs and fleece to keep us warm and provide ourselves with cover. I have a great feeling of affection for them. For the time being, they are the children I do not have."

The newsman nodded understandingly, and continued. "As your flocks are growing significantly larger each year, I assume it's safe to surmise this is why you continue to buy land and watering rights."

"Yes, for both my sheep and horses. Most of the land I buy is from homesteaders enticed out west by the railroads who filled their heads with nonsense about how lush and bountiful this part of the country was. Some throw in the towel at the first sight of what they bought into. Others give up after a year or so when they find out the only things that thrive around here are jackrabbits and sagebrush." Brown snorted his contempt for the railroads. "They put good, decent folks through all sorts of misery just to line their pockets with a few pieces of gold." His voice rose in disgust. "The whole thieving lot of them should be horsewhipped. Or better yet, put out here to try and make a living like those people they have cheated and swindled.

"I'll tell you something else," Brown went on, warming up to his subject. "The homesteaders who haven't gone broke yet are being run off their land by big out-of-state corporations like Riley and Hardin's Double O, The Pacific Livestock Company, French-Glenn and others like them. They don't care about people, or the land they acquire. All they're interested in is the bottom line and how much profit they can make while times are good." Brown's voice grew louder. "Take the Swamp Lands Act, for instance. It was enacted to help the settlers reclaim useless swampland, which they bought for a dollar an acre with ten years to pay off their debt. The big outfits in Harney County made out like tall dogs on that one. The settlers got swamp all right, but the California corporations, with the help of their shyster lawyers, bought thousands of acres they claimed was swamp land but wasn't. To top it off, when the homesteaders made something out of the poor land they purchased, their wire was cut, their planted fields trampled by cattle and their wells were fouled. Those that weren't frightened off went broke trying to fight the bogus lawsuits that were filed against them. Others either mysteriously disappeared or were called out and shot down in cold blood." Brown emphasized the word mysteriously. "That's why Peter French was shot and killed by Ed Oliver, a small land owner who had been pushed against the wall by French-Glenn. Oliver only had two choices: fight back or pack up and leave. I don't hold to violence of this sort, but there's a case of poetic justice if ever there was one."

Brown went to his chair and slumped against the cushions, exhausted by his diatribe against those he felt were exploiting decent, law-abiding citizens.

"Bill," the reporter asked, "Johnny Overstreet was with one of the companies you mentioned, wasn't he? This is the story I came to get, so I guess now is as good a time as any to hear what you have to say about the affair."

99

Whereas Brown had been loquacious and open before, his demeanor quickly changed. He now became taciturn and tight-lipped Obviously, the subject was one he did not wish to dwell on, and he would have hurried through the accounting were it not for the probing of the journalist.

"Overstreet was one of the Double O's hired hands." Brown spat out the words Double O as if saying them left a sour taste in his mouth. "He and I tangled over a waterhole west of Wagontire Mountain. I was bringing some sheep to water, and there he was with about forty steers. At my hole."

"But, didn't Riley and Hardin, the owners of the Double O, claim in their suit that the water was on open graze and available to all?" Crowell asked.

Brown came as near to swearing as he did that day at the small pond in the desert when Overstreet pulled a gun and made him crawl through the grass. Overstreet's words were burned in his mind and still rang in his ears: "Brown, you're a low-down snake to claim this water, so get down off that horse and crawl like one before I mistake you for a rattler and shoot you out of the saddle." And Bill Brown had done just that, much to his shame. Even though no one had seen this, or knew about it, the memory of the incident flushed his face with blood.

"Confound them! They are liars to the bone. I bought that parcel of land, and the waterhole on it, from the Willamette Valley and Cascade Mountain Road Company. It was a known fact, and I have the papers to prove it," he said defiantly.

Crowell nodded. "But Overstreet didn't know this, I gather, and was just following orders to water his cattle there."

"If you mean I should have shown him the papers, I don't carry them with me. I'd need a mule team to carry the files of legal documents I have for the land I own," Brown snapped back. He had told Overstreet it was his hole, and felt the Double O rider should have taken him at his word.

"Bill," the reporter asked gently, seeing the anger that consumed the man he was interviewing, "I read the transcript of the trial proceedings. In them you stated you didn't have a gun when Overstreet drew on you, but you were on trial for shooting and killing him."

"That's a moral fact."

"Yet he was shot and killed. And you did it?"

"Another fact, and I've never denied doing it."

"But . . . "

"There are no 'buts' about it," Brown interrupted. "I was taking my sheep to my own water when Overstreet rode up and told me to stay away. When I wouldn't oblige him, he drew on me. I had no choice but to leave. My saddle gun was a quarter of a mile away where I had set-up camp."

"So you went back to camp, got your rifle, and returned?"

"That I did. With my saddle gun across my lap in plain sight. When Johnny Overstreet spotted it, he shot at me three times. One bullet came so close, it sounded like a hornet going by. The jury saw the gun he used. It was a .44 long barrelled Colt, and three spent cartridges were in it, just like I swore to."

"What did you do while he was shooting at you?" the journalist asked.

"Why, first I sat there open-mouthed at the man's audacity. Then I raised my carbine and shot him."

"How many times did you fire?"

An expression of amazement came over Brown's face, surprised that anyone would question his ability to shoot. "Just once. Got him right above his right eye, where I aimed. He was dead before he left his saddle."

"Then what did you do?"

"Tied him to his horse, pointed it west, toward the Double O, and swatted it on the rump with my hat." Brown picked nervously at a hangnail, then bit it off. "After that, I rode back to where my tender Gomez was putting up some lambing tents and told him to take care of the sheep. After that I rode to Canyon City and turned myself in."

"The rest I know," Crowell said. "The evidence was gathered, a trial was held and the jury brought in a verdict of not guilty."

"That's a fact," Brown stated proudly. "It took them less than five minutes to acquit me, and the vote was unanimous on the first count." The reporter strained to hear Brown's voice, which had drifted lower. "But I do regret the matter had to be settled with violence."

.

A two-hour ride northwest of Bill Brown's Buck Creek Ranch, between Camp Creek and Hampton Buttes, twelve cowhands were celebrating the fact it was Saturday night and the end of the work week. They had pooled their money to buy three jugs of local moonshine, which was beginning to take effect. They were full of boisterous energy, but it was too far to ride to Prineville or Paulina, the nearest towns, and too early to turn in for the night. Even though it was close to midnight, going to bed was the last thought in their minds.

"I shore wish it weren't so durn far to Prineville," a lanky rider said, slurring his words as he weaved about. "I'd hit them cathouses, one after another, then start all over again."

"One's good enough for me, Mo," a red headed youth sitting by the fire hooted back. "I'd walk up to old Nikki Hyde, lay down ten dollars and say 'keep bringing on those fancy ladies 'till my money runs out'."

"Ten dollars! Where would you get ten dollars, Art, much less ten cents," another of the group called out. "We spent all our money on this here panther piss," he raised the jug he had been drinking from high in the air, "Unless you been holding out on your buddies."

"I guess I would give her an I.O.U." the redhead replied, giggling hysterically.

"Well, I plumb got to do somethin'. Sittin' here with you bunch of turkey gobblers is getting bor-ring," Mo said as he squatted to sit, misjudged his position and fell over backwards.

"I agree with Mo," a puncher called Shorty cried out, pulling out his six-gun and firing it into the air. "Let's wake up the coyotes and join them in a song." He gave a series of howls, then went into an off pitch, off-color rendition of Buffalo Gal.

"Kee-rist, Shorty, sit down and shut up," a bandy-legged puncher called Abner said, pushing his companion who stumbled clumsily and fell into the sage and juniper fire they had built to keep warm and provide some light. Shorty yelped and rolled in the dust to smother the hot embers while the rest of the group gathered around and laughed as if he were putting on a show for their benefit. Spilled liquor from the jug Shorty had been holding caught fire with a whoosh and its fiery fingers spread around the legs of his audience. They danced around, swatting at their pants, hooting and hollering as if they had stepped on a red anthill.

"Whooee," Abner cried out. "Now I know why they call it white lightnin'.'" He reached down, grabbed Shorty by the arm pits, and lifted him up.

"Durn you, Abner, you did that a-purpose," Shorty cursed as he swung at his companion, missing by a good two feet. The momentum of his blow swung him around and he fell flat on his back. As he lay there, he stared at the stars above and wondered why they were all revolving in a giant circle.

"I ain't seen anything that funny since granny got her tit caught in a wringer," a rider called Hiram exclaimed, laughing so hard tears ran down his face.

The revelry continued for another hour until, one by one, they began to sprawl around the fire. It would have ended there had not one drunken rider named Dusty Wagner jumped to his feet with a rebel yell, which he ended with the shouted statement, "This night's turning dull. Capital D-U-L-L."

The shout roused Abner. "So, you got any idee's, Dusty?" he asked.

"You bet your britches I have," Wagner answered. "Bill Brown's got a bunch of sheep on graze an hour's ride from here. I say we go touch 'em up a bit."

The next day, a neighbor rode to the Buck Creek Ranch to tell Bill Brown that 487 of his sheep had been slaughtered. The neighbor told a friend several days later, "Aside from a funeral I went to once, that was the first time I ever saw tears in a grown man's eyes."

It was just a coincidence, but the same Saturday night that Bill Brown's sheep were killed, two planned sheepkiller raids took place. One was a half-mile west of the town of Mitchell where Billy Nelson's wool-filled sheep sheds were burned to the ground. Two hours later, four miles away on Newsom Creek, Dick Koopman's sheds were also burned, along with his house and a barn filled with new cut hay.

Five days later, in broad daylight, James Jones, a well-liked sheepman from Spray was killed, along with 150 head of his sheep, on the south fork of the John Day river.

CHAPTER 13

When Tim McNally entered the room, he knew that what he was going to say would not please most of the men there. He squared his shoulders and walked stiff-legged and erect to the empty chair that was waiting for him at the head of the long walnut table.

Twenty others were seated and waiting as he stood before them. He remained standing and gripped the back of the chair before him with both hands, nodding soberly at each face in turn, occasionally calling out a name.

McNally, a solidly built, bandy-legged rancher was in his mid-fifties, but there were few grey hairs in his tousled shock of wiry, reddish-brown hair—a gift of Irish ancestors. Nor did he look his age. He was often mistaken for a man ten years younger.

The cattlemen who were there to hear him speak were not dressed in regular working clothes, for it was Sunday. Most wore ill-fitting suits that only saw the light of day when they went to church services or a funeral.

McNally cleared his throat. "I appreciate your coming to my place on such short notice, and on a Sunday to boot when we should be spending time with our families." He grinned wryly, and his next remark brought a chuckle. "At least that's what my own wife tells me." He paused and his face turned grave. "But we're here for a purpose, and I guess you all agree or you wouldn't have shown up today."

McNally shifted his weight from one foot to the other. "I'm not much for small talk, so I'm going to get right to it. You don't have to ask where I stand because I've let my feelings be known to each and every one of you." He glanced around the table and saw a few heads nod in agreement, then he continued, leaning forward toward them. "My decision was not an easy one to make. Not only because everyone at this table is my friend, but because I know, as you all know, what damage sheep are doing to our grazing land.

"I haven't been to your last two meetings because my mind was already made up." His voice became stronger. "I also know, or feel anyway, that you wouldn't be here today unless there was some doubt in your own minds about forming a Crook County Sheepshooters Association."

McNally slid his chair aside with a booted foot and leaned on the table. "I have asked you here, and thank you for coming," he added, "for the purpose of pleading with you not to turn to violence, but to turn to talk."

A voice interjected. It was Jack Kitching of the Circle K. "What's left to talk about, Tim? We've got to act."

McNally thought a moment before answering. Then he said, "That's the whole point, Jack. As far as the sheepowners are concerned, it's been all action and no talk. A half-dozen times that I know of they have offered to sit down and see if we couldn't work things out, but the only man among us who was willing to do so is sitting right there." He pointed a finger at Tom Pickett, then continued. "We have turned every one of their offers down flat. And why? They're our neighbors, and many of them are our friends. Are we going to shoot them down like the Paulina shooters did to Jim Jones? You can count on it if we form a sheepkillers group of our own."

The Irish stockman's words hit home. Most of the men in the room shifted in their chairs and glanced at each other uncomfortably. They had known and liked Jones, the first owner to die because he had turned to sheep to make his living. One of them in particular was ill at ease because his daughter had married Jones' brother.

McNally recognized the mood of the men in the room had shifted and he took advantage of it. "All I'm asking," he pleaded, "is for a little more time and that we not go off half-cocked and make a decision we may later regret." He reached out, pulled his chair to the table and sat down. "I appreciate your hearing me out. I've had my say, now I think every man in this room should let his feelings be known. But first, if it meets with your approval, it might be helpful to hear what the delegation of sheepmen who visited Tom had to say."

McNally then used a ploy that always worked for him and never failed to bring a little humor to a tense situation. He said, "All opposed to hearing Tom out, raise your hand." Then, before anyone had time to respond, immediately turned to Pickett and said, "As no one is opposed, Tom, the floor is yours."

A ripple of laughter filled the room. McNally's Irish sense of humor had won the day again.

Tom stood, and with a straight face said, "I appreciate the fact that none of you have any objection to my speaking next." He glanced at McNally and smiled, "Particularly as it was done in such a democratic manner." His statement brought another round of laughter, and what might have turned out to be a bitter and acrimonious meeting became one of mutual respect and understanding. Realizing his audience was now listening with an open mind, Tom recited honestly and in detail what had transpired when he acted as host to the seven sheep owners who spent a night at the Triple C discussing their feelings about the sheepkillings.

He deliberately avoided mention of Rachel Williams' efforts to get the state capitol involved, fearing this information might alienate some of the men in the room. His rationale for not bringing this matter up was simple. If the cattlemen and sheepmen could work out their own grievances, there would be no need for the legislature to act.

When Tom finished, there was silence in the room. Then a stooped and bent figure stood. It was Poe Follette, whose ranch adjoined that of Sid Stearney in the Crooked River valley. Follette, along with Stearney, was one of the more vocal advocates of those who wanted to form a Crook County sheepshooters group. He had a reputation of being blunt, irascible and outspoken when it came to letting his feelings be known. Tom and Tim McNally both held their breath, expecting the worst.

"I don't know who the piss ants were that killed Jones," Follette said angrily. "They should be sought out and hung. Jones was a good Christian man, and one I had no complaint with." He unconsciously reached up to smooth the grey tufts of hair that ran in a semicircle around the base of his bald skull. Wrinkles in a weather-beaten face seemed to deepen as he continued. "I have to admit, his death made me stop and think. Those sheep

106

he was grazing were the only means he had to take care of his family. Our quarrel is with those who are running thousands of sheep over our grasslands, destroying everything in their path, not a man who keeps a few head on his own property."

Follette stood, searching for his final words. His eyes sought out Tom Pickett, then moved to Tim McNally. "I don't know how everyone else feels, but if sitting down together and talking will help, I'm willing to give it a try."

McNally and Pickett began to breathe again.

One by one, the ranchers expressed their views. Some rose when they did, others remained seated. They were men who were used to saying what was on their mind, so none of them wasted time getting to the point. In less than forty minutes everyone had spoken. A vote was taken and, by a vote of 20 to 1, they agreed to try and settle their differences with the sheepowners through negotiation, not violence. The lone holdout was Sid Stearney.

The motion was also made, seconded and unanimously approved to make Tim McNally their chairman, both during future meetings of the group and in sessions with the sheepmen.

Pickett lingered behind as the others filed out of the room. When they were alone, he gripped McNally's hand and held it firmly. "Tim, without you this would never have come about."

"It wasn't just me, Tom," McNally answered. "Poe Follette turned the tide. If he had stood against us, the vote might very well have gone the other way."

Tom's lips tightened and he nodded in agreement. "That's one we owe him, Tim. And Jim Jones, too," he added softly, referring to the dead sheepman.

CHAPTER 14

The front page of the July 21st issue of the *Crook County Journal* carried the banner headline, **CATTLE-MEN AND SHEEPMEN AGREE.** This headline and the sub-head below, **Meeting Held to Fix Range Lines in the Blue Mountains**, took up half the front page.

The story that followed filled the remainder of the page.

Sheepmen Allie Jones, Jack Edwards, Dr. David Baldwin, Will Lord, Andy Morrow, Jim Keenan and Joe Bannon returned yesterday from their trip into the Blue Mountains where they went to meet a contingent of twenty cattlemen to settle differences between sheepmen and cattlemen over the range. They report that their conference with the cattlemen was very satisfactory, and the best results are hoped for from the meeting. Prominent cattlemen from the Ochoco, Crooked River, Willow Creek and Mill Creek areas were present to meet them. In respect to the wishes of the cattlemen, none of their names will be used in this story.

After a hearing of both sides of the question, lines were arranged which will be satisfactory to all. Concessions were made by both sheepmen and cattlemen, and the boundary they agreed upon runs as follows."

The paper meticulously listed the creeks, ridges, mountains, ranches and springs that comprised the perimeter of the boundary. The story concluded:

Within these lines, no sheep will be allowed to range.

The committee appointed by the sheepmen's association is to be congratulated upon the success of their mission, which will end the range troubles in the Blue Mountains if the lines are strictly observed as they should be. This paper also wishes to add our congratulations to the cattlemen, and the committee they formed to deal with this matter.

We are told the conference between the two groups was conducted in the friendliest manner, and the spirit of fairness manifested on both sides made an agreement much easier to arrive at than was anticipated.

It was also reported to us that everyone involved expressed the opinion that one man was chiefly responsible for the outcome, and that was Timothy McNally whose ranch lies along the banks of the north fork of Crooked River. It is said that Mr. McNally dedicated himself to arrive at a peaceful and fair settlement between the two groups.

What hadn't been told, but would appear in later issues of the *Journal,* was the fact that months of meetings and negotiations preceded this announcement. And each and every one of these was attended by McNally, whose pleading and cajoling had gotten the two sides to settle on a tentative agreement before they met to sign the Blue Mountain pact.

It had not been easy to patch together the differing conflicts, and there were moments of deep despair for McNally when he thought all of his work might be in vain. Only the firm conviction that what he was doing was right, and the support of a few people on each side, kept him going.

McNally spent weeks away from home, travelling from one end of the county to the other. He was a patient listener who never lost his temper, and an even more persuasive debater. As time dragged on, the quest for peace between his neighbors became an obsession that consumed him. The first few months, McNally thought he was fighting a losing battle as the sheep killings continued, but he saw a thread of hope in the fact no other owners, herders or tenders had been killed since Jim Jones' death. This was the light at the end of the tunnel that kept him going. That and the constant encouragement and support his wife gave him. Without her help and understanding, he knew he could never have gone on, or driven himself as he did.

The newspaper really hadn't given McNally the full credit he deserved. He was the blacksmith that forged the pact and the glue that held it together.

There were threats on the dogged Irishman's life, but he ignored them. They usually came in the form of a note delivered late at night. He was not a brave man but he believed, with a conviction his friends did not share, that the purpose of the notes was to try and scare him off, not to harm him or his family.

At other times he was verbally threatened. When this happened, he would pull one of the abusive messages he had received from a pocket, hold it out and ask, "Did you send this?" Or even more effectively, thrust a fistful of them at the man facing him and growl, "Read these, then tell me: How would you like to get notes like this in the dark of night with your wife and children huddled around you, trembling and crying with fear?"

As a result of McNally's passionate belief that an equitable settlement could be reached, even his staunchest opponents began to listen, and, more important, take what he had to say seriously. For if there was one thing these men of the frontier respected it was courage, and men who stood up for their beliefs despite the odds against them.

McNally knew the Blue Mountain accord was a fragile thing. He had been there when handshakes sealed the agreement, and saw the visceral hate toward sheep that still smoldered deep in the hearts of some of the cattlemen present. He and Tom Pickett had talked about it afterward as they rode home from the ceremony. Tom, who had accompanied him on his visits with the most obstinate ranchers, gave voice to McNally's own misgivings when he said, "You know, Tim, you still have a big job cut out for yourself. The fight isn't over yet, it's just beginning. What was done today needs nurturing and care. As much as we would like to, neither of us can walk away and say the job's finished."

As McNally mulled these words in his mind, Tom added, "I guess you know, Tim, you're the only one who could have pulled this off. I honestly admit I couldn't have, nor can I think of another man in the county who could. It's an awesome responsibility, but it's going to be up to you whether this accord holds together or not."

Deep inside, McNally knew what Tom said was true, but it was something he did not want to admit, even to himself. What he really wanted was to go home, be with his family, and pick up his life where it had been before all of this started.

After a month, the truce still held. There were a few minor incidents, but Tim McNally, working patiently with representatives of both sides, was able to resolve the problems that did occur.

In mid-August, Tom Patterson, a small ranch owner who pastured forty sheep between land owned by the Baldwin Sheep and Land Company and the Bruner Cattle Company, was killed and his sheep were found missing. At first, it was suspected the killing had been done by David Bruner, owner of the cattle company, and one of the original supporters of forming a Crook County sheepshooters organization. Then a witness, a Basque herder came forward, and in heavily accented English testified he saw a group of riders shoot Patterson and drive his sheep away. The herder followed them into the Ochoco Mountains, then turned back to seek out the sheriff. A posse of both sheep and cattle men was formed and the rustlers were tracked into the deep canyon recesses of the Strawberry Mountain wilderness, a few miles south of Canyon City. There, the posse not only found Patterson's missing sheep, but also several hundred head of stolen cattle the rustlers intended to butcher and sell to beef and mutton hungry miners in the surrounding gold country. The four men guarding the animals were caught by surprise, and before they were hanged confessed to taking advantage of the wave of violence in the county by running off small bands of both cattle and sheep. Because of their isolation, none of the rustlers was aware of the Blue Mountain peace agreement

Another incident took place the following month, and for awhile it looked like the range war might ignite again.

Roderick Grant, a Blue Mountain sheepherder was shot in the back and his body was left for the buzzards. Strangely, not one of the sheep he was tending at the time was maimed or killed. Again a crisis was averted by Tim McNally, who brought representatives of opposing sides together. An

111

investigative committee was formed and they soon discovered Grant's horse was missing. It was later reported seen, fifty miles away, at the homestead of Henry Harven. The committee sent four riders to investigate. They encountered Harven on the road to Fossil and asked him to produce a bill of sale for the horse, which he was riding. He cursed at them, and at the dead Grant, saying he would be damned if he would, then drew his gun. Before Harven could fire, he was blown out of his saddle by a shotgun held in the arms of one of the riders facing him. Ironically, after his death the Izee sheepshooters, who had renamed Big Spring to Dead Dog Spring, made known publicly they intended to call the spring near which Rod Grant had been murdered, Grant Spring, in memory of the sheep man.

For Tom and Rachel, the cessation of the violence that had spread over almost two-thirds of the state meant they would be able to spend more time together.

As soon as Rachel received word of the Blue Mountain Agreement, she called the Poindexter Hotel and left a message for Tom to let him know she was winding up her affairs in Salem and would be leaving for home in three days. The telephone, Prineville's first and only, had caused a sensation when it was installed. People came from miles around to gather in the hotel's lobby just to see how it worked. When the desk clerk took Rachel's call, several people were there to watch and listen. Because a Marks Creek neighbor of Tom's happened to be at the hotel, Rachel's message was passed along within three hours after it was received. The neighbor left straightaway and rode to the Triple C ranch to deliver it. Everyone else who was in the lobby at the time of the call also got to hear what was said because the clerk, due to the telephone's weak reception, had to shout into the mouthpiece to be sure he had written the words down correctly.

By Sunday, when the latest news was exchanged after services at the community's two churches, there were probably only a handful of people in town who hadn't heard that Tom and Rachel were "interested in each other".

When Tom received word that Rachel was returning, he spent the remainder of the day with Reub going over a list of jobs that needed to be done while he was gone, for he intended to leave early the following morning to meet Rachel en route.

The sun had just broken over the top of the Ochoco mountain range when Tom passed through Prineville, for he left before dawn. He slowly climbed up the steep trail leading to the rimrock cliff that towered over the town and valley where Ochoco Creek met Crooked River. At the top of the mesa, he stopped to give his horse a rest. After dismounting, he stretched his muscles, then reached into his saddle bag and removed a piece of jerky and some day-old biscuits he had taken from the cookhouse. He strolled to the rimrock edge, and as he ate his line rider's breakfast, gazed down at the snake-like contours of Crooked River, leisurely winding its way north. How a few months can make a difference, he thought. It was just last April that the stream, swollen by spring floods from a melted snow pack, had cut itself a new path and changed its main course from West Second Street near Deer to a new location west of town, just below the rock formation on which he stood.

No longer would the river's current turn the huge wheel of Stuart and Pett's flour mill where he had spent many a long evening in the second floor of the grain storage tower, waiting to see if the vigilantes would choose that night for one of their midnight raids. His mind wandered back into another time when he first saw this wondrous country, then he shook his head, clearing these thoughts away. "Mustn't dwell on the past," he told himself. "It's the future that counts."

Later in the day, when he crossed the Deschutes River and passed through the area where Grey Wolf's band of Indians and Frank Allen's men, led by Luis Baca, had joined forces to destroy the herd he and his partner were bringing to central Oregon, his mind drifted to the past once again. A wave of depression swept over him as the thought of Allen brought back the memory of his bad dreams. Then the realization came to him. "I haven't had that nightmare since Rachel took care of me after I was knifed!"

Thinking of Rachel and remembering he would soon be seeing her erased all negative thoughts from his mind. He pulled himself erect in the saddle, relaxed and turned again to enjoying the primitive beauty of the land through which he rode.

Rachel and Tom met just east of the summit of the Cascade Range, near what would soon be known as the town of Sisters. That night they camped in Glaze Meadow under a full summer moon that starkly displayed the still snow-covered peaks of Mt. Washington, Mt. Jefferson and Three Fingered Jack. They had just finished a simple meal of steak and potatoes that Tom brought with him, along with a coffee pot and the coffee they were now sharing. They talked well into the night, and at such length they both began to slur their words between yawns.

Tom rose and spread his saddle blanket on the ground. "I guess we don't have to get all of our talking done in one night," he said. "You've had a long day, and we could both use some shut-eye."

Rachel, who was hugging her knees and staring at the fire, gave a small nod of agreement.

Tom spoke over his shoulder as he left the fire's small circle of light. "I'll give the horses a last check."

When he returned he was pleased to see Rachel had placed her bedroll next to his.

After they had slipped under their blankets, Tom reached for her hand. She squeezed it and murmured sleepily, "Tom, this truce just has to work. I hope and pray we have seen the last of the violence." She paused and moved to him. "I so desperately want be able to spend more time with you."

Neither of them could ever have guessed that an incident, soon to take place at the Poindexter Hotel, would completely shatter this wish.

CHAPTER 15

March, the following year

His name was William Vasbinder and he was a timber buyer from Sigel, Pennsylvania.

He had just completed a purchase of timber near a double bend in the Deschutes River, fifty miles southwest of Prineville. The Indians called the spot Wychick, but to migratory settlers who paused there it was known as Farewell Bend—not because it was a place they bid their goodbye's, but because it was a spot where they could get their wagons across the river safely, and it was a pleasant place to camp. They 'fared well' there, hence the name. In the early years of the century to follow, the name would be shortened to Bend.

Vasbinder and four companions left Farewell Bend for Shaniko, where they planned to spend several days looking at timber on one of the western spurs of the Blue Mountain range. This was intended to be the final leg of their tour. From Shaniko, they would ride north to The Dalles and take a train back to their homes in Pennsylvania. On their way, they stopped to spend the night at the Poindexter Hotel in Prineville. It was a blustery March day and a cold, persistent rain had thoroughly soaked them all.

That evening when he and his companions gathered at the hotel's bar, Vasbinder begged off joining them for dinner. He complained to John Newcombe, a physician travelling with his group, that he had a sore throat and was extremely tired. Newcombe offered the diagnosis that Vasbinder might be catching a cold, and agreed early retirement and a full night's sleep would probably be the best remedy.

The next morning, Vasbinder joined his companions for breakfast but just sipped at a cup of coffee, leaving his meal untouched. The timber seeker's face appeared flush and he told Newcombe that he thought he might

115

be running a fever. Still, he expressed the opinion they should all continue on as planned.

By the time the five men reached Shaniko and checked into the Columbia Southern Hotel, Vasbinder had a chill and a high temperature as well as a rash on his face. Again, Dr. Newcombe recommended bed rest.

When Vasbinder didn't appear for breakfast the following morning, Newcombe went to his room. Ten minutes later, pale and shaken, the physician joined his fellow travellers in the hotel's dining area. They sat, hunched together at the breakfast table as the doctor whispered to them. Silently, they rose and hurriedly left the room, the food on their plates barely touched.

For several minutes, Newcombe sat by himself, composing his thoughts. Then he stood and walked stiffly to the hotel's cluttered reception desk where he addressed a young woman who was making notes in the hotel ledger. He cleared his throat to catch her attention. "My name is Dr. John Newcombe," he said in his most professional manner. "William Vasbinder, one of the fellows I am travelling with," he paused to wipe away some beads of sweat that had formed on his upper lip with a pocket handkerchief, "seems to have come down with a serious case of poison oak. Unfortunately," again he paused, and licked his lips nervously, "his companions and I have to leave right away on urgent business." He seemed to gain more confidence by the respectful attitude of the clerk, who was listening attentively, and finished in a more self-confident manner. "I wonder if you would be so kind as to have the local doctor look in on him at noontime."

The receptionist, a young girl just turned seventeen, gushed at being given a task of such responsibility. "I'll be more than happy to do so, Doctor. Will you be checking out soon?"

Seeing that the rest of his group had arrived with their luggage and were gathered behind him, Newcombe replied, "Immediately. I'll go pack my bag while the others settle their bills."

As Newcombe turned to leave, the clerk reached forward to touch his arm. "It's several hours until noon, would you like me to check your friend before then in case he might need something?"

116

"No," Newcombe snapped sharply, startling the well-intentioned clerk, who immediately drew her arm back. "No, he's sleeping now and it would be better not to disturb him." After a quick glance at his three waiting companions, Newcombe hurried up the stairs to his room.

Twenty minutes later, after they passed Shaniko's last building and were on the stage road leading out of town, the four men who had been travelling with William Vasbinder urged their horses into a fast gallop.

As soon as Doctor Newcombe and the men who checked out with him left the Columbia Southern Hotel, the girl at the counter went to the manager's office and explained she had to leave the desk for a few minutes to find Frank Perlroth, a veterinarian who also acted as the sheeptown's only doctor. When asked why, she explained that one of their guests had poison oak and needed Perlroth's attention. The manager nodded and replied, "I'll keep an eye on the desk, just don't take too long tracking him down."

"Thank you, Mr. Sweeney," she said with what might have passed as a curtsy. "I won't be long."

Ten minutes after noon, Dr. Perlroth appeared in the lobby. His cracked and worn medical bag was gripped tightly in one hand. "Now, Betty," he said to the girl behind the counter, "tell me what room the guest with poison oak is in and I'll have a look at him."

"Room 226, Doc."

The veterinarian turned and walked to the plushly carpeted stairs and wearily mounted them. He had been up all night trying, unsuccessfully, to deliver a breech birth foal at a horse ranch in Antelope, and had arrived back in town only minutes before he was told about the sick guest at the hotel. As there were several patients waiting in his office, he was unable to get the few hours sleep he had counted on. After this visit he would have the breakfast he missed, then he would go home and take a nap.

Perlroth knocked lightly on the door of room 226 and entered without waiting for a reply. A few rays of light escaped around the sides and bottom of drawn shades, and a kerosene lamp, whose wick had been lowered, burned dimly on the bedside table. The doctor reached out and turned up the wick, fearing if he opened the blinds the sudden bright light might startle the sleeping figure.

Perlroth peered closely at Vasbinder's face, then untied and pulled aside the part of the nightgown that covered the man's throat. After this cursory examination, he left the room and returned to the desk. "You say his doctor told you he had poison oak? At the girl's nod, he said, "That would be my diagnosis, too. I left some calamine lotion on his dresser. You might look in on him in an hour or so, and if he's awake have him put some on his rash. I'll check back around supper time to see how he's feeling."

Five hours later, refreshed by four hours of sleep, the doctor returned to the hotel. The young clerk was just preparing to leave her shift.

"Glad I caught you before you left, Betty. How's our patient doing?" he asked jovially.

"He's still sleeping, Doc. I checked an hour after you left, then again thirty minutes ago."

A frown creased Perlroth's face. "Best I have another look, then."

The sour smell of sickness filled Perlroth's nostrils as he entered the room. He hurried to the bed and stood, looking down at his patient. Then he rolled up the blinds and opened the window to let in some fresh air. This done he returned to the bedside, bent his head and placed his left ear on Vasbinder's chest, which he had covered with a clean towel from the wash stand. The heartbeat seemed regular, but extremely weak.

Next, he pulled up a chair and placed his bag on his knees. He rummaged through its contents until he found the thermometer he was looking for. He unscrewed the top of the case it was in, shook the mercury down and thrust it under the sick man's tongue. Perlroth took out his pocket watch and waited the prescribed three minutes, after which he replaced the watch and removed the thermometer, bending toward the light to read it better. What he saw alarmed him. The gauge read over 104 degrees.

Perlroth pulled the sheets over the foot of the bed and peeled back Vasbinder's nightshirt to reveal a body covered with a fiery red rash whose pustules were secreting a yellow mucous-like fluid. Perlroth reached into his case again and pulled out a magnifying glass. After carefully examining

118

the skin, he came to the conclusion that it certainly looked like poison oak, but if so, it was the worst case he had ever seen. He applied the calamine, then slumped back in the chair. Would it be best to wait out the night and see if the patient was better in the morning? he asked himself, or try to contact the state physician who might give him some advice. That would disturb his evening, he thought, so he decided to wait.

When Perlroth checked back the following morning, his patient was comatose. Even more startling to the uneducated doctor were the boil-like eruptions that covered Vasbinder's body from the top of his scalp to the soles of his feet.

Alarmed by what he saw, Perlroth raced down to the lobby to use the town's newly installed telephone.

When Wood Hutchinson, the State Physician, got the call at his office in Salem, he listened attentively, then told the veterinarian he would arrive by stage the following morning. Meanwhile, no one other than Perlroth was to enter room 226.

After Hutchinson put the telephone receiver back in its cradle, he leaned over his desk and put his head in his hands. He was almost certain he knew what the disease was, but he was reluctant to give such a serious diagnosis to someone trained to deal only with ill and injured animals, or at the most, broken bones and open wounds of humans. He needed to see the sick man himself and cursed under his breath that Shaniko did not have a proper doctor and Perlroth had not called him sooner. There was little doubt in his mind that what he heard required the personal and immediate attention of the state's highest medical officer.

As promised, Dr. Hutchinson arrived on the morning stage. He was met by an upset Perlroth who told him Vasbinder had died during the night. The state physician asked to be taken directly to the Columbia Southern Hotel, firing questions as they walked. When they arrived, Hutchinson took one look at the body and silently nodded. His suspicions were now confirmed. He turned to the sweating man beside him and said firmly, "Absolutely no

119

one must enter or leave this hotel, starting right now. In my satchel there are some quarantine signs. These must be posted at all doors to the hotel without delay. After you have done this, you, but only you, are to leave and find the sheriff. Tell him to put as many deputies as are necessary to keep those people who are here, in, and any who have not been in the hotel for the last three days, out. Be sure and emphasize to the sheriff that neither he nor any of his men are to enter this hotel. After you have done this, return here. We must find out who was staying at the hotel when this man checked in and try to locate them."

After he had finished giving these instructions, Hutchinson looked questioningly at Perlroth. "I don't suppose you have any fresh vaccine in town?" he asked.

"Vac . . . vaccine?" the veterinarian stammered. "For. . . for what?"

Until now, the state physician had refrained from criticizing or speaking down to Perlroth, realizing the ignorant doctor was over his head and his background had not prepared him for the crisis that was to come. But even a student in the first week of his first year of medical school would have recognized immediately what he was dealing with. Hutchinson's composure broke as he looked at the blank face staring back at him. He spat out the words contemptuously, "Smallpox, you damned fool!"

CHAPTER 16

The day Vasbinder and his companions left Prineville for Shaniko, two maids were cleaning Vasbinder's room at the Poindexter Hotel. It was late in the morning and they were behind schedule. A group of cattle buyers had arrived on the early stage and were impatiently waiting for their accommodations.

Jo Mann, a redfaced Irish woman in her late sixties, was making her thoughts about J.N. Poindexter, the owner of the hotel, known to her helper Molly Buckley, a young farm girl from the small community of Post. Molly was living in town for the winter while attending the newly established high school, and worked at the hotel on weekends to earn spending money. The only thing she did not like about her job was having to listen to the sharp-tongued Jo Mann all day long.

"Sure, and I don't know who Himself thinks we are," Mann prattled on. "He treats the hired help around here like a bunch of just-off-the-boat Chinamen. Twelve beds to look after and just the two of us to do all the work." Throwing an armful of dirty towels on the floor in a fit of anger, she muttered a mild Irish curse. "Begorra, it's not right. And to top it off, there hasn't been a sip of whiskey to be found in any of the rooms we've done so far." With an exaggerated wail, she turned to her helper. "What's the world coming to when a poor lass from Galway has to go through half the morning without a nip? 'Tis an abomination."

The teenager tried to ignore the Irishwoman's remarks and bent to strip the sheets from the bed. "Hold on, now," Mann's raspy voice stopped her. "The bucko who used this room last seemed clean enough." She bent for a closer look, squinting through rheumy eyes, then exclaimed, "Leave 'em be. No one will know the difference and it will save us re-doing the bed and washing the sheets."

121

"But," the young girl started to protest.

"No buts about it," Mann cut her off. "You'll do as Jo tells you or there will be trouble between us." She eyed the youngster menacingly. "Just remake the bed and be quick about it." Molly Buckley, intimidated by the older woman, and not wanting to jeopardize her job, managed a weak "Yes'm," and did as she was told.

Fifteen days later, the two maids, as well as a drummer who used the room after they made it up, came down with high fevers and a rash. Two days after that, four more people who had been at the hotel developed the same symptoms: The daughter of an employee of the hotel, a local rancher who had occupied the room across the hall from Vasbinder, and who had spoken to him in the hall, a carpenter who was doing some repair work on the second floor and a waitress in the dining room.

Smallpox, the deadly virus that killed or maimed millions since it appeared in Africa ten thousand years before the first white man set foot in the Pacific Northwest, swept through the community of Prineville like wildfire.

Three weeks after William Vasbinder spent the night at the Poindexter Hotel, eighteen cases had been reported. A week later this figure doubled, and within four weeks half of the town's 700 residents had contracted the dreaded disease. Two months later, this figure rose to 70%.

Unlike Shaniko, whose inhabitants had to rely on a veterinarian for medical help, Prineville had two medically trained physicians: Dr. Horace P. Belknap and Dr. John Henry Rosenberg. Belknap attended medical school at the University of Michigan, then went on to Bellevue Hospital in New York to pursue his internship. Rosenberg, a young man in his mid-twenties, who was currently serving as Prineville's City Physician, graduated from the University of Oregon's Medical School in Portland. Both doctors immediately recognized the symptoms of their first patients. Together, they hurriedly established a three part program to combat the virus: Quarantine and isolation for those already infected; fumigation of all persons and buildings that had been in contact with the "spotted death"; and vaccinations to stop its spread.

To isolate those who had already contracted this highly communicable disease, the City Council unanimously voted to purchase a home on East First Street from Mrs. S. J. Follette and turn it into a pest house. At first there were numerous complaints from the taxpayers that an expenditure of $50.00 to buy the dwelling was extravagant, but these ended as more and more cases were diagnosed. No one uttered a word of protest when, a few weeks later, a second residence on East Second Street was acquired to house additional victims. When it became obvious both buildings could not hold the increasing number of people who became ill, a tent camp was set up at the site of the racetrack on the outskirts of town. Here the worst cases were brought and left unattended. Food and water were delivered to a containment line that marked the quarantine area, and left. Those interned within the confines of this line were expected to take care of themselves, and each other, without outside help. The few who managed to survive under these conditions were forced to immerse themselves in barrels of strong disinfectant, left just inside the boundary, before they were examined and allowed to return home.

In addition to the pest houses and quarantine camp, one of Prineville's two houses of ill-repute turned itself into a hospital and the madam and her charges acted as nurses. The second whorehouse, run by Nikki Hyde, closed its doors. Hyde herself fled to California.

In the beginning, the efforts of the two physicians were hampered by both of the town's newspapers who downplayed the seriousness of the situation. This stand was encouraged by local merchants who did not want their town isolated and cut off from trade. But when the Prineville and Occidental hotels, the two livery stables and the barber shops were closed, followed by a quarantine of numerous retail stores, the *Prineville Review* and the *Crook County Journal* could no longer maintain the pretense that, "Only a few isolated cases had been recorded," as they had previously been reporting.

As the contagion grew, the town and county came to a standstill. Schools, the circuit court and churches were closed to the public and gatherings of any kind were forbidden.

Dr. Rosenberg, who preferred using his middle name, Henry, personally supervised the second part of the plan, which was to arrest the spread of the pestilence, and organized a city-wide fumigation of all homes, businesses and social gathering places where the disease had appeared. Individuals were not spared, either. If they had been touched or contacted by anyone who was infected, they were sprayed thoroughly from head to foot with a solution of full strength formaldehyde after their clothes had been removed and burned.

Even incoming and outgoing mail was fumigated and left to sit in the post office for 48 hours before it could be handled. Each day, from 11:00 a.m. until 1:00 p.m., the post office was closed and mopped with a chemical disinfectant. In addition, all passengers arriving on the stage, as well as those leaving, had to be fumigated with eye searing fumes from the smoke of burning sulphur while they waited for the inside of their stage to be scrubbed with a strong solution of lye.

To add to the problem, several cases of scarlet fever broke out and, in most instances, could not be properly diagnosed until the febrile disease had sufficiently developed. These people were also quarantined—sometimes, by mistake, with the victims of smallpox.

Those who had not contracted smallpox were required to have a vaccination, but this precautionary step was frustrated by the town's lack of sufficient vaccine. In the past, local druggists had carried a few points for emergency use, but they had little call for it, and because smallpox vaccine spoiled after a short period of time, they found it unprofitable to stock. Consequently, the epidemic raged for a full week before vaccine could be obtained from other cities west of the Cascade Mountains.

In spite of these obstacles, the doctors and city fathers were doing everything they possibly could. In addition to suffering the costs of the pest houses and race track quarantine station, the Council of the City unanimously agreed to underwrite the cost of the vaccinations. The magnitude of Prineville's disaster was reflected in the city's budget. In late March, when the first case was reported, the town had total debts of $146.15. Two months later this figure increased to the staggering sum of $4,554.51. The city treasury was close to bankruptcy, and, to make matters worse, businesses that had thrived and contributed taxes to the city coffers began closing their doors. Ranchers and settlers who usually bought what they needed in Prineville were now travelling to The Dalles and Eugene City for their supplies—trips that took a full week to make.

Shaniko and Prineville were not the only communities affected. Travellers carrying the pestilence spread it throughout Oregon and to such distant spots as Chicago, Ohio and Pennsylvania—where Vasbinder's companions had fled.

In an effort to confine the contagion, neighboring counties stretched rope across all roads leading into Crook County. These barriers were guarded day and night by armed men. At the border that separated Crook from Lake counties, stage coaches were not allowed to pass, and even fumigated mail was refused and turned back. Crook County, like those individuals who had contracted smallpox, was itself now quarantined.

The number of dead increased daily, and notices that appeared in Prineville's two papers under the heading "The Grim Destroyer Death" read like a who's who of original settlers and their families. The movement of bodies to the graveyard during the day became so depressing the Committee on Resolutions, a group formed to deal specifically with problems created by the epidemic, ruled the coroner could only transport corpses at night.

Then, as suddenly as the disease started, it came to an end. On the first day no new cases were reported, a ravaged figure knocked on Dr. Henry Rosenberg's office door. When he opened it, the physician stared in shock at the face of a man so horribly disfigured by rotting carbuncles he no longer looked human. Blood seeped from open sores and the hand he held out for help was so decayed it looked like rotten fruit. The pathetic figure tried to speak through chattering teeth, but the sounds that came out were mumbled and unintelligible. Rosenberg knew the man standing before him did not have long to live. "Easy now, easy," the young surgeon said, trying to repress a shudder as he gently guided the pathetic figure to the examining chair in his office. These past few months the doctor had treated some disfigured horrors, but this was the worst he had yet seen.

Once he was seated, the ill man reached inside a vest pocket and, with a shaking hand, extracted a folded piece of paper which he held out to

Rosenberg. Red-rimmed eyes beseeched the physician to take it. Fever blistered lips tried to frame words, but failed. Then the man's head dropped limply on his chest. He jerked twice and collapsed to the floor.

Rosenberg knelt and placed two fingers on the prone figure's neck. Feeling no pulse, he rose wearily and went to the wash basin to rinse his hands with disinfectant. There was something familiar about the man. He had the nagging feeling he was, or might have been, someone he had seen on his rounds, or knew. Then a cold chill ran down his spine as he realized who it was.

"My God," he uttered aloud, turning to look at the body. "It's Tim McNally."

After wiping his hands on a clean towel, Rosenberg reached for a pair of forceps and picked up the note McNally had tried to give him. He took a surgeon's knife in the other hand to use as a tool and carefully unfolded the paper, being careful not to touch it. Rosenberg could barely read the almost illegible scrawl, but as he deciphered the words his breath caught in his throat.

It read: "Sheep pact to be broken. Warn Tom. Tell him watch out for Stearney and Pervez"

The two names trailed down the side of the page, the message unfinished by a dying man no longer able to write.

CHAPTER 17

The paper on which Tim McNally had written his warning was fumigated for 48 hours by Dr. Rosenberg before he had a rider take it to Tom Pickett at the Triple C ranch. Along with McNally's note, the overworked and exhausted doctor included a message of his own.

Dear Tom:

The enclosed letter was given to me by Tim McNally shortly before he died in my office. I truly don't know how he stayed alive long enough to deliver it, but somehow he managed. To my deep regret, I could do nothing for him. Even though he was so consumed with the smallpox poison that he was unable to speak, his eyes, so alive to the task he had set out to do, gave a sense of urgency to the words he wanted to say.

It is the second day now that no new cases of the dreaded virus that struck down the vitality of this town have been reported. Both Dr. Belknap and I feel the epidemic has burned itself out, but we have decided to wait another week before lifting the quarantine. If, indeed, this scourge has run its course, the courts, schools and local businesses will be reopened by this time next week. I pray that this be so.

I am greatly saddened by the news carried in Tim's letter and know you will do everything in your power to see that the sheep killing madness does not start all over again, and that all of Tim's work will not have been in vain.

I remain,
your obedient servant,
J.H. Rosenberg, M.D.

When Rosenberg's letter and Tim's cryptic note were delivered to him, Tom Pickett was working some iron in the blacksmith shop. "Bad news I'm afraid," Ted Black, the rider who had brought them, said as Tom washed up in a barrel of clean water.

Tom slowly dried his hands and arms on his shirttail and reached out to take the envelope that was handed to him. "Thanks for riding all the way from town, Ted. Cooky just made some fresh apple pie. Tell him I said it was all right to help yourself."

Black respectfully touched the brim of his hat. "Don't mind if I do, Tom. Thanks. If you'd like to send a message back to town, let me know."

Tom nodded absentmindedly as he opened and read Rosenberg's letter, then the note from McNally that had been folded inside. Looking up at Black, Tom slowly shook his head. "You're right about the bad news, Ted. Guess no answer is necessary. Just tell Doc Rosenberg I appreciate what he has done." Tom slowly turned and headed for his house. When he got to the front steps, he paused and wearily sat down. A heavy sigh escaped from his lips as he gazed at Lookout Mountain, whose top was covered with a mantle of dark, rain-laden clouds.

The wind picked up, rustling the messages he held, then began a slow moan as a summer storm front moved its way from the northeast. The breeze turned cooler, bringing with it the heavy scent of rain. In the distance, thunder rolled and flashes of lightning filled a darkening sky, too far away yet to make its crackling sound heard.

Tom looked down at the notes. Both were yellowed and stained by the sulphur fumes used to cleanse them of any live smallpox virus. He sat on the letter from the City Physician to keep it from blowing away in the wind and gripped the message from McNally tightly in both hands. He read it again, slowly, as if he might have missed something the first time. Then he stared, unseeing, at the building pillar of churning cumulus clouds that were beginning to form over the Ochocos. Tom realized that Tim McNally had literally dragged himself from his deathbed to deliver this warning, so it had to be taken seriously. How much more had Tim known? And who other than Stearney and Pervez might be involved? A host of names flooded his mind.

Poe Follette? Dave Bruner? Henry Snodgrass? The list went on and on. He glanced once again at the scrawled writing. Why had things changed, and what action was being planned by the sheepkillers? And even more important, where and when was it going to happen?

If only Tim had been able to talk. Was there some clue in Tim's message that he had missed? He glanced at the sheet of paper in his hand once more. As he did, a fat drop of rain fell on one name, smearing it and spreading the ink so thinly the original impression of the pen point became clear and distinct. Tom jumped to his feet. Of course! Tim had been able to write the names of two men before he was unable to continue, but what he had taken as the convulsions of a dying man had been Tim's attempt to underline the larger of the two. Pervez.

Rajat Pervez was fairly new to central Oregon, and had arrived when the vigilantes were at the height of their power. He came from Goose Lake in southern Oregon with less than fifty head of scrawny, wild steers. That was in early spring, Tom remembered. By the end of summer, Pervez had increased his herd to well over 200 steers and was able to put enough money down to buy the old Peterson place on the middle fork of Crooked River. At the time, no one connected him directly with the vigilantes, but it was a known fact he sympathized with them and was often seen in their company. Tom slapped a leg as the thought struck him. The land Pervez had acquired was directly in line with the route the vigilantes used to move rustled beef south to Linkville and the Klamath basin. And he had a large pasture in a valley surrounded by protective rimrocked hills, to which the only access was by the road past his ranchhouse. He could easily have hidden rustled cattle there.

No one knew much about Pervez, or where the money came from that he used to increase his stock and pay for the ranch. He kept pretty much to himself, but toadied up to anyone in a position of power or wealth, ingratiating himself with these people wherever and whenever he could. Due to his slight build and dark brown skin, it was first assumed Pervez might have Mexican blood, but his temper would flare if this was ever mentioned in his presence and he would snap, "My ancestors came from a land where rajahs

129

rule and where a prophet watches over our lives." As a result of this remark a few people began calling him "prophet," but the name didn't stick. Another one soon took its place, however, and it fit perfectly. In fact it was a natural combination of his personal appearance and his first name. Pervez was slight, with a beard of wispy whiskers, above which was a sharp, prominent nose. He had dark eyes, high cheekbones and practically no chin. His hair was black and straight, giving even more emphasis to his thin, pointed face. A pair of wire rimmed spectacles accented these features. The first time Rajat Pervez was referred to as "Rat" Pervez, the name stuck.

To Tom, the connection between Pervez and Stearney made sense. Stearney had a large ranch, but was gullible and not too bright. He could be used by Pervez and still be made to feel he was running things, while Pervez could remain behind the scenes in the shadows he preferred.

Tom couldn't have been more right in his assessment of Pervez. Barely more than a week before McNally died in Dr. Rosenberg's office, Stearney and Pervez were huddled over a trestle table at Stearney's Bar S ranch. An open bottle of rye and a half-empty glass sat before Stearney. Pervez gripped a cracked mug of steaming black coffee.

"Pervez, sometimes I take offense at your not drinking with me. It's hard to trust a man that won't join you for a snort now and then."

A brief flash of anger crossed the dark brown, almost black, eyes of the man he addressed. Pervez replied coldly, in clipped words, "I told you before, Sid, my beliefs do not allow me to take alcohol."

Stearney snorted. "Your beliefs? You're always flapping your lips about what you believe. It's not normal." He leaned forward until his face was inches from the thin man with the hawk-like nose that sat across the table from him. "Pervez, do you know what I believe?"

"No, Sid, what do you believe?" Pervez answered in a low, condescending voice, drawing out each word.

Stearney lifted his glass in the air, studied it, and drained its contents in one gulp. "I believe I'll have another drink!" After setting the empty glass down, he pounded the table and laughed uproariously at his own joke.

A forced smile appeared on Pervez's face. "Sid," he said, "I'll tell you something else I believe."

"What's that?"

"I believe you are a very funny man."

"You're damned tootin' I am," Stearney replied. "A darned sight funnier than you and that's a fact."

Pervez's dark eyes clouded. He hated dealing with this fool, but Sid Stearney was the only cowman in Crook County that he had been able to manipulate. "You're right, Sid," an insincere grin passed over his face that Stearney mistook for a real one, "I see very little humor in the fact we have lost thousands of acres of good grazing land in the Blues to a bunch of whining sheepmen. And that you in particular got the short end of the stick." He was referring to the fact Stearney had to pull several hundred head out of the area that had been designated for sheep. He knew this rankled the man at the table with him.

Stearney exploded in rage. He jumped up and stormed around the room, cursing all sheep, sheepmen and those who had agreed to a truce with them.

Pervez's following remark only added more fuel to the fire burning inside Stearney. "All of your neighbors are beginning to feel sorry for you, Sid." He smirked as he added, "What with you having to sell off half your stock to meet your debts, and with not enough land to feed those cattle you have left. I suppose they will be passing the hat soon to keep you out of the poor house."

Stearney swung toward Pervez, both fists cocked. If there was one thing he couldn't stand it was being pitied. He hadn't had to sell half his herd, and didn't need money to meet his obligations, but one thing his thin, brown companion had said was true. He did need more pasture. Drool ran from the corner of his mouth as he shouted, "Whoever said I had to sell my cattle is a damned liar. I'm square on all my debts!"

"Of course what they're saying is a lie," Pervez answered mockingly. "But they wouldn't be saying it if they didn't believe it."

Stearney moved a step closer to Pervez. "Well they're dead wrong. Just as wrong as they were when they gave in to that sniveling bunch of sheeplovers."

What Stearney didn't know was that Pervez himself was in desperate financial trouble. Pervez had borrowed heavily from the Cattlemen's Bank the preceding winter to buy three thousand head of yearling Durhams. His plan was to fatten them up during the spring and summer months, then sell them in the fall market and pay off his loan. With the profit, which would have been substantial because of the demand for beef in the East, he was going to leave this land of heathens, return to the poverty stricken country he came from, and live like one of the rajahs he talked about so much. But he had been foiled by the Blue Mountain Agreement. The land he counted on using to graze his cattle had been turned over to the woolgrowers. As a result, he was forced to sell half his stock at a loss to pay for the hay he had to buy to feed the others. Now his money was gone, and if he couldn't move his cattle to free range before the end of summer he would be bankrupt. To make matters worse, a loan payment was due in two months and he knew the bank wouldn't grant him an extension if they found out about the trouble he was in.

Pervez had lost the fortune he was counting on. Now his only hope for breaking even lay with the man he was trying to taunt into action. Pervez knew that it would take only one violent raid against the sheepmen to break the pact, but it would have to be a big one and with his very survival at stake it would have to be soon.

He baited Stearney again. "It's too bad no one had the guts to stand up to them."

"What do you mean no one stood up to them," Stearney fumed. "I did. I was the only man in the whole cowardly bunch to vote against allocating any land for sheep."

"Yes, you *voted*," Pervez deliberately emphasized the word. "Voting's nothing. That's not standing up to them, that's giving in to them."

Stearney had just picked up the bottle from the table and was pouring himself another drink when Pervez made this comment. With a roar, Stearney threw the bottle against the cabin wall. His voice, slurred by the effects of too much liquor, rose to a shout. "Sid Stearney gives in to nobody. Particularly a bunch of egg-sucking sheepherders."

"Nor do I," Pervez hissed, realizing he had gone just about as far as he could in provoking the drunken rancher. "We've gotten nowhere with the cattlemen in Crook County, but who needs them. We know how the owners of the spreads around Camp Creek and Silver Lake feel. They're ready to fight, and have been since the pact was signed. If you're man enough to stand up for what you believe in, and have the guts to do what needs to be done, sit down and listen. I have a plan."

CHAPTER 18

The next morning, Pervez and Stearney left the Bar S to act on the plan they had discussed the night before. They carried rations of bacon, hardtack and coffee, for they expected to be gone several days. Their first stop was at the H/H ranch, just west of Camp Creek at the base of the Maury Mountains.

Harold Harrison, the owner of the H slash H, greeted them as they rode into his yard, scattering a dozen chickens that had been foraging for food in the dirt. Harrison stepped down from his porch veranda and watched them shrewdly, his eyes measured each man, then rested on the packs strapped behind their saddles. Rearranging a wad of tobacco from one cheek to the other, he leaned over and spat on the ground. As was customary, Stearney and Pervez waited until he made his welcome known before they got out of their saddles.

Harrison hooked two thumbs behind the straps of a pair of worn suspenders, spread his legs apart, and spoke. "Just passing through or do you two have something on your minds?" he asked.

Sid Stearney, fuzzy headed and ill-tempered from too much liquor the night before, looked down at the muscular rancher and curtly replied, "A little of both I reckon, Harold. We'd like to talk to you, but not out in the hot sun."

Harrison nodded in agreement. "Come inside then, there's some coffee left."

Before following Harrison into the one room shack, both riders stopped to knock the dust from their pants with their hats.

"Ain't no need to do that," Harrison remarked. "I'm not much for housekeeping. My wife used to take care of that before she died. Did it mostly to keep herself happy, I suspect, 'cause it never did matter much to

134

me." He went to the sink and pulled two cups from a pile of dirty dishes, then filled them from a smoke-stained enamel coffee pot that sat on a round-bellied iron stove. "Hope you don't mind lukewarm coffee. The fire died out and I wasn't expecting company." He handed the cups to both men and pointed at a pine table that was covered with more dirty dishes. "Push those plates aside and have a seat. Then tell me what this visit is all about."

Pervez started to take a sip from his cup, but stopped when he saw a dead fly and stale coffee grounds floating on top of the oily liquid. He shifted a greasy plate in front of him that looked like it had been used for several meals and sat the cup down.

Harrison dumped the remains of a cup that he had used for breakfast in the sink, refilled it, then joined them. He slapped a knee and cackled in delight. "Sid, that must have been some toot you were on last night. Your eyes look like two pee holes in the snow." Before Stearney had a chance to respond, Harrison jumped to his feet, went to his unmade bed and pulled an earthenware jug from under it.

He returned to the table and sat it in front of Stearney. "What you need is a little hair of the dog." In response to Stearney's grateful look, he added, "It's good stuff. I make it myself." He swung his glance to Pervez. "I understand you're not a drinking man. Some preacher convince you that a sip of whiskey now and then condemns you to eternal damnation?" Without waiting for an answer he peered intently at the slight, dark man across the table from him. "Ever try the stuff?" At Pervez's negative shake of the head, Harrison clicked his tongue. "Then you don't know what you're missing, does he Sid?"

Stearney, who had drunk straight from the jug, wiped his lips with the back of a hand. "That's what I keep telling him, Harold, but he says it's against his religion."

"Well," Harrison answered, reaching across the small table to take the jug from Stearney's hands and pouring a generous amount in his cup, "there's no accounting for taste, I always say." Leaning back, he eyed them both suspiciously. "I've got a load of work to see to, so let's get to it. What's in your craw that brings you two birds here?"

135

Stearney glanced at Pervez, who had remained silent the whole time. Then he shifted to look at Harrison. "We figure it's time to do something about all those sheep grazing in the Blues," he said bluntly. "I guess you know where I stand—both of us stand," he corrected himself, tilting his head toward Pervez. He paused, waiting for a reaction from Harrison. Getting none, he continued. "We've heard talk the ranchers around Silver Lake and Camp Creek may be ready to form their own sheep killers group like the Izee and Paulina ranchers have done. That's what we're here to find out. You're our first visit."

A wary look creased Harrison's face. "The first of many you intend to make, I suspect, judging from the size of your grub bags."

Stearney jerked his head down in a quick nod.

Harrison pushed the jug back to Stearney and rose to his feet. He slowly walked to the stove, picked up the pot, and returned to the table. He stopped to refill Pervez's cup, but seeing that it was untouched, gave a barely noticeable shrug and poured more for Stearney and himself. On his way back to the stove, he stopped and looked back. "Do me a favor, Pervez. See if you can find my foreman and bring him here. He's a big fella with a harelip he tries to hide with a wispy mustache. I expect he's trying to separate some calves from their mommas, just across the pasture." He waved an arm. "Toward Wolf Creek."

Pervez's jaw set. Inwardly he seethed at being treated like a hired hand and resentment flushed his face. He had seen men by the corral as they rode in and knew Harrison could have called out to one of them to fetch the foreman. But he also realized Harrison would play a key role if their plan was to succeed. He had too much at risk to say no, so he swallowed his pride and grudgingly rose to his feet. "What if he's not there?" he asked sullenly.

"Oh, he'll be there," Harrison said pointedly. "He always does what he's told."

As Pervez left, Harrison returned to the table and took the seat across from Stearney. He pushed some plates aside to give him room to place his elbows on the table. Leaning forward, he said intently, "Sid, why is Rat riding along with you? I've got to be honest, I have never liked that man."

"Why, he feels the same as I do, Harold." Stearney replied, somewhat taken aback by the question.

"Like a rat's ass he does, Sid. He's never taken a position one way or the other before. How come all of a sudden he does now. I outright don't trust him."

A confused look spread over Sid Stearney's face. He stammered a reply. "I, I don't know Harold. I just guess he decided it was time to get involved."

"No, I expect there's more to it than that. He never has talked straight and he wouldn't be sticking his scrawny neck out now unless there was something in it for him."

Not wanting to admit it was Pervez's idea to make the trip they were on, Stearney straightened. "He agreed to accompany me on a visit to the ranches around here and Silver Lake. And he's the only one in upper Crook County willing to do so. I imagine that's worth something."

Harrison mulled over Stearney's remark before he spoke. "I still don't trust him, Sid, but I'll go along with you for the time being. Meanwhile, and keep this under your hat, you're right about the ranchers in this part of the county being unhappy with the Blue Mountain Agreement. We've been doing a lot of talking amongst ourselves, but so far it's been just that. Talk. Maybe the two of you can bring it to a head." He rose and went to a battered roll top desk, cluttered with papers, that sat in a corner of the dingy room. Rummaging around, he found a stub of a pencil and an old receipt for some goods he had purchased at Wurzweiler and Thompson's in Prineville. He started writing on the back. "I'm going to save you some trouble. There are cattlemen around here who don't think like we do, so it would be a waste of your time to see them." He returned to where Stearney remained seated and handed him the paper. "On the back of this receipt is a list of people to contact. Tell them you talked to me and I agree with what you are trying to do." He turned the paper over and tapped the letterhead with his index finger. "This is just between the two of us, but they're a hundred percent behind us."

"Wurzweiler's?" Stearney stared at Harrison in amazement.

"Yup. When they say 'The Cattleman's Friend' under their names, they don't mean the sheep owners' friend. We've already..." Harrison stopped as

Pervez entered the room with a dusty, sweat stained figure who wore a red bruise on his upper right cheek. The bruise, a recent one, was just starting to swell and distorted one side of the wrangler's face. When Harrison saw this, he broke out laughing. "Don't tell me, Harlan, let me guess. Some momma cow just plain took offense at your wanting to take away her young 'un."

His answer was a sheepish grin and a mumbled reply that his boss had guessed right.

"Shake hands with Sid Stearney. You've already met Rat . . . Rajat Pervez," Harrison said, correcting himself, but not soon enough. A flash of anger spread across the dark man's face. Harrison continued, "I'm going to take you away from all those unhappy ladies for the rest of the day. I want you to ride with Sid and Rajat to John Webb's place. Tell him I thought he should hear these boys out, and that I sent you to let him know they can be trusted." He turned to Stearney. "John's a little touchy. There have been rumors the governor has hired some Pinkerton agents to seek out the names of the sheepkillers with the intent to make an example of them. I think it's just that—a rumor, but John has it set in his mind that it's a fact. Who knows, though, he could be right. The two of you could ride in without any trouble, but if he didn't believe your story, you just might not ride out. That's why I'm sending Harlan along." Harrison paused and looked meaningfully at Stearney. "Webb's also the man who carries the matches in case you might want to start that fire you were talking about."

As they all filed out of the shack, Harrison draped an arm over Stearney's shoulders. "Good luck, Sid." He then slapped Pervez on the back, "Always good to see you, too, Rat. Stop by anytime."

Pervez swallowed bile as the door closed behind him and he heard Harrison's laughter. This was not the time, but sometime, somehow, the owner of the H slash H would pay for his insults.

By noon, the three men had entered Webb's land, which was natural cattle country. Wandering creeks, whose tree-lined banks provided both water and shade for the cattle, stretched as far as the eye could see. Gentle hills, covered with pine, rose and fell like waves on a quiet sea. Abundant grass, nourished by water from dozens of springs that seeped through the ground, grew lush and green even in the blistering heat of a summer day.

Soon, they passed small groups of steers resting in the shade of dense growths of ponderosa pine, their tails constantly in motion as they swished the flies away.

In another hour they entered drier and browner pasture where small groups of riders were ushering bands of cattle to better grass. As soon as they were spotted, one rider broke from the group and headed east at a fast gallop. "Going to warn the boss that he has visitors, I expect," Harlan said. "The ranch and bunkhouse lie just beyond that saddleback in front of us."

Harlan's guess proved to be true. In less than twenty minutes a line of armed men rode over the ridge he had indicated. The riders paused just long enough to locate the strangers coming in, then formed a skirmish line and rode toward them. "Best we just stop and wait," Harlan warned them. "Might also be a good idea to put both your hands atop your saddle horns. As Mr. Harrison says, this bunch is pretty touchy."

Twenty riders pulled to a halt in front of them. Their dust filled the air. The H/H rider squinted through the choking alkali powder at the leader of the group. "Quinn, is that you? It's Harlan."

The man at the front of the line of riders rode forward, the butt of a 30-30 rifle rested on his thigh.

"Harlan? What in Sam Hill brings you here on a working day?"

"Brought two folks to see your boss. Mr. Harrison figured I'd better tag along with them in case one of you might have an itchy trigger finger and shoot first with the idea of asking questions later."

The man called Quinn rode up to them, saw Harlan's grin and jammed his rifle back into its scabbard. He half turned and shouted over his shoulder. "It's all right, boys, you can get back to what you were doing. I'll escort these gents in." Without a word, the line of riders swung their horses and rode back the way they came.

Quinn slouched in his saddle, reached into a shirt pocket for his sack of Bull Durham and deftly rolled a smoke with one hand. Licking the paper in place, he put the cigarette in his mouth, then reached out and handed the cloth bag to Harlan who did the same. Harlan then held it out to Stearney and Pervez who shook their heads, but voiced their thanks.

"Quinn's way of passing the peace pipe," he told them, returning the tobacco pouch. He and Quinn made small talk while they finished their smokes, then Harlan took a last long pull, spat in a gloved hand, drowned his smoldering stub, and dropped it to the ground. "Now that you two have been delivered, I'd best get back to work. Quinn here will see you to Mr. Webb." He turned to the Flying W hand. "Mr. Harrison said to pass the word these two birds have seen him and they can be trusted to keep their mouths shut."

John Webb's ranch house was large by eastern Oregon standards. It was well built and furnished in good taste, the complete opposite of Harrison's shanty Pervez observed enviously. This is how he would live when he returned to India. Everything was neat and in its place. Throw rugs covered an oak floor that gleamed with wax and tastefully framed pictures decorated the walls. A large grandfather clock ticked steadily in the reception area, then tolled the hour in deep tones. Quinn deferentially removed his hat as he knocked on the door of John Webb's study. It was answered almost immediately by an elderly, grey-haired gentleman nattily attired in a three piece suit. A string tie with a turquoise stone hung from the collar of a freshly starched white shirt. Quinn leaned forward and whispered in the man's ear. Webb nodded once and said, "Thank you, Quinn. You may go now, but first would you ask Mrs. Parker to bring us some fresh coffee."

Webb turned to his two guests. "This is an unexpected pleasure. Would you please come in." He stepped aside and gestured toward the room.

Stearney quickly removed his Stetson, crushing it in both hands in his nervousness. He had never met John Webb, but he had heard many tales about him, and the man who invited them into his study was not what he had expected. He knew Webb had ridden with both the Izee and Paulina sheepshooters on some of their most violent raids. He had anticipated a fiery, rough and tumble rancher, not the well-mannered and genteel person who greeted them. Perhaps this was Webb's clerk. He was about to ask, but was saved from embarrassment by Pervez who extended a hand and said in his most solicitous voice, "Mr. Webb, my name is Rajat Pervez, and this," he indicated his companion, "is Sid Stearney. We would appreciate a few minutes of your time."

"Certainly, gentlemen. It is my honor. Please come in and be seated." He indicated several armless leather chairs clustered before a huge mahogany desk. Seating himself in a large fan-back swivel chair behind it, he glanced toward the door as a prim, dark-haired lady entered. She was bearing a tray on which was balanced a silver coffee service and three bone china cups and saucers. She placed the tray on a corner of the desk and stood waiting.

"Would you care for coffee?" their host asked.

"Sure," said Stearney, rising to help himself.

Webb held up a hand. "Don't disturb yourself, Mr. Stearney. Mrs. Parker will do the serving. Mr. Pervez?"

"Thank you," Rajat Pervez purred. "With cream and sugar, please. And I believe Sid likes his black."

"Yeah, black," Stearney mumbled, sitting back in his chair.

"I'll have the usual, Mrs. Parker. And thank you for being so prompt."

After the three had been served, she left the room. Webb's eyes followed her, then returned to the two men seated before him. "My housekeeper. Absolutely irreplaceable. I don't know what I would do without her. She runs the staff with the precision of the antique German clock you heard as you entered." He seemed not to notice as Stearney gripped his cup at the rim with his fingers and slurped noisily.

"Now," he said, reaching into a vest pocket and removing a large gold watch which he placed on the desk before them. "My schedule is really quite full today." The clock in the hall chimed the quarter hour, as if to emphasize the importance of his statement. "You have fifteen minutes to explain what it is you wanted to see me about."

The way he said it made Pervez's blood run cold. He had dealt with men like this in the country he came from. Wealthy, powerful men, hiding behind the pretense of manners, yet capable of ordering lesser men to death without blinking an eye. Yes, John Webb was definitely a man not to be crossed. Pervez also realized Stearney had been taken in by Webb's surface charm and was not aware of the true nature of the man they had come to see.

Rajat Pervez cleared his throat and spoke in a tone he would have used when addressing one of the rajahs in the country he came from. His voice purred with servitude. "Mr. Webb, you are generous in receiving us and we will not take any more of your time than you have allocated." He briefly and succinctly described the reason for their visit and concluded by saying the two of them and Harold Harrison felt the time to strike was now. A quick glace at the timepiece showed him twelve minutes had elapsed.

John Webb sat in silent contemplation, his chin resting on the steepled fingers of both hands. After two minutes of silence, Stearney fidgeted in his chair and leaned forward as if to speak. Pervez jammed a booted heel on Stearney's foot, pressing hard to get his attention. When he had it, he glared and shook his head slightly. He relaxed only when Stearney slumped back in the chair.

Webb's voice broke the silence. "You have stated your case well, Rajat."

Pervez's heart soared. The use of his first name meant Webb would support their efforts. He wanted to shout aloud, but he kept silent and continued his pressure on Stearney's foot.

Webb continued. "Visit all of the names on the list Harold Harrison gave you, and tell them exactly what you have told me here today. No more, no less. I will write a letter that you can carry with you. It will pledge my participation. Show it to each man you talk to." He leaned forward, an intent expression on his face. "How long do you think it will take to see them all?"

"Four days, Mr. Webb."

"Good. This is Monday. In the letter I will ask that they gather here next Sunday to vote on an organization to be called the Silver Lake and Camp Creek Sheepshooters." Webb's eyes burned with a fanatic's fervor. "When the vote passes, and you have my word it will pass gentlemen, I know the exact spot we will make our first attack. And it won't be in the Blue Mountains, so there will be no outcry that the treaty has been broken. But I can guarantee you this." His eyes were ablaze with the fire that burned inside him, "It will be a massacre the likes of which has never been seen before, and its end result will be a broken treaty."

He rose to his feet as the grandfather clock chimed the half hour. "Now, if you would wait in the hall, I will prepare the letter. If you would like more coffee, or perhaps something to eat, please advise Mrs. Parker." They were dismissed with the wave of a hand.

CHAPTER 19

The morning after he got Rosenberg's letter and Tim McNally's note, Tom was saddled and ready to ride. His foreman, who was seeing him off, patted the neck of Lady, the mare he was riding, then walked around the horse examining the cinch and bridle.

"Reub, all your fussing around is making me nervous," Tom said with a twinkle in his eye. "You would think I was some four year old taking his first ride with all that checking you're doing."

Hassler looked down and scuffed the ground with the toe of a worn boot. "I guess you're right, Tom. I just don't like your riding off by yourself. I wish you would change your mind and let me go with you."

Tom leaned from the saddle and patted his friend on the shoulder. "Reub, we've gone all over that and you know how I feel. I'll make better time alone. And, you're the only one I can trust to see to things while I'm away. Besides," he added, seeing the disconsolate look on Hassler's face, "I shouldn't be gone much more than a week."

"Well, watch out for yourself," Reub said gruffly as Tom swung into the saddle.

"I will, Reub. Front, back and sideways. Just remember your promise. I don't need any nursemaids tagging along behind."

Reub Hassler had to bite his tongue not to tell Tom that's what he said the last time and look what happened, but he kept silent.

Tom lifted his hand in a wave and trotted down the road. A trail of dust followed him. When he reached the Mitchell stage route, he turned left. His plan was to visit the ranchers who had attended the first meeting at McNally's ranch when all but Sid Stearney voted to hold off forming the Crook County Sheepshooters Association and to try and settle their differences with the sheepmen through negotiation, not violence. He also remembered Perez had deliberately not been invited to this meeting because he was so disliked by his neighbors. Tom did not intend to see Stearney for fear of tipping his hand, so he would be making eighteen calls. He knew he would be lucky to complete his rounds in a week, but he would try. He intended to stop first at Poe Follette's, whose ranch was next to Stearney's on Crooked River.

Follette would be the key, Tom realized. He recalled how Poe had been one of those actively involved in trying to form a local sheepkillers group, but who, after listening to Tom and Tim McNally, had helped swing the vote for a peaceful settlement. Had Poe changed his mind? Tom shook off the thought. No sense worrying about where Follette stood until he got the facts. He knew Poe was a straight shooter and would give him an honest answer, so he would know soon enough.

As Tom rode west toward a skyline of rimrock, he chose to bypass Prineville and take the rougher but shorter route south of Cadle Butte and down Wickiup Creek.

It was early afternoon when he spotted Crooked River and the complex of Poe Follette's buildings near its bank. As he rode in, he saw Follette talking to a group of riders by a wood-fenced corral. When Follette saw Tom he waved and limped over. Follette had been thrown from a horse he was trying to break ten years ago, and had been stomped hard before two of his men had been able to reach him and wave the horse away. Follette had stubbornly refused to see a doctor, so his broken back had mended without being set, leaving him with a permanent stoop. He was still able to carry on normal activities even though there were times he suffered from intense pain, something he rarely admitted, even to his wife.

"Howdy, Tom. What brings you out on a scorcher of a day like this?" As if to make a point of what he said, Follette removed his hat and wiped sweat from a balding head with a red bandanna which he thrust back into a hip pocket. "Light down and we'll go in the house and have something cool to drink. I was going to help the boys bring in a couple of sick cows, but you saved me a hot ride."

"Don't let me keep you from any work, Poe. What I have to say can wait until it's done."

"Nonsense. I was only going because I had nothing better to do. Now that you're here, we can visit. I haven't seen a soul outside of my own crew since the pox hit the county. The paper quotes Doc Belknap as saying it's over. That true?"

"Guess it must be," Tom replied. "I got a letter from Henry Rosenberg. He wrote they had no new cases and expected to lift the quarantine if no one else came down sick. That was three days ago."

"Hallelujah," Follette said quietly. A questioning look immediately crossed his face. "Anyone get the bug at the Triple C?" Then after a short, meaningful pause, "Or at Rachel Williams'?"

"No," Tom replied. "We made it through, and I saw Rachel last week. No one got sick at her place, either. We both stayed clear of town soon as we heard what was happening."

"We were lucky here, too, as were most of the ranches in the valley. Only one case I know of, and that was Cy Burnett's wife. She pulled through, but has scars all over her face and arms. I guess she and Cy don't mind though, considering the alternative. Surviving is what counts."

Tom doffed his hat as they entered Follette's cool adobe home. "Afternoon, Mary," he addressed Poe's wife who came out of the kitchen to greet him.

"Why, Tom, how nice to see you. What brings you this far on such a hot day?"

"I have some business to discuss with your husband," Tom replied.

"Well then, let me get you some cool cider. I'll bring it to you in the front room, then I've got to get back to my apples. I'm cutting them up to put out to dry, but I'm starved for news, so don't just talk business with Poe." She turned to go back to the kitchen, then stopped. "Mercy sakes, what's the matter with me. If you've come all this way you must be starved. I'll fix you a bite to eat."

"Thank you, Mary. Just the cider will be fine. I ate on the way."

"Ate," Mary Follette sniffed. "You men. I'll bet I know what your meal was. Cold biscuits and jerked beef or salt pork most likely." She grinned slyly. "I don't suppose you're too full for a piece of hot apple pie, are you? Maybe with some barrel cheese on top?"

"No, I don't suppose I am," Tom matched her grin.

"Good. You two go on into the living room and I'll be back shortly. I don't have to ask Poe if he would like some pie or not. After twenty-three years of living under the same roof, I know what his answer would be."

"Twenty-three years?" Tom turned to look at Follette.

"Yep." He saw that Mary had not left yet and answered in a louder than normal tone, "Twenty-three last August, but it seems more like fifty." Chuckling, he pointed to an overstuffed armchair whose fabric displayed a pattern of roses. "Take the comfortable chair, Tom. I have to sit on one with a straight back. If I slump into soft cushions I have a dickens of a time getting up."

For twenty minutes they chatted about the smallpox epidemic and what was happening on the ranches around them. Mary Follette came in with two plates of pie and their cider. "If you'd like more, Tom, just let me know."

"How about me?" Poe voiced. "I might like some more, too."

"You might like some more, but you're not getting any more. It might spoil your supper," Placing the pie and cider on the table near Tom, she said, "We'll expect you for supper, too, Tom. There's plenty."

"Thanks, Mary, but I can't stay."

"Then I'll pack up something you can take with you," she said before leaving the room.

Poe shifted in his seat to ease his back. "I don't expect you just came for small talk, Tom. What's on your mind?"

Pickett reached into a shirt pocket and silently handed Poe the letter from Rosenberg and the scrawled note from McNally.

As Follette read them both, his jaw dropped. "I hadn't heard about Tim," he said in a whisper. "He was a good man. Ma has to know about this. I expect she'll want to prepare some things and go visit Mrs. McNally and Tim's young 'uns right away." He struggled to his feet. "Excuse me a minute. I'll go tell her."

Tom heard a cry of shock from the kitchen, then Follette returned. He straddled the chair and said apologetically, "Easier to sit this way."

There was silence between the two, then Follette spoke. " I don't think any of the men at the meeting who voted to work something out with the sheep owners have any intent to break the pact. I would have heard. I gather you're out to see all of us. Have you talked to anyone else yet?"

"You're the first."

"Well, don't take my say for it. Make your calls. But if you do find one of us is working toward this end, let me know. If a man can't keep his word, he's not worth much," he said coldly.

Follette reached for his cider and slowly drained the glass. Not so much because he was thirsty, but to give him more time to think. As he replaced the tumbler, he commented, "Now Stearney is another matter. And as for Rat Pervez, I wouldn't trust him any farther than I could throw my horse. Hang on!" He said suddenly as a thought struck him. "One of my punchers has a buddy who works for Sid Stearney. He might know something." Follette pushed himself to his feet and left the house. He was back shortly with a barrel-chested rider whose work pants looked as if they might slip down his slim hips at any moment.

"Randy, you know Tom Pickett, don't you?"

"Sure do," the ranchman said, stepping forward and extending his hand. "How are you, Mr. Pickett?"

"Fine, Randy," Tom replied.

"I filled Randy in on the way back," Follette said. "He says he did hear something that might be of interest to us."

Randy shifted his weight and tugged at his pants, which had been dangerously close to falling off. "I was over at the Bar S about two weeks ago to see Lefty Gomez about borrowing some wagon wheel metal until we could get to Eugene City to get some of our own. He said he couldn't lend us any without talking to his boss who was on a trip with Rajat Pervez. Anyway, we got to talking and I asked him when Stearney was going to be back. Lefty said he didn't know for sure as Stearney told him he was going to visit most of the ranches around Camp Creek and Silver Lake, and not to expect him for at least a week. Is that any help?"

"It certainly is, Randy," Tom replied. "More than you know."

After his rider left, Poe Follette faced Tom. "There's your answer. It don't take too many brains to figure out what Stearny and Rat Pervez are up to." He rubbed at a day's growth of whiskers. "I guess it's still worth seeing the others. You may learn something more. Would you like me to ride with you?"

"No thanks, Poe. It's not necessary and I expect Mary will be counting on you to go with her to the McNallys. I'll make the rounds and if I hear anything you should know about, I'll be in touch." He picked up his hat from the floor and settled it on his head when Mary re-entered the room, a filled flour sack in her hand, which she handed to him.

"There are some roast beef sandwiches in there Tom, and a couple of apples from our tree. Also another piece of pie, so don't mash it." After an awkward pause she said, "We're grateful to you for bringing the news about Tim. I just feel awful that we hadn't heard sooner. We'll leave first thing in the morning, which will give me a chance to bake up some things." Not forgetting her manners, she added, "Come visit us again soon. And next time bring that nice Mrs. Williams with you."

After Tom completed his tenth call, he felt he had all of the information he needed. None of the ranchers he talked to intended to break their word unless the sheepmen broke theirs, and, like Poe Follette, they didn't know of anyone in their group who expressed any disagreement with the pact. They had all heard the Camp Creek and Silver Lake ranchers were openly unhappy that the southern portion of the Blue Mountains was no longer available to them for summer and fall graze, and most were aware that Sid Stearney and Rajat Pervez had been visiting these ranchers, but for what purpose they weren't sure. Only one of the ten had heard about McNally, and to a man they expressed concern that without his guiding hand resolving any future conflicts between cattle and sheep men would be difficult. It also became apparent to Tom that not only were none of them willing to take McNally's place, they looked to him to do it.

Tom had been away from the Triple C longer than he planned, not because it took so long to travel from ranch to ranch, but because he couldn't turn down the invitations to spend the night from cowmen and their wives, isolated for months by fear of the smallpox virus, who were thirsting for news about their neighbors and the county.

After his last stop, which was at the Brennan ranch on Maury Mountain, he decided to ride home by the Willamette Valley and Cascade Mountain Wagon Road and have dinner at the stage stop a few miles southeast of Post. This route took him past old Camp Murray and toward the flats that lay at the foothills of the Ochoco Mountains. It was here, at the crest of the slope directly in front of him, that Lieutenant Stephen Watson had led a charge against wily Chief Paulina and a small band of Snake braves who were camped at the top of the ridge. Lieutenant Watson, with more courage than sense, charged the high ground with his 1st Volunteer Cavalry at dawn only to become mired in a vast area of swampy land. As their horses foundered, he and two privates were killed and five other soldiers were gravely wounded. After the Volunteers retreated, Paulina and his braves horribly mutilated the bodies, then withdrew during the night. Paulina knew this country and had chosen his spot well, deliberately luring the unsuspecting Watson into battle by camping in the open on the northeastern side of the swamp. Now the hillside, once the scene of a savage battle, was covered with peacefully grazing cattle.

Before he reached the dusty, rutted trail that ran from The Dalles to the now deserted military camps of Harney, Wright and Curry, Tom stopped to water his horse at one of the year-round streams that fed Beaver Creek.

What a history of violence this country has seen, he mused. First trappers fighting amongst themselves and the Indians for furs, then the bloody series of Indian wars which were followed by the Rosslyn Robbers and after that the vigilante reign of terror until, most recently, the cattle-sheep war. What is it in the nature of man that makes him want to eliminate his own species, Tom wondered, and, like those before him who have pondered the same question for centuries, he did not have an answer. He just knew that he had to live life by his own set of rules, and guessed Paulina must have felt the same way. In the grand scheme of things, who was to say which of them was right.

"Lady," Tom reached out to pat the neck of his mare, "when you figure it out, let me know."

On hearing her name, the dun swung her head from the creek and nuzzled Tom hard enough to push him off balance.

"Hey, don't take me so seriously. I was just kidding. I don't expect our Maker even knows for sure, else there wouldn't be so many religions preaching so many different things." He picked up the reins and stroked the wet muzzle. "Let's just drop the whole thing and move along. I don't know about you but my stomach's beginning to think my throat has been cut."

When Tom arrived at the large log structure that served as a rest and meal stop for stagecoach passengers travelling to southern Oregon and Nevada, he noticed a larger than normal group of horses tied to the hitching rail. Loud laughter echoed from inside the building.

Tom dismounted and checked the brands. He recognized them all. They were from ranches around Camp Creek and Silver Lake.

He led Lady to a stable behind the stage stop and was met at the door by a tousled hair boy of grade school age. Tossing him a silver half-dollar, Tom said, "Give her a good rub-down and some grain. I'm going to grab a bite to eat and expect to be on my way in an hour."

"Thanks, mister," the boy said examining the coin. Then he looked up with a wide grin that showed a missing tooth, "you can count on me. She'll be ready and waiting."

As Tom entered the coach station, all conversation came to an abrupt stop. There were eight men at the bar, he noted, and another five seated at a table near the fireplace. He recognized some faces and nodded to them. They acknowledged his greeting with one of their own, then returned to their conversations in more subdued tones. Occasionally, one would subvertly glance up to look in his direction.

John Bridges, the proprietor, hurried up to Tom, a welcoming smile on his face. He wiped both hands on a stained apron that once might have been white and extended a hand. "Tom, welcome! I haven't seen you in a coon's age. Looking for food, whiskey, or," he added, "both?"

"Just food, John. I could eat a horse."

"Then come on back to the dining room. I haven't butchered any horses lately," he joked, "but I am cutting up a bunch of nice T-bones for a load of

151

travelers that will be stopping here in a couple of hours. I guess I could spare one for a wandering wadie."

"T-bone sounds great," Tom said, following his portly host into a room that held a long, oil-cloth covered table that had already been set.

Bridges waved toward it. "Pick any spot that suits your fancy. What would you like with your steak?"

"How about some beans and biscuits with gravy?"

"No sooner said than done. I have some canned peas, too."

"Sounds good to me. Anything special for dessert?"

"You bet. Chokecherry, rhubarb or apple pie and bread pudding."

"I'll take the cherry pie. And make that steak rare."

"Rare it is," Bridges chortled. "That's the only way I know how to cook them." He hurried away to prepare the meal.

By the time Bridges returned, the men in the other room had left. Through an open window Tom saw them ride away and noticed they were all travelling in the same direction.

"It looks like you lost all your customers," Tom observed as the steak was placed before him.

"Yep. They just stopped to wash the dust out of their throats. There's some kind of meeting going on at John Webb's place. It must be mighty important because they're the second batch by today. Lots of travelling going on since the quarantine was lifted. Even Sid Stearney and that little runt of a rancher from the North Fork were here this morning."

Bridges glanced at the plate, unaware of the information he had just given Tom. "Steak rare enough for you?"

CHAPTER 20

The cattlemen who were gathered at John Webb's ranch were in his spacious, high-ceilinged living room to celebrate the decision they had just made, which was to form their own sheepshooters association. Liquor was flowing freely, and they were in a boisterous mood.

After the vote, a shaken Rajat Pervez sought Webb out and pleaded with him for a few minutes alone.

Tears glistened in Pervez's eyes as he faced the older man in his study. Webb, aloof and confident, sat rigidly behind his highly polished mahogany desk, a crystal glass half-filled with bourbon rested on a silver coaster in front of him. Although a full decanter and several glasses stood on a sideboard just steps away, he did not offer Pervez a drink.

John Webb joined his hands over an embroidered silk vest and tilted back in his chair. He spoke slowly, enjoying the moment. "Let me recap what you have just said, Rajat, to be sure I have it right. You want me to hold another vote because you do not like the one that was taken?" He swirled a finger in his glass, then sucked the drops of amber liquid from it, relishing the discomfort of the man standing before him.

"No, no. I have no problem with the vote to organize a sheepkillers association. It is the date." Pervez removed a kerchief from his pocket and wiped his sweat-covered face. "We must change the date."

"Must?" said Webb, enjoying the game of cat and mouse he was playing. "Must, you say? Explain why we *must*, Rajat."

"It's as I told you, Mr. Webb. Unless I can get my cattle into the Blue Mountains before summer ends, the bank will foreclose on my mortgage and I will lose everything." Pervez began to tremble. "All I'm asking is that the raid you have planned not be delayed until next spring. That will be too late. The vote must be to act now."

Webb rocked back and forth in his chair, his eyes as hard as ice. "There's that word '*must*' again, Rajat. Just because you bit off more than you could chew, why do you expect the rest of us to save your hide?" He rose to his feet, placed the knuckles of both hands on the desk top and leaned forward. His voice was low and menacing. "Pervez, I have been planning this killing for months. To do it any sooner than next spring would be meaningless. When we strike I want thousands of sheep dead, not the measly few that haven't, as yet, been taken out of the hills." He sat back and his harsh laugh filled the room. "You little pipsqueek," he snarled. "Just because you got too big for your britches, don't expect me, or anyone else, to pull your fat out of the fire."

"Please, Mr. Webb. Everything I have worked for and dreamed about will be gone. I will do anything you ask if only you will see that some action is taken now. I beg you."

Webb held up a hand to stop him. "Pervez, you are pathetic. A man doesn't beg. Nor does he crawl. He takes the hand he is dealt and either folds or gambles. You gambled your hand and lost." Webb's voice filled with contempt. "I can assure you, there will be no change of plan. I suggest you either join me and our friends or leave my ranch." Stiffly, and in measured strides he left the room without looking back, leaving the shaken Pervez alone.

As Webb paused at the top of the steps that led into the room where his neighbors were now enjoying the buffet he had prepared for them, he was spotted and a cheer went up. A drunken voice rang out, "A toast. A toast to John and the Camp Creek/Silver Lake Sheepshooters." A roar filled the air as glasses were held high.

Webb was handed a full tumbler of rye. He stood patiently for a moment, then raised a hand for silence. "Gentlemen, a toast in return." He held his glass out toward them. "To next April and the death of all sheep east of the Cascade Mountains." He put the glass to his lips. As he did, the sound of a single shot came from his study and echoed throughout the drawing room.

CHAPTER 21

April, the following year

Two Irishmen, a herder and tender, had set up camp in the desert between Silver Lake and Camp Creek, by Benjamin Lake. They knew they were trespassing on the cattlemen's side of the dead line, but still they brazenly grazed a band of 2400 castrated rams. These wethers were being pastured to fatten them up for the mutton market by three central Oregon sheepmen. These sheepmen, one of whom had signed the pact that restricted sheep to certain areas in the Blues, had spread the word their herd would be guarded and issued the warning that, "We are well armed and not much afraid. If the cattlemen want trouble, they are welcome to come pay us a visit."

Their mistake was in issuing this challenge prematurely. The rams had been moved into one band, but the armed men had not, as yet, arrived to protect them.

At the bottom of a gentle slope, the two Irishmen had erected a single, two-man worn canvas tent whose rope supports were staked firmly to the ground. In front of the tent was a dirt-covered fire pit, lined with rocks and hot coals, in which bread was baking in a Dutch oven. A few feet from the tent flap were the ashes of an open fire, contained by a circle of rocks. Over the now dead fire, hung two smoke-blackened kettles. One of these was half-full of mutton stew that would be their meal for the next few days. The heavy iron kettles were suspended from a stout juniper branch which was attached by baling wire to two heavier poles sunk firmly in the ground. The bonfire had been positioned to provide both light and warmth to the inside of the tent.

155

Sage, bitterbrush and stunted junipers surrounded their campground and spread up the grass rich slopes of the grazing area they had chosen. A pleasant scent of spring flowers filled the air.

The herder and tender had just completed their rounds. Satisfied that all was well, and that their two sheepdogs would alert them to any threat of danger, they resumed gathering and piling weather-smoothed rocks for the large monument they planned to build. Carefully, they searched for stones of all sizes; larger ones for the base, medium size rocks for the middle and smaller ones for the top. There was no real purpose in erecting this pillar, it was just a way of passing time. If they made permanent summer camp at this spot, they might even exceed the fifteen foot tower they had built the previous summer.

As the shadows began to lengthen, the two men abandoned their rock gathering and, with the aid of the dogs, bunched the wethers, for it was the hours after sunset and before sunrise that were the most dangerous. This was the time when coyotes and mountain lions made their kills.

As darkness fell, the herders started a fire and stirred in the fat that had congealed on the surface of the stew. This, fresh baked bread and a rationed cup of raw whiskey from a stave barrel would be their meal.

They had spoken little throughout the day, for theirs was a lonely life and one that required a minimum of conversation. Both men were sending money back to their families in Ireland, and both longed for the day when they had accumulated enough cash to start their own herds. Eventually, perhaps, if life was good to them, they might even be able to have their wives and children join them in this vast land of opportunity.

Because it was a warm night, they dragged their bedrolls from the tent and spread them out in the fragrant grass. With nothing on their minds, nor any problems to torment their thoughts and keep them awake, they fell asleep immediately.

From a ridge that overlooked the gentle valley where the wethers had been grazing, a prone figure stretched to ease his cramped muscles, then rose stiffly from the ground. He hurried to the horse he had picketed in a gully below him, removed its hobble, then mounted, and, before he rode west, circled the area. A bright moon helped light his way.

An hour later, the lone rider caught sight of a flicker of light through the trees. Carefully, he worked his way toward it. When he was fifty yards away, he stopped and called out, "Halloo the camp," adding, "it's me, Hank. Hank Brown." His horse fidgeted nervously and nickered as he waited for a reply.

A dark figure holding a Winchester rifle stepped from behind a tree to his right. "You alone, Hank?"

"Alone?" Brown snorted. " What do you mean am I alone? Of course I'm alone. What kind of a fool question is that?"

"Don't get so all-fired testy. That's what John Webb said to ask, and that's what I asked. Go on in." The guard mumbled his displeasure, "Me, I have to stay out here until I'm relieved. Whenever that is."

Brown dismounted and walked his horse into the circle of light from the fire. He ground reined his horse and knelt before the flames, spreading his hands to warm them. A figure limped up to him and held out a plate of cold beans and biscuits. "The boss said to feed you when you came in." He handed over a tin cup and gestured toward the coffee pot by the fire. "Consider yourself served," he said gruffly as he departed.

Hank Brown wolfed the meal and washed it down with hot coffee. Sensing a presence, he glanced over his shoulder, then struggled to his feet. "Evenin', Mr. Webb." He nodded at the two men standing by John Webb. "Mr. Harrison, Mr. Snodgrass."

"What did you see?" Webb snapped, wasting no time on formalities.

"It's just as you said, Mr. Webb. They're running sheep over the boundary. I'd guess between two and three thousand head. And there are only two sheepherders guarding them. I scouted most of the day and didn't see another soul. It looks like they're alone." He paused and a wicked grin spread over his face. "They spent the better part of the day piling rocks for their own tombstone."

Snodgrass's eyes narrowed. He ignored the comment about the rocks. "You're sure you didn't see any armed men hiding out?" he asked.

Brown replied, "Nope, and that's for darned sure. I rode so many circles around the sheep and Benjamin Lake that I almost got dizzy." He straightened to his full length, tucked his chin back and said proudly, "I made the last sweep after dark, just as you said to do, Mr. Webb. And I didn't see no campfires."

Webb slapped the Flying W hand on the back. "Good job, Hank. Grab some sleep, we'll be leaving before dawn." He addressed the others. "Guess we'd better do the same. It looks like tomorrow is going to be a full day."

Harold Harrison, who had remained silent, spoke out. "Before we do, I have to say this, John. I've got to hand it to you. The sheepmen did exactly as you said they would last summer—delivered a couple of thousand sheep or more to us, right on our front doorstep." Harrison shook his head in wonder. "I had my doubts they would do anything this foolish, particularly after they won such a big hand with the Blue Mountain Agreement."

Neither Harrison or Snodgrass saw the mad gleam in John Webb's eyes as he turned and gazed into the darkness that surrounded them. Nor did they hear his whispered reply, "This is just the beginning, just the beginning."

An hour before dawn, eleven men rode out of the coulee where they had spent the night. Nine were from the newly-formed Camp Creek/Silver Lake Sheepshooters Association. With them were Mac Logan, who represented the Paulina Sheepkillers and Henry Snodgrass of the Izee Sheepshooters. It was Snodgrass who had spoken before the group of Paulina cattlemen in the middle of the night, out in the desert, when they met to vote on forming a sheepkillers association of their own seven years ago.

A cloudless night, lit by a half-moon, helped guide their way. They rode easily, without talk, in single file. John Webb led the way. There was little underbrush to impede their progress and the grey-bodied pines through which they rode cast surreal shadows on the ground around them. Every now and then the tremulous warble of a nighthawk broke the silence as it caught its meal of insects on the wing. The spongy surface of pine needles muffled the horses' feet, and except for the clicking of bridle metal, or a horse expelling air, they made no sound.

When they had crossed the notch in the canyon that led to the flats of Benjamin Lake, where the sheep camp was located, Webb raised a gloved hand. They all stopped and dismounted, then gathered around him. He pointed toward a scattered grove of ponderosa, beyond which was an outcropping of centuries old lava. "We'll circle that ridge and come at them from two sides," he whispered. "If the herders are unarmed, take them alive. If they put up a fight, gun them down. You five come with me." He indicated a group in the circle around him. "The rest of you follow Henry." He nodded toward Snodgrass. "When it's light enough to see, start the dance."

They separated. One group circled north, the other, led by Webb, swung east. As they crested the ridge where Hank Brown had spent the afternoon and evening watching the activities of the herders below, a hint of grey replaced the blackness that had hung over the tops of the towering pines on the mountains in the far distance. The stars began to lose their brightness as the band of dim light stretched higher into the sky.

Mac Logan, the Paulina rancher who was with the group led by Webb, urged his mount forward until the two men were side by side. Webb was peering intently at the lantern lit tent below. "Still too dark to see much," Logan commented. "But with all those sheep blatting and those dogs barking, I would say the herders are already up and about. There aren't any shadows moving around in the tent, either."

"It makes no difference, Mac. It would be nice to catch the woolies bunched up, but they're as easy to kill this way. It just takes a little more ammunition. We'll have enough light before long." He swung his horse around and issued a whispered command to the men behind him. "Spread out and wait for my signal. Logan and me will take care of the herders."

In the magic moment just before the sun rises over the horizon and a gentle light covers the land, Webb drew his pistol, raised it, then thrust it forward. The six mounted riders raced downhill toward the milling sheep, yipping and yelling.

When he saw them coming, the tender, who was putting out the campfire, stood frozen in shock. Then, gathering his senses, he raced for the tent where he had left his rifle. Webb, a bandanna covering his face, knocked him sprawling with the shoulder of his horse. Leaning over the saddle, he cocked his Colt and pointed it at the frightened Irishman, who was getting to his feet.

"Your choice," Webb growled. "Live or die."

He could have said anything, for the tender couldn't hear the threat because of all the firing and yelling, but he did have sense enough to know a cocked and loaded gun was aimed straight at him. He raised his hands.

A tight smile of satisfaction appeared on Webb's face as he reached inside his shirt and threw down a gunny sack and short length of rope. He leaned down and shouted, "Put that over your head." The sheepman quickly complied. Webb got down, tied the sack tightly under his victim's chin and guided his captive past the tent and up the continuation of the sloping pasture until they reached a single white pine. Webb bound him tightly to the tree and returned to his horse.

Logan, who had also donned a mask, rode up, dragging the herder behind him. Webb waved toward the man he had trussed to the tree. Careful not to mention Logan by name, he said, "Take him on up to where his friend is. I'm sure they won't mind keeping each other company while we go about our business. But before you do, we need some answers. Then put the sack on his head." Webb walked to the herder who had wrapped himself in a ball and was huddled in the dust. Grabbing the frightened man by his leather vest, he jerked him to his feet and snarled, "You wouldn't mind me asking a question or two would you?"

" 'Tis all right by me, your honor," the man stuttered. "Oi'm not a brave man."

"Then listen carefully. I want to know two things. First, how many animals are you watching over, and second, where are all the armed men who were supposed to be guarding you? You have two seconds to tell me."

A look of panic spread over the herder's face, and he shook so violently his teeth chattered. His answer blurted out in an Irish brogue so thick that neither Webb nor Logan could understand. Patiently, Webb asked again, and pushed the pistol under the quivering chin. "Now you have one second. Speak slowly, and tell the truth if you want to live to see the day out."

The Irishman swallowed hard, and in a heavily accented voice said they were watching almost 3,000 four and five-year-old castrated rams, and armed men were expected to arrive later that day to help guard them.

A sigh of relief escaped from Webb's lips. He looked at Logan, who had cupped an ear to hear because of the intensified gunfire below them. "The timing couldn't be better. We'll be finished and gone before they get here."

By mid-morning, 2,500 dead and dying sheep littered the field; those that had escaped were scattered in the hills. The killers had spared the dogs who were frantically running among the bodies, whining and waiting for some command from one of their masters as to what to do.

On their way home, the grimy, exhausted group of sheepshooters stopped at a nearby creek to slake their thirst and wash the blood and viscera from their faces and hands. Webb pulled an unopened bottle of rye from his saddlebag and passed it around. He was pleased with the job they had done, and told them so. He also advised, "We can't afford to stay here much longer as armed riders are on their way. Go home by different routes, and be careful that no one sees you until you are on your own land. If anyone asks where you were today, tell them you never set foot off your property." After a thoughtful pause, he added, "Reshoe your horses and beat the metal into iron you can use for something else. We don't want our tracks identified, or any shoes left around to be found."

The bottle had made its rounds and was handed to Webb, nearly empty. He examined its contents, drained it in one swallow, then crashed the glass on some rocks alongside the creek.

"We'll meet again, Friday of next week, where we planned," he said. "Oil up your guns and bring along plenty of ammunition. Then we'll visit some more sheep that are eating cattlemen's grass."

CHAPTER 22

Ten days after the slaughter at Benjamin Lake, the same group of cattlemen from the Izee, Paulina and Camp Creek/Silver Lake sheepshooters, struck again in southern Oregon, near Silver Lake, where they killed more than 3,000 sheep and lambs belonging to Charles McKunes. Then, after they had disposed of the sheep, they burned McKunes' corrals and wool sheds at his ranch in nearby Thompson Valley. The two armed tenders watching the sheep were killed.

Three weeks after the McKunes raid, again in the vicinity of Silver Lake, 2,300 merinos belonging to Grubb & Parker were slaughtered. This time the sheepkillers used a technique they had not tried before: Instead of firing from their saddles, they dismounted, and, to save bullets, kneeled to shoot into the sides of the bunched animals. This way they were able to kill or wound several with one round. A herder who ran into the line of fire was shot, and a camp tender badly trampled.

Emboldened by their success, and the lack of resistance they faced from the woolgrowers, the three sheepkilling associations became more open in their efforts to enlist new members. They were successfully helped by two important factors: The price of wool, which had skyrocketed and resulted in more sheep being pushed onto grasslands being used by cattle, and an unexpected and sudden decline in the market price for beef. Frustrated by these events, more and more Crooked River Valley and upper Crook County cattlemen began talking about breaking the Blue Mountain Agreement and forming a sheepshooters organization of their own to take back the land they had lost. To complicate matters, many cattlemen faced bankruptcy because of the low price being paid for their cattle, and to save their ranches and feed their families, began raising sheep. Thus, a split was driven between those who refused to acknowledge there was a place for sheep in central

162

and eastern Oregon and those cattlemen who became sheepmen in order to survive. The rancor between these two groups would flare into further violence, and the ill-feeling it created would pit family against family for generations to come.

To make things even worse, miners, whose diggings and placer fields were being overrun and trampled by growing hordes of sheep, joined together with farmers and small ranchers whose fences were being pushed down and their fields of hay and vegetables destroyed by foraging woolies. When posted notices and armed guards no longer could stem the flow of migrant sheep, the miners either lent their support to the existing sheepshooters organizations or supported the efforts of those trying to establish another sheepshooters group in the north and northwestern part of Crook county.

Early in June, a few ranchers from the Ochoco Valley who had suffered recent losses from the encroachment of sheep on their privately owned pastureland, acted.

Their victim was Allie Jones, one of the woolgrowers who had met with Tom Pickett at the Triple C. Jones had also been one of the sheepmen who met with Tim McNally and the group of influential cattlemen who established the Blue Mountain Agreement.

The attack took place on Jones' land, a few miles from Prineville. Although only 65 head of sheep were killed, the consequences of this action would lead to even bloodier violence.

Within ten days, despite the efforts of Tom Pickett and Poe Follette to stop it, a Crook County Sheep Shooting Association was formed. Later, when the Crook County Shooters, as they called themselves, joined forces with the three other sheepkiller groups, they became the Inland Sheepshooters.

Two days after the Crook County Shooters met, they issued a rambling letter that was published in the *Crook County Journal,* whose editor supported the cause of the cattlemen. Though portions of it were vague and confusing, this notice voided the Blue Mountain Agreement and reinstated the original dead line boundary that had been drawn up earlier by the Paulina Sheepshooters.

The message to the newspaper, dated June 17th, read as follows:

TO THE CROOK COUNTY JOURNAL!

Conflicting range territory in Crook County led to the slaughter of sheep last Monday when masked men shot and killed sixty-five head belonging to Allie Jones, a sheep owner residing fifteen miles east of Prineville. The killing occurred on Mill Creek in the vicinity of the "dead line", the men threatening a greater slaughter if the herds in the confines of this line are not removed instantly. The continued and increased intrusion of sheep in this part of the country resulted in the wanton slaughters which have recently occurred near Silver Lake, and marks the first steps in the range difficulties which are likely to be encountered here during the coming season. The scene of the killing is in the territory where an effort was made to establish lines for sheep and cattle, called The Blue Mountain Agreement. *The sheepmen have violated this agreement, therefore we no longer consider it to exist and by our decree it has been rescinded.*

While it is hoped that open hostilities will not break out between sheepmen and cattle owners in this territory during the summer months, it is asserted that an encroachment upon this disputed region by nomadic sheep will be the signal for forcible resistance. The "dead lines", or "death lines" as they will become known to invading sheep or herders, will be strictly enforced which means sheepmen will not be occupying a peaceable neighborhood.

We so publicly decree on this date.

THE CROOK COUNTY SHEEPSHOOTING ASSOCIATION

The following Thursday, two large advertisements appeared in the weekly *Prineville Review,* whose views tended to favor sheepmen.
One, from the Oregon Woolgrowers announced:

$1,000 REWARD
THE OREGON WOOLGROWERS ASSOCIATION

Will pay the above reward for such information as shall lead to the arrest and conviction of any person or persons guilty of shooting, killing or maiming any member of the above Association, or any employee of such member, while engaged in their duties in attendance on the herds of a member, or guilty of killing, maiming, or otherwise unlawfully and with malicious intent of destroying the sheep of a member.

J.H. Gwinn
Secretary, Oregon Woolgrowers Association
Pendleton, Oregon

H.C. Roper
Secretary, Antelope Woolgrowers Assoc.
Antelope, Oregon

The second ad, placed by the Antelope Woolgrowers was set in bold type. It read:

$1500 REWARD

IN ADDITION TO THE $1,000. REWARD OFFERED BY THE OREGON WOOLGROWERS ASSOC., THE ANTELOPE WOOLGROWERS OFFERS A FURTHER REWARD OF $500. FOR THE ARREST AND CONVICTION, OR FOR SUCH IN-FORMATION AS MAY LEAD TO THE ARREST AND CON-VICTION OF ANY PARTY OR PARTIES WHO MAY BE GUILTY OF KILLING, MAIMING OR INJURING ANY MEM-BER OF THE ANTELOPE WOOLGROWERS ASSOCIATION, OR ANY PERSON EMPLOYED BY SUCH MEMBER, WHILE ATTENDING TO THEIR DUTIES IN CARING FOR THE

SHEEP OF A MEMBER, OR FOR KILLING, MAIMING OR OTHERWISE UNLAWFULLY DESTROYING THE LIVE-STOCK OF A MEMBER.

Signed

ANTELOPE WOOLGROWERS ASSOCIATION

J.D. McAndie, President

H.C. Roper, Secretary

Shortly after the ad ran, only one man was brave enough—or foolish enough—to try and claim the rewards by informing on a local cattleman who was a member of the Crook County Shooters. He was found dead, in the desert, with several bullet holes in his back. After a hearing in the county courthouse, the jury, composed solely of cattlemen, soberly delivered a verdict of "Death by suicide."

Less than a week after the cattlemen ran their warning in the *Crook County Journal,* a small band of Crook County Shooters made good on their promise to enforce the dead lines by attacking a camp on Old Baldy Mountain, where they killed or scattered 2,300 sheep belonging to Miles Lee. The herder in charge, G. W. Brooks, had just arrived at camp and was preparing supper when he heard several shots fired close to camp.

The *Prineville Review* reported his eyewitness account of what happened:

"I rushed out of my tent, rifle in hand, and saw several men firing upon the sheep, which were banded together. Some of the attackers had kneeled to make their killing more effective. Others had not, and were shooting from horseback.

They all were shooting as fast as they could pull their triggers.

"I got behind some trees and opened fire on them, but they spotted me and returned a heavy fire. I only had 11 cartridges, and when these were done, I tried to crawl to where I had more ammunition cached. When they saw I was out of bullets, they made it so hot for

me I had to flee for my life by dodging behind rocks and trees until
I got away."

When asked by the paper's reporter if he could identify any of his assailants, Brooks replied, "It was dark and they was all masked. Only thing I know for sure is there were five or six of 'em. I heard one of them yell, 'find him and kill him', but I hid in a badger hole and they never did catch me. I was lucky they didn't. I was even luckier the badger wasn't home."

By early July, a violent range war was raging throughout central, eastern and southern Oregon. By mid-summer more than 10,000 sheep had been killed. Thousands more would meet their deaths in the months to come, for the sheepkillers had discovered a new and faster way to kill sheep—and save ammunition. It was the same method used by the Indians in Montana at the beginning of the century, before they had firearms. The Indians called it buffalo jumping. The technique they used was to force a herd of buffalo to the rim of a high cliff, gather behind them with beating drums and branches of fire, and crowd the frightened and confused animals over the edge to their death on the rocks below.

Quite by chance, eight Crook County Shooters found they could do the same thing with sheep. Only the sheepkillers didn't use drums or torches. They simply surrounded a large herd on three sides and fired into them as they raced forward. The frightened animals bolted to escape by using the only route left open and followed each other over the edge of the steep rimrocked cliffs. The sheepkillers had a name for this new and efficient way of killing sheep. They called it 'rimrocking'.

CHAPTER 23

Throughout the summer months, violence in the range-
lands east of the Cascade Mountains increased as mem-
bers of the three sheep killing organizations from Izee, Paulina and Camp
Creek/Silver Lake joined forces with the recently formed Crook County
Shooters. They struck at sheepmen in individual groups and as organized
units. When members of all four of the sheepshooter organizations rode
together, they called themselves the Inland Sheepshooters. Only those
woolgrowers who kept their sheep on their own private land were spared as
the sheepkillers now laid claim to all open range land.

In July, Andrew Morrow and Jim Keenan, two other woolgrowers who
had met with Tom Pickett, lost more than 1,000 Shropshires in the rolling
hills that lay adjacent to Willow Creek, just 18 miles north of Prineville. By
counting the empty cartridge boxes found at the scene, they determined over
1,500 bullets had been used. The empty boxes also showed something
else—the name of the Prineville firm of Wurtzweiler and Thompson, which
had been stamped on each with India ink.

The lone sheepherder who had been guarding the flock was bound to a
tree. A rough gunny sack had been tied over his head. Keenan's son, who
had been with him, escaped and hid among the rocks until the attackers left.
He later described them as being 20 in number and unmasked, but said their
faces had been blackened, either with axle grease or charcoal from dead
campfires, to hide their identity.

Three days after the slaughter of Morrow and Keenan's sheep, ten
masked riders killed 200 blackfaces owned by V.S. Cowles. The sheep had
been bunched together for market on Mill Creek at the foot of Wildcat
Mountain, 26 miles east of Prineville.

A day later, a few miles east of Paulina, a woolgrower had moved 2,000 head of sheep onto his ranch at Grindstone. These were killed or scattered by six hooded riders.

Two days after that, less than two miles from Paulina, 1,000 sheep were attacked and slaughtered as they were being driven from public land to private pasture by a single Basque herder and his dog.

In addition to the method of 'rimrocking', which was now being used extensively by the four sheepshooters groups, an even more vicious method of killing sheep was introduced. It was first used on a herd owned by the Keerin brothers of Izee—former cattlemen who had taken to running sheep to survive the drastic fall in beef prices. Their tender rode in on a sweat-lathered pony to bring them the news that hundreds of their merinos, which had been gathered at Swamp Creek, were dead or dying for no apparent reason. After seeing for themselves that this was true, the Keerins sent for Prineville's veterinarian. After examining the sheep, the sober faced animal doctor cut open the body of one of the dead animals and looked at its throat, stomach and intestines. Then he examined the grass on which the animals had been feeding, smelling a handful of blades cautiously. After this he asked to see where the salt licks had been placed and, at each, he touched a wet finger to the salt and then smelled his finger carefully. At one salt block, he cut a piece off with his pocket knife, put it to the tip of his tongue and made a sour face. He spat on the ground and turned to the Keerins who were anxiously watching.

"Are you two using blue vitriol or saltpeter for anything?"

They looked at each other dumbly, then shook their heads in unison. Owen Keerin said, "No. We don't even stock the stuff. What makes you ask that?"

The vet took a deep breath and the muscles in his jaw tightened. "Because that's what is killing your sheep. It's been spread on the grass and put on your salt licks." He shifted uneasily as he glanced first at one brother, then the other, and swallowed hard. "I'm sorry, but you won't be able to save any of them." Putting his hands on their shoulders he examined their stricken faces. "You'd be merciful to shoot those that are still alive. Ingesting poison is an extremely painful way to die."

169

By the start of winter, tens of thousands of sheep had been shot, bludgeoned to death, rimrocked or poisoned. In addition, 22 herders and tenders were known to have been killed or wounded. Another eight had vanished and were unaccounted for. No woolgrowers had been harmed, but they were constantly being harassed in the middle of the night by riders who fired shots at their homes and burned their outbuildings.

To add insult to the havoc they were creating, a taunting letter, signed "The Sheepshooters' Headquarters in Crook County", dated December 29th, was sent to The *Portland Oregonian*, which had been issuing regular reports on the violence in the eastern part of the state.

The letter was addressed to the editor:

Morning Oregonian
Portland, Oregon

Mr. Editor:
Seeing that you are giving quite a bit of publicity to the Sheep-shooters of Crook County, I thought I would lend you some assistance by giving you a short synopsis of the proceedings of the organization during the past year. Therefore, if space will permit, please publish the following report:

Sheep Shooters' Headquarters, Crook County, Oregon, December 29, 1904—Editor Oregonian: I am authorized by the four sheep-killing organizations, known jointly as the Inland Sheepshooters, to notify the Oregonian to desist from publishing matter derogatory to the reputation of sheepshooters in Eastern Oregon. We claim to have the banner county of Oregon on the progressive lines of sheep shooting, and it is my pleasure to inform you that we have a little government of our own in Crook County, and we would thank the Oregonian and the Governor to attend strictly to their business and not meddle with the settlement of the range question in our province.

We are the direct and effective means of controlling the range in our jurisdiction. If we want more range we simply fence it in and live up to the maxim of the golden rule that possession represents nine points of the law. If fencing is too expensive for the protection of the range, dead lines are most effective substitutes and readily manufactured. When sheepmen fail to observe these peaceable obstructions we delegate a committee to notify offenders, sometimes by putting notices on tent or cabin and sometimes by publication on one of the leading newspapers of the county as follows:

You are hereby notified to move this camp within twenty-four hours or take the consequences. Signed: Inland Sheepshooters.

These mild and peaceful means are usually effective, but in cases where they are not, our executive committee takes the matter in hand, and being men of high ideals as well as good shots by moonlight, they promptly enforce the edicts of the association. Our annual report shows that we have slaughtered thousands of head of sheep during the last shooting season and we expect to increase this respectable showing during the season to come—providing the sheep hold out and the Governor and Oregonian observe the customary laws of neutrality.

In some instances the woolgrowers have been so unwise as to offer rewards for the arrest and conviction of sheepshooters and for assaults on herders. We have heretofore warned them by publication of the danger of such action as it might have to result in our organization having to proceed on the lines that "Dead men tell no tales". This is not to be considered as a threat to commit murder, as we do not justify such a thing except where flockowners resort to unjustifiable means in protecting their property.

Signed: Corresponding Secretary,
Crook County Sheepshooters.

CHAPTER 24

A day after the Crook County Shooters' letter appeared in *The Portland Oregonian,* Governor George Chamberlain called an emergency meeting in his walnut panelled office at the state capitol in Salem.

Those attending were the state Attorney General and the majority leaders of both houses. In addition to these state officials were two others the governor had invited: Rachel Williams and an investigator for the Pinkerton Detective Agency.

All were seated around the governor's solid circular cherry conference table, which pundits frequently referred to as the "Round Table." Considering all the problems the state was having with land fraud claims and suits brought against the Willamette Valley and Cascade Mountain Wagon Road, as well as the cattle-sheep war, Chamberlain often wished that it truly was King Arthur's Round Table, and that he had a magician like Merlin, who could resolve the problems of the state as easily as the sorcerer had for Arthur.

Governor Chamberlain sighed as he stood. As important as this meeting was, he knew he had to keep it short for another was scheduled in forty-five minutes. Sometimes it seemed as if all he did was attend an endless series of meetings that never left time to get any real work done. He often wondered, as he had when shaving this morning, why he had given up the placid life of a school teacher for public office.

Expectant eyes turned to the tall, imposing figure with bushy sideburns who had risen from the post of accounts clerk to become a member of the state legislature, then on to become the state's first Attorney General and finally governor of the state.

Chamberlain leaned forward and placed his hands on the highly polished surface of the table. "Thank you for coming on such short notice. We all have busy schedules so I'll come right to the point. Most of you know Mrs. Williams." He nodded in Rachel's direction. "She has been actively seeking our help for almost two years now." He gave her a rueful smile. "Starting with my predecessor T.T. Greer, Mrs. Williams has been diligent, to say the least, in her efforts to have us take some form of action to solve the problem that has been plaguing us in the eastern part of our state. I doubt if there is a legislator in Salem who has not had the opportunity to talk to her. Or," he chuckled drily, "not to have been able to avoid talking to her. That is one reason I have asked her to be with us today.

"The other gentleman who has joined us this morning you have not met. With the exception of our Attorney General, that is. His name is Roy Freeman. I will tell you why he is here in a few minutes, but first, I would like to get your opinions on this," he sputtered in anger as he held up a copy of the *Oregonian's* editorial page, "abominable letter from the Crook County Shooters that ran yesterday." The governor's face had turned florid and flushed. "Their audacity is beyond belief."

L.T. Harris, the Speaker of the House, raised his hand for recognition and after receiving a nod from Chamberlain, rose to his feet. "Governor, I have discussed this matter with my honorable associate George Brownell," he bent his head toward the President of the Senate, "and I think it is safe to say I can speak for both of us." He stopped for a moment to receive an acknowledged grunt from his colleague. "We are in a sensitive area here. Both Houses are well represented by cattle interests in the fifteen counties of central and eastern Oregon. As you well know, the cattlemen are very influential and," the speaker licked his lips nervously, "very generous in their donations to congressmen who support their cause." He spread his arms in a hopeless gesture. "Frankly, I don't know what we can do, if anything." He cast a furtive glance at Rachel Williams before saying, "Even though the residents of the eastern part of the state are a small minority when it comes to a statewide vote, they do carry considerable clout." He shifted nervously, deliberately avoided looking at Mrs. Williams, and sat down.

"Mrs. Williams," the governor's deep voice broke the awkward silence, "would you care to reply to what the Speaker just said?"

All eyes focused on Rachel, who fought to control her emotions. "Yes," she said, remaining seated. There was a sharp edge to her voice. "Votes, money and influence. That's all I have heard since I have been in Salem." She rose to her feet, eyes snapping. "Gentlemen, whatever became of the words justice, honor and the law? Killing is against the law, as is burning a man's property and violating his constitutional rights." Anger overcame her as she looked at each of the politicians in turn. "If none of you has the intestinal fortitude to pass legislation that will stop such violent acts, then at least have the courage to enforce those laws that do exist." She knew she had gone too far, and should stop, but frustration from the many months she had spent at the state capitol boiled to the surface. Her voice rose in intensity. "My fellow woolgrowers and my friends said it would be a waste of time to look to our elected representatives for help. I hate to admit it, but they were right and I was wrong." Drained by her outburst, she dropped into her chair.

The governor leaned back in his seat and clapped his hands. "Well put, Mrs. Williams. I have often felt the need to say what you have just said, and I applaud you for it. But, being a realist as well as a politician, I can recognize the problem the leaders of both Houses are facing. We are a democracy, and if a democracy has one failing it is that passing new legislation is a painfully slow and tedious process." A crafty look transformed his face. "That's why in their infinite wisdom, our founding fathers also gave equal power to the executive and judicial branches." He pushed himself to his feet, paused dramatically, then continued. "Gentlemen, and Mrs. Williams, it is now time to tell you why I have asked Mr. Freeman to join us." He gestured at the silent figure seated to the left of the Attorney General.

"Mr. Freeman is a special investigator employed by the Pinkerton Detective Agency. I'm sure you have all heard of the Pinkertons, have you not?" He paused then continued. "Their motto is, 'The eye that never sleeps', and if Mr. Freeman is an example of the rest of their detectives, I can safely vouch for that credo. I might add that Mr. Freeman is more than just a special investigator. He is in charge of their Denver office and reports directly to Robert Pinkerton, one of the sons of Allan Pinkerton the founder of the agency.

"Roy Freeman comes with impeccable qualifications. His latest endeavor was working with Tom Horn to bring "Peg Leg" Eskridge and Dick McCoy and his sons Tom and Joe, to justice."

Seeing the favorable reaction he had expected from the mention of these names, the governor went on. "Roy has also been personally involved in substantially reducing the number of train and stage robberies that have plagued the west this past decade."

Chamberlain leaned forward, knowing he had everyone's full attention. "You are undoubtedly wondering why Mr. Freeman is with us. Let me explain. In 1866, the governor of the state of Oregon was given special powers to deal with exigent emergencies by a hastily called general session of the state legislature. These powers were granted to deal with the Indian problem at that time, but they were never repealed. In fact, they were forgotten until Chief Justice Moors called them to my attention." He paused momentarily, then continued. "Consequently, as governor, acting under these powers, I retained the services of the Pinkerton Agency to infiltrate the sheepshooters' organizations for the specific purpose of gathering enough evidence to bring them to trial. In fact, unbeknownst to all of you but the attorney general, the Pinkertons, in cooperation with the United States Secret Service, began their investigation shortly after my inauguration."

The governor turned to face Rachel Williams. A broad grin lit his face. "So you see, Mrs. Williams, all of your efforts have not been in vain as you just suggested."

Seeing her violent blush, he held up both hands and jokingly suggested, "I think it's best to say no more, don't you agree?"

Struck dumb by the governor's surprise announcement, she could only nod her head in agreement.

More than pleased with himself, the governor directed his gaze at the leaders of both houses. "I apologize for keeping the two of you in the dark. It's not that I don't trust you. Far from it. I just felt, until the time was right, the fewer people who knew about this, the better. In fact," the tone of his voice dropped lower, "that's why the leaders of the minority party weren't invited to sit in with us this morning."

He needed to say no more, for it was a well-known fact both of these politicians had been openly receiving large sums of money to block any legislation that might be detrimental to the members of Oregon's Cattlemen's Association, an organization funded mainly by cattle interests in eastern Oregon.

Outside, the sun escaped from a cover of low clouds, its oblique rays reaching through the room's bay windows to seek out the golden watch fob on the governor's vest. From there it traced a path along the brocade covered walls, then disappeared. The governor placed both arms on the table, and leaned forward conspiratorially. He spoke with such intensity they weren't aware they had all stopped breathing to better hear his words.

"I have asked Mr. Freeman to give us a progress report, which he is prepared to do. But first I must ask that you pledge not to reveal—to anyone—what you are about to hear." His eyes sought out each person around the table. After receiving an acknowledgement from everyone, he said, "After you hear what Mr. Freeman has to say, you will know the necessity for this promise. Sir," he addressed Roy Freeman, "if you please."

Freeman rose and paused just long enough before speaking for those around the circular table to make their own evaluations of him. He did not look like a Pinkerton detective. His demeanor was congenial and pleasant. His wool suit was well-tailored, but comfortably rumpled. Both suit and vest were complemented by a conservative tie whose knot showed it had been hastily done by a man who knew he had to wear one, but would have preferred not to. When he spoke, his voice was soft and well modulated, giving a hint of an eastern education. Unless they knew his occupation, they would have guessed him to be a cattle buyer or a representative of an out-of-state company looking for investment opportunities in the west.

"Thank you, Governor Chamberlain," he began, jerking a nod at the expectant faces before him. "First, let me explain our policy. Pinkerton agents operate independently. Once our objective has been assigned, we rarely report to those who have employed us until our job has been

176

completed. However, at the request of Governor Chamberlain, and in view of the circumstances, we have agreed to make an exception in this case." He gripped his velvet vest with short, pudgy fingers, breathed deeply, and exhaled a burst of air. "There is one condition the governor agreed to and it is that I will accept no questions. The reason for this is obvious. The less you know about our operation, the better our chances are for success."

As they watched and listened, a transformation took place in Freeman. The man they first took as someone they would not give a second glance at in a crowd became a professional killer and hunter of men. His eyes and voice hardened and held them riveted as he revealed the most intimate details of the four sheepkiller organizations, who their members were and even some of the future raids they had planned. He recited by memory a long list of their supporters, from informants who supplied the cattlemen with inside information on when and where herds of sheep were being moved to merchants who supplied them with ammunition and poison. He concluded with a list of politicians who had secretly sworn to oppose any move against the cattle interests and the amount of funds each had received.

"My God," the Speaker of the House breathed aloud, echoing the sentiments they all felt.

"Yes, I expected that would be the reaction most, if not all, of you would have," Freeman responded. "There is more that I could tell you, much more, but you have heard all you need to know. All but one thing, that is."

It was a dramatic moment. Freeman knew this and he played it out as he pulled a Havana cigar from a leather case he withdrew from an inside coat pocket. I wonder what their reaction would be, he thought, if they knew the letter to the *Oregonian*, signed by the corresponding secretary of the Crook County Sheepshooters, was written by one of my agents. The purpose had been to gain public support for the governor's action in hiring the Pinkertons when the time came for it to be known. Even the governor was not aware of this, but that's how the Pinkertons worked. Their methods were unconventional, just as their successes were legend. Freeman was pleased at how well the letter had worked and the immediate public outcry that followed its publication.

The Pinkerton agent brought his mind back to the moment and emphasized his last statement. "Yes, one thing. Our operatives, as you may have guessed by now, are active members of the Inland Sheepshooters. Each one has reported back that the one cattleman the four organizations fear the most, and who has stood against them from the beginning, is going to be killed." Genuine sadness covered his face as he gazed out the window, momentarily lost in thought. Sorrow filled his voice as he turned his attention back to them. "They want to make an example of him, and unless we tip our hand—which we cannot do if we are going to bring these murderers to justice—we can only sit back and watch his death."

Governor Chamberlain jumped to is feet. "Dammit, man, we can't just..."

Freeman held up a hand, stopping the governor in mid-sentence. "I said 'we' could do nothing, meaning the Pinkerton Agency. I didn't say someone else couldn't. Their intended victim can be warned, but it must be by a person he knows and trusts. And this individual cannot, must not, reveal where this information came from."

For the first time, the Attorney General spoke, expressing the thought that was on all of their minds. His voice was hard and deliberate. "Just who do they plan to kill, Roy?"

Freeman looked directly at Rachel Williams. His reply brought a stricken look to her face and she involuntarily threw a hand to her mouth and uttered a small cry when he answered, "Tom Pickett, of the Columbia Cattle Company."

CHAPTER 25

Frosted breath surrounded Tom Pickett's face as he swung a saddle on a sturdy cow pony named Patch. Pickett planned on taking the rough stage route to Mitchell, 26 miles away, and felt the roan, with its compact body and short, stout legs could handle the rugged terrain better than Lady, his regular mount.

He left the Triple C and headed north toward the Blue Mountains and the stage road that followed Scissors Creek into the Ochocos. He chuckled aloud as he thought of the note he had left for his foreman Reub Hassler that said, "Have gone to Mitchell to see the bull Abe Childs wants to sell. Plan to take the stage route and should be back for supper".

He felt a little guilty because he left shortly after Reub had gone to bring in a dozen cows that had wandered through a fence some wild horses had knocked down. By the time Reub got back, which should be around noon, it would be too late for his foreman to send someone after him. Tom's chuckle turned into a laugh as he thought of Reub, who would be stomping around, telling anyone who would listen that the owner of the Triple C should not have ridden off by himself. But Tom felt a desperate need too be alone with his thoughts. It was January, and he had been cooped up with his crew for three months. He was restless and needed to get away, if only for a few hours.

He also missed Rachel, who was spending the winter months at the state capitol in Salem. They had been able to get together for three days at Thanksgiving, but that was over two months ago. She had been discouraged at not making any progress and confided to Tom that unless she could get the legislators to take some form of action she was going to give up and return to central Oregon. Tom knew Rachel had dedicated herself to accomplishing what she had set out to do and realized defeat would be a bitter pill for her to swallow. He had wrestled with mixed emotions. Although he wanted her back, he knew what she was doing was very important to her, and he hoped that she would succeed. Slowly, he had come around to her point of view, and after the Crook County Sheepshooters Organization was formed, realized the only sensible solution to ending the killing that was pitting neighbor against neighbor was by getting the state to act.

By mid-morning Tom had reached the mile high summit that looked down upon the Ochoco and Strawberry Mountain ranges. He paused to give his horse a breather and to admire the view. An unobstructed wind urged him to raise the collar of his sheepskin coat to protect his neck. Patch blew out great gusts of vapored air as he shifted to put the bitter wind to both of their backs, then the stout animal reached down to nibble at some frozen bunchgrass that had been blown free of snow.

Tom gazed over the thick stands of fir and pine toward the two isolated peaks that rose out of the valley below him. White and Black Buttes. They had been aptly named by an early trapper. The one on his left, bare and covered with a coating of gray-white shale, glistened in the sun. The other, a dark lava cone which was also bare of trees, stood black as night. Exposed as they were to the sun, neither carried more than a few small patches of frozen snow.

A surprised snort interrupted his reverie. Below, to his left and no more than fifty yards away, stood a magnificent bull elk. Tom began to count as thirteen elk cows passed the bull and slowly wended their way down the steep slope. They all wore their silver winter coats that would turn brown in April or May. As silent as ghosts, another herd of forty or more Roosevelt elk, chaperoned by two more bulls, crossed a barren ridge below him. "Guess they must have cabin fever, too, Patch," Tom murmured, more to himself than his horse. He looked back at the huge bull he had first spotted. They stared at each other intently, then after a full minute of eye contact, the large mammal pawed the ground, gave a parting snort, and followed his charges.

"You rascal," Tom called after him. "You wouldn't be so slow in moving if you thought I was looking for meat." He rubbed the neck of his horse and gave it a pat. "Time to move on, Patch." He jerked hard on the reins to pull the pony's nose out of the grass.

From the peak where they had rested, they left the frozen ruts of the stage road and dropped into a protected valley that was surrounded on all sides by broken ridges of lava. Tom worked left of the two mountains and crossed a small ice-crusted stream to follow a valley that led into a series of low, rock-covered hills that were dotted with stunted juniper. He stopped at the next stream to water his horse and stretch. As he dismounted, he failed to notice a reflected glint of sun on metal that came from the rimrock above.

An hour's ride later, the canyon deepened and led to East Creek, which, fed by a number of tributary streams, would soon join Deep Creek, a stream that ran through the small town of Mitchell. Tabled plateaus of stratified rock towered above them, blocking out the sun and bringing a deep chill to the air. The fogged breaths of both horse and rider became more pronounced and blended with the leafless and stark cottonwood branches that slapped at their faces and barred their way. As the barrel-chested cow pony cautiously worked its way around the slick, ice-covered rocks it stumbled, tried to catch its footing, and fell. At the same time, Tom heard a sharp crack. His first thought, before he was thrown from the saddle, was that the gelding had stepped on a broken branch which tripped him and made the snapping sound. He lay in the shallow, icy stream, momentarily stunned until the sharp report came again. A rock exploded, just inches from his face. The rolling echo that rang down the canyon told him what was happening. Someone had shot his mount and was now trying to kill him.

On hands, knees and feet he stumbled to the nearest protection he could find; two large boulders which were nestled against the solid granite wall of the canyon. As he dove for the safety of this shelter, two more shots rang out in quick succession. One took the hat from his head, the other plucked at his torn jacket. Tom cursed as he took stock of the situation. He could see his horse, which, he now realized, had taken a bullet meant for him. There was no way he could get to his saddle carbine without exposing himself. He grimaced when he thought how ineffectual his six-gun would be against longer ranged rifles.

181

He cursed again as he realized the cover he had chosen would expose him to deadly ricochet fire. But he had no choice. From the shouts of the men above, and the location of the smoke from their guns, he estimated there were six to eight of them, and they had him covered from every angle. In spite of the freezing temperature in the ravine, sweat ran down his face.

Time was the only ally he had. In four hours it would be dusk, and if the men above didn't realize the situation he had put himself in, he might be able to hold them off and sneak away after dark. This hope was soon dashed as a fusillade of shots lashed at his hiding place. Rock chips stung him as lead slugs buzzed by like angry hornets. He pulled himself into a ball, crouched in one corner and instinctively covered his head with both arms. "Like that will do a lot of good against bullets," he thought to himself as he tried to draw into an even smaller target.

It took a few seconds before Tom realized the firing had stopped. Cautiously, he hugged one of the huge boulders and slid to a position where he could peer out. Heavy gunfire erupted again. As he dove back to the corner that had given him protection before, the shooting increased as more men seemed to have joined in the attack. Then he became aware no bullets were entering the cave-like shelter in which he was trapped. "What are they up to now?" he muttered as his ears, which rang from the intensity of the firing and the whine of ricocheting lead, tried to make out the shouts he heard and the sound of booted feet running over rocks.

Suddenly, it came to him. The reason for the sudden barrage of fire was meant to pin him down. Now they were attacking, hoping to take him by surprise. "You won't catch me napping," he growled aloud, drawing and cocking his .44 Colt. "When I go, I'll have the pleasure of knowing some of you will be going with me."

He stepped from his shelter in a crouch and aimed directly at a massive figure running toward him, no more than twenty yards away. At this range, he knew he couldn't miss. His finger squeezed the trigger and bucked in the air as he fired. The man racing at him stopped as if he had been pole-axed. His mouth flew open and a shocked look spread over his face as the rifle he was holding dropped in the water. It was Unk Tanner, one of Tom's crew.

CHAPTER 26

As they rode home, Unk Tanner filled Tom in on what had happened. "Not long after you left, a rider came racin' in to the ranch on a horse so lathered I don't figure it will make it through the night. The feller came all the way from Salem and had ridden half the day yesterday and all night. He changed horses wherever he could find one." Tanner paused to reflect and gather his thoughts. "I'll bet he must have left a half-dozen dead horses behind if the horse he came in on was any example." The thought of anyone treating a horse like that caused Unk to lean over and affectionately pat the neck of his own mount. "Anyway," he said, getting back to the story, "when he heard you went riding off by yourself, he liked to have had himself a conniption fit. Said we'd best arm ourselves and high-tail it after you as the message he was carrying said your life was in danger and you were to have a guard at all times."

Tanner thought over what he had said to be sure he had not missed anything, then continued. "Reub was away and there was no one else could give orders, so I rousted the boys from their noon meal and came to find you. I guess the feller was right, 'cause we were a half-mile away from where you was holed up when we heard the first couple of shots. Then a whole bunch more. When we arrived, we found Patch lyin' in the crick and figured they must be after you, so we cut loose on 'em. Surprised 'em I expect, as they took to their horses and lit out. We lung shot one. Before he died he said he wanted to meet his maker with a clean conscience and admitted they had been waitin' in the hills for most of a week to catch you by yourself." Tanner jerked his head at the horse Tom was riding. "That's his mare, compliments of the IZ ranch accordin' to the brand."

Tanner rested an arm on the saddle horn and leaned sideways to face Tom and finish his story. "After seeing that cranny you was hidin' in, I figured you was either dead or would be leaking blood like a sieve. I was in such an all-fired hurry to get to you that I didn't think to call out."

"That's all right, Unk," Tom replied. "I was half-deaf, so probably wouldn't have heard you anyway."

Tanner jerked his head in a quick sideways motion and clicked his tongue. "You like to have scared me to death. I know how straight you can shoot. I thought for sure I was a goner."

Tom didn't reply. He hadn't been sure he had pulled his gun up in time when he recognized Unk, in which case Tanner would truly have been a 'goner'.

Unk added a final comment. "I couldn't decide whether to send some of the boys after them when they skedaddled or not, but the country around here is so durn rough, and there're so many places to fort up that I was afraid they might ride into a trap."

"Unk," said Tom, "you did everything just the way it should have been done. I'm grateful to you. I guess you know you saved my life."

Tanner straightened in the saddle and stuck out his chest. He was pleased at the compliment his boss had just given him, and replied honestly and proudly, "Yep. I guess I did at that."

Several minutes went by, then Tanner spoke again. "Won't Reub be hog-tied when we get back and he hears what happened?"

"Yes," Tom replied, smiling, then a broad grin split his face as he thought of Reub's reaction. "That he will."

"I imagine Mrs. Williams will be pleased, too." Before Tom could respond, and ask what he meant, Tanner added, "I plumb forgot to tell you. The rider she sent on ahead said she was leaving right after he did, so I 'spect she'll be waitin' to meet us."

They opened the gate and passed under the Triple C arch, a group of tired and cold riders. As they drew closer to the ranch house, Tom searched for a sign that Rachel was there. Then he saw her, standing on the veranda, shading her eyes to watch them come in. Tom spurred his mount forward and slid to a stop in front of where she stood. Before he could dismount, she ran down the steps to him. Looking up, she placed a hand on his leg.

For a long moment, neither spoke. Then, in a husky voice, Tom said, "I guess this is twice you've had to look after me."

Eyes glistening with tears, she nodded and replied in a voice choked with emotion, "It seems that way, doesn't it?"

Tom jumped from the saddle and she went into his arms. They held each other tightly, oblivious to the surreptitious glances of the ranch hands as they rode by. They didn't even notice Unk Tanner come up to lead the IZ horse away. Nor did they see one of the last riders hand Reub Hassler the hat Tom had lost.

Still holding each other, Rachel and Tom entered the house. A roaring fire was going in the living room and the cook, who had been setting a table for two, discretely left the room. Tom pushed back a lock of Rachel's hair and studied her face. She leaned to him and tilted her head back, taking his face in both hands. Then their lips met. Their kiss was long and tender. With a slight shudder of happiness, Rachel put her head on Tom's chest as he held her closer. "Damn you, Tom Pickett. If this keeps up, I'll be a white-haired, worry-wrinkled old woman long before my time."

He kissed the top of her head. "I guess I'd still love you anyway."

Rachel pulled back suddenly, a look of surprise on her face. "Why Tom, that's the first time you ever told me that." Teasingly, she added, "Does this mean we're engaged?"

Tom flushed a bright red. "I suspect you might have guessed by now how I felt about you," he stammered awkwardly. "I'm not much for putting things like this in words, but if being engaged is . . ."

Rachel put the fingertips of one hand to his lips. A smile lit her eyes. "Yes, I suspected how you felt, just as I guessed you knew I felt the same about you." Then she covered her mouth with both hands and giggled. "Here we are, two middle-aged people acting like a couple of fifth graders who have just decided to go steady.

"As for being engaged," she said mischievously, "that's something we should think about for awhile." Standing on her toes, she gave him a peck on the mouth. "Right now, I suggest we both have a fresh bath and a change of clothes. After that we'll eat and I'll share some exciting news with you."

After supper they were snuggled comfortably together on the large brown leather sofa that faced the rock fireplace. Hiner, who had joined them, was stretched out on the hearth rug, occasionally interrupting their low-voiced conversation with a long, contented groan.

Rachel filled Tom in on the meeting in the governor's office, and the need to keep the news of the Pinkerton Agency's appointment confidential. "The governor said I could tell you, but no one else. He also asked that you not tell anyone." She paused in her story, then added, "He has given the Pinkertons a $10,000 advance, so I know he's serious."

Tom gave a low whistle, which caused Hiner to raise his head and look back at them over his shoulder. When there was no further indication the whistle was meant for him, he slumped back to the floor. "That's a lot of money, Rachel. But I guess he figures if it gets the job done it will be worth it. But how can he spend that much money without everyone in the state capitol knowing it?"

"Some discretionary power granted by the state legislature in the Sixties to deal with the Indian problem at that time. It allows the governor to act on his own if he feels there is an emergency to deal with. After the law was enacted George Woods, the governor at that time, formed a unit of voluntary cavalry to fight the Paiutes and Bannocks. The volunteers never did fight any Indians, and the legislation was never rescinded."

"He must have had a battery of lawyers look that up," Tom said in admiration.

"No," Rachel replied," the Chief Justice stumbled upon it. But," she pushed herself to a sitting position, and took his hand. "He has a legal team working on it now. He also said he took action two weeks after I first talked to him about the need for Salem to do something to stop the sheepkilling. Can you imagine that, Tom! And all along I have been thinking that nothing was being done. But it was!"

Tom started to reply, to tell her how pleased he was, when a knock, followed by a forced cough, interrupted him. They looked up to see Reub Hassler standing at the entrance to the room. He was holding Tom's battered Stetson in both hands.

186

"I hope I'm not interruptin' anything. I waited until you two had finished supper, but I can't wait any longer. I got some words that need sayin' before I turn in."

A pang of guilt hit Tom. He had been so absorbed in seeing Rachel that he had completely forgotten to seek Reub out and tell him what had happened. He realized this must have hurt his old friend deeply, and was made even more aware of this by the formal tone in Reub's voice.

Tom got to his feet and went to him. "Reub, I owe you an apology. With Rachel being here and all, I just plumb hadn't gotten around to seeing you yet. Please come in and join us."

While Tom had been talking, Rachel went to the table and poured a cup of coffee, adding two heaping teaspoons of sugar and a splash of cream. She carried it to the Triple C foreman. "Do join us, Reuben. You know how much your company and friendship means to both of us." She held out the coffee. "Two sugars and cream. As I recall, that's the way you like it."

Hassler looked at her gratefully, but before taking the cup held up the hat. One of his index fingers was stuck through a hole in its crown.

"Thought you might like to have your John B. back." The term referred to its manufacturer, John B. Stetson. "As you can plainly see, had the hole been an inch lower, what little brains you have would have blown right through it." He dropped the hat on a nearby chair, undecided as to whether to leave or say what he had on his mind.

Rachel sensed this and, still holding the coffee, took him by the arm and gently led him to a chair by the sofa. "Please sit down, Reuben. I think you have something more to say, and I think we. . . Tom, should hear it."

"What I have to say, I'll say standing," Reub said. Then the words that were bottled up inside him came rushing out in a torrent. "That was a darn fool thing you did, riding off alone. You almost got yourself killed again, and you would have if it hadn't been for Mrs. Williams here. I don't know what makes you think there are a bunch of angels hovering over your head, watching out for you. The only angel you're going to get is a stone one atop a grave marker. If you weren't so pig-headed stubborn you'd have figured that out for yourself by now."

187

Reub stopped and looked at the coffee Rachel handed him. He became even more flustered as she clapped her hands in applause.

Tom remained silent for a moment, taken aback by Reub's unexpected outburst. Then he responded. "Reub, have a seat and let's discuss this." He sat on the edge of the sofa, facing his friend. His hands were clasped tightly together. "I can't argue with a word you've said because you are right." Not wanting to reveal the confidential information he had gotten from Rachel, he went on. "You warned me a long time back, when Stearney's hand and the IZ poke stopped by here, that I should watch my back and not go riding off alone. I didn't listen and got cut up bad. And there hasn't been a time since then that you haven't argued with me when I left the ranch by myself."

Tom paused to let what he had said sink in. "I've been acting like a wet-behind-the-ears greenhorn, and I admit it." He locked his fingers, put his elbows on his knees and leaned toward Reub. "Obviously, the sheep-killers would like me out of their hair, and will probably try again. So how about this. I put you in full charge of the security of this ranch, as well as my own protection. I also promise not to ride out alone, and you can assign whomever you like to ride with me."

Tom settled back in the cushions, his voice rang with sincerity. "Reub, you are the only person I know, other than Rachel, that I would trust with my life. And the only one capable of doing the job. Will you do this as a favor to me?"

Reub's eye's searched Tom's face, and, after deciding his boss was serious, stood up. "If you'll shake on it, I'll start tonight. If you do, I guarantee you won't be able to step out of the house without someone watching your back."

Later, as the coals of the fire began to die and shadowy fingers filled the room, Rachel rose from the sofa and stretched. "Tom, it has been a long day for both of us. I think it's time for bed."

"Rachel, I wish you would stay more than a couple of days before you ride back to Salem."

"I know, Tom. I wish I could, too. But Governor Chamberlain is going to need all the help he can get once he decides to present the Pinkerton reports to Congress. In the meantime, I can still keep working on those key legislators whose votes he is going to need."

Later that night, unable to sleep, Tom was lying under the covers of his bed, both hands behind his head, watching the full moon through his bedroom window when a shadow passed before it. He rose on both elbows, fully alert, then relaxed and fell back on his pillows as a hint of jasmine filled his nostrils. He heard the rustle of bedcovers, then a warm and fragrant body slid to him. As he reached out, Rachel whispered teasingly, "I guess it's all right as long as we're engaged."

The words had just left her mouth when a jar shook the end of the bed.

"What was that!" Tom said, rising up in alarm.

Rachel snickered as she wrapped herself around him. "I think that was Hiner joining us."

CHAPTER 27

Had there been a grave marker, it would have read, "Leonidas J. Douris". However, no one would have recognized him by that name for he was known to one and all as Shorty Davis. But there was no tombstone for Shorty Davis. He rode from his homestead one day with his dog and was never heard from again.

His disappearance became a legend that was told and retold through future generations to come. There were many versions of what happened. Some thought he had tired of frontier life and returned to his native Greece. Others felt, as Davis was a cattleman who had turned to raising sheep, that a letter he received carried a threat and he left the area to begin life under another name in Nevada. Still others speculated that he had been killed by a fellow sheepherder who held a grudge against him. Another theory was that he had been slain by the sheepkillers and buried, along with his dog and horse, in a spot that had never been found. Only two men knew the true story. His killer and the man who found the evidence left behind.

Shorty Davis was an immigrant from Thessaly. At the time of his disappearance, five of his six brothers were still living in Greece. Davis had the reputation of being somewhat of a recluse. He kept to himself and bothered no one. He was not known to have any enemies and went out of his way to avoid trouble.

Shorty's ranch was on Crooked River, an hour's ride from a few buildings that comprised the town of Post—named after its postmaster Walter H. Post. Every Tuesday, as regular as clockwork, Davis would appear at the store that also served as a post office for supplies and to pick up any mail that might have arrived. When three weeks had gone by without Davis making an appearance, Walter Post became worried. Fearing that Davis might have been hurt, or was ill, he rode out to Davis's section of land to check on him.

After knocking and calling out, Post lifted the latch and pushed open the door of Davis's rough-hewn cabin. The musty odor of an unused room and spiderwebs that blocked his entrance and covered the single, glass window, indicated to Post the cabin had been vacant for some time.

Post had never been in the one-room shack before, and noticed it was divided into a bedroom and a kitchen area. A stone fireplace served for heating the cabin as well as preparing food. Motes of dry ash, disturbed by the door's draft, hung in slanted rays of light from the paned window.

The room was spartan and plain. Hand sawn pine planks covered the log walls and a slab of wood on two short sawhorses served as a kitchen table. The walls were covered with yellowed pages of *The Morning Oregonian* and the *Prineville Review* to serve as insulation. On a bench against one wall were scattered pieces of harness and a stirrup that needed mending. Above the bench an assortment of smoke-stained pots and pans hung on rusty nails. A single shelf held some tinned goods, a few cracked crockery plates and two tin cups. An un-made bed was built against the third wall. At the foot of the bed was a leather-strapped chest that, Post discovered, held a jumble of rumpled and unfolded clothes.

Post roamed the room, searching for any clue that might indicate where Davis had gone. It was certain enough that he did not leave in a hurry as there were no dirty dishes and everything seemed to be in its place. The postmaster did some mental calculations. Davis had been in to pick up a letter the first of February. It was now the 22nd. If the letter was still here, it might provide some clue as to Shorty's whereabouts. Post searched diligently, even looking in the pockets of the clothing in the chest. Then he took a piece of kindling and carefully poked the ashes for a tell-tale scrap of unburned paper, or even the whole ash of burned pages or an envelope. He found nothing.

As Walter Post returned home, he mused over the dust that had accumulated in the cabin as well as the thick webs of industrious spiders. Had Shorty Davis returned home after picking up his mail? Post pulled up before the building that served as his store, the post office and residence for his family. As he dismounted, the thought struck him. He had seen sheep grazing as he rode through Shorty's property! Davis would certainly not leave his sheep unattended. Something was definitely wrong. Tomorrow he would send his eldest son to Prineville with a note for the sheriff.

Three days later, Charlie Congleton, the Crook County Sheriff, announced his arrival by the jingle of the spring bell above the front door of the store. Walter Post, who had been stuffing mail in a dozen square open-boxed shelves, turned to look over his shoulder. Congleton spoke first, "Mornin', Walt. Sorry I wasn't able to get here sooner, but I had to pick up a couple of horse thieves in Lamonta and just got your message yesterday. This county is getting so gol-durned big, I need to be twins to cover it all." He stopped and his nostrils flared. "Is that coffee I smell?"

"Fresh pot," Post replied. "Come on back and I'll pour you a cup." He held back the curtain that separated the store from where he and his family lived and waved the lawman in.

Congleton slid easily into a kitchen chair and thrust his booted feet out as he poured cream in the mug Post handed him. Then he added a heaping spoonful of sugar. "I've got a full day facing me, Walt, so let's get right to it. Has Shorty Davis shown up yet?"

"No, he hasn't. I had my youngest ride out there yesterday afternoon. No horse, no dog, no Shorty." Post told him what he had seen at Davis's cabin, and closed his accounting by saying he expected foul play might be involved as Davis hadn't told him he was going anywhere.

"You say he was last in here the first part of February?"

"Yep."

Congleton stirred his coffee, then took a cautious sip to test how hot it was. After a deep swallow, he said, "It's not like Shorty to let his sheep wander loose, and if his dog was with him, I don't imagine he planned to stay away long." He stared at his coffee for several seconds, then asked, "Didn't that fire at old man Chance's place start about that time?"

Post's face screwed up in thought. "I think so. Chance stopped in here the same week Shorty did. He bought a drum of kerosene. Said he had some slash to burn." Post stood up. "It'll be in the ledger. Want me to look up the date?"

"I would appreciate it, Walt. If it's not too much trouble."

"No trouble at all. I'll be right back." Post returned, carrying a large, fabric covered journal. Setting it on the table, his finger traced up the entries. "Here it is. Came in the second of February."

Congleton nodded. "The day after Shorty was in."

"I reckon so."

"Have you seen Chance lately?"

"As a matter of fact, I have. He stopped by last week to try and sell me some coyote pelts. The crazy old coot. I've told him a dozen times there's no market for them, but he keeps coming back."

"He still running cows?" Congleton asked.

"A few mangy head of doubtful ancestry. Probably no more than five or six. Lets 'em run in the hills behind his place."

"How did he and Shorty get along?"

"Like two tomcats."

"Did one of them ever threaten the other?"

"Not in so many words, but I did hear Chance tell Shorty one day that if he ever found sheep on his land, he would take a pickaxe to 'em."

"What did Shorty say to that?"

"Told him if any did show up they wouldn't be his, then turned his back and walked out."

Congleton rose, stretched, and hitched up his gunbelt. "Guess I'll ride out to Shorty's and have a look around for myself. Then I'll swing by Chance's place and see if he knows anything."

"If you want to talk to Chance, you'll have to go to the Valley. He told me when he was in last that he was going to Brownsville to see his brother and wouldn't be back for a couple of months."

"Guess I'll not talk to him, then, " Congleton replied. "Thanks for the coffee. And for sending word. If Shorty does show up, let me know."

When he left Post's store, the sheriff took the route that led to Shorty Davis's property. As soon as he was out of sight, he changed course and headed west toward the Maury Mountains where Abner Chance had filed his homestead. Post had told him all he needed to know, so a search of Shorty's cabin would be a waste of time. The sheriff remembered Chance's fire. It had burned for ten days and the smoke was so intense it could be seen in Prineville, twenty miles away. Thinking it might be an uncontrolled forest fire, Congleton had sent one of his deputies to investigate. The deputy reported back that Chance was doing considerable burning, not slash but good-sized fir logs and small growth green pine. The deputy asked if Chance was clearing timber and the old man had replied, "It's none of your business what I'm doing," and ordered him off the property. As Chance was violating no law, and the fire was contained to a small area, the deputy wrote up his report which was filed away and forgotten. In his accounting, the deputy mentioned the fire was so hot, he couldn't come within fifty yards of it, and that the snow around the fire had melted up to a hundred yards away.

The sheriff also remembered that Chance was among the first to join the Crook County Sheepshooters, and made it known to anyone who would listen that he did so to protect his cattle. He was often heard saying that any sheepman that threatened his grass would "Burn in Hell." Those who knew Chance knew he wasn't right in the head, so his remarks weren't taken seriously.

As the sheriff rode over the ridge that faced Chance's meadow, he saw the large, blackened area where the fire had been. He rode around it to reach Chance's lean-to shack and, to announce his presence in case the crazy old man was there, called out loudly several times. When he had determined there was no one around, he searched the tool shed for a rake and shovel. He also found a pair of knee high gum boots, which he put on. Grunting displeasure, he waded through several inches of old ash to where he figured the center of the fire would have been.

Six hours later, covered with a layer of soot and grime, he trudged to the nearby creek to wash up. Then he returned to the edge of the burned area and knelt to carefully examine the objects he had found: a lump of metal that once might have been a horses bit, a length of black steel with a deformed trigger guard and what remained of a misshapen and barely recognizable set of false teeth.

A great weariness fell over Sheriff Congleton. He now understood what had happened to Shorty Davis. He also realized no court in the world would convict Chance on the meager evidence that lay on the ground before him.

What's more, as he had no concrete proof these items were related to Davis in any way, he would never be able to bring Chance to trial, or, worse than that, even tell anyone what he had found.

CHAPTER 28

The male clerk sniffed in disdain as he peered over his wire rimmed reading spectacles at the disreputable looking figure that stood before his desk.

"You say you *have* to see the governor?" He asked incredulously. "My dear sir," the contempt in his voice was obvious, "it is necessary to make an appointment to see Governor Chamberlain. He is a very busy man. Besides," he started to say there was little chance you have of seeing the state's top elected official, but there was something in the man's eyes that warned him off. He finished instead by concluding, "The governor is working on an important speech and has given strict instructions not to be disturbed."

It was true the governor was preparing a short talk, but he had said nothing about not being interrupted. The clerk had taken it upon himself to make this comment because of the unkempt appearance of the caller, who was shifting impatiently from foot to foot. The man actually reeked, and it was obvious he hadn't seen bath water for several weeks. Nor had his clothes.

The immaculately dressed and clean shaven employee of the state hissed, "Perhaps I can direct you elsewhere?" In his mind and by his manner, he meant out of the state capitol and into the street.

"Yes, you can," the man growled belligerently. "To the governor's personal secretary."

The young clerk visibly bristled. "The secretary to the Governor of the State of Oregon is home ill today, and I have the honor to be taking his place." He opened the leather bound appointment book on his desk and ran his fingers down the scheduled hours. "I see no entry for an appointment this afternoon." He paused to look at the unshaven man before him and started to rise from the cushioned swivel chair in which he had been seated, "Mr?"

"Freeman. Roy Freeman," the visitor hissed as he bent over the desk and roughly shoved the governor's temporary secretary back onto the chair so hard the chair rolled sideways and backwards until it and the surprised bureaucrat slammed into the wall. "Don't bother to announce me, sonny, I'll do that myself." He strode to the door that led to the governor's office and violently threw it open as the flustered clerk recovered the glasses that had fallen into his lap and struggled to get to his feet.

Governor Chamberlain, who was seated at his desk, jumped up as he saw what appeared to be a madman burst into his office, followed by a sputtering and disheveled secretary.

"What is the meaning of this intrusion?" the Governor asked, leaning sideways to open the desk drawer where he kept a loaded revolver.

For a moment, Freeman froze as he saw the handgun leveled at him. Then he burst out in peals of laughter, much to the surprise of both the governor and his assistant.

"Don't bother with the pistol, Governor," Freeman chuckled, wiping tears from his eyes with a stained and soiled kerchief he pulled from a back pocket. "I guess if I could fool you, I could fool anyone." He slumped into a leather chair that faced the desk. "I sure could use a glass of that whiskey you keep over there." He gestured at a false-fronted bookcase that held the governor's liquor supply.

"How did you know where. . ." the governor started to ask, peering intently at the intruder's face. Then he burst out laughing himself as he said, "No! It can't be! Is it really you, Roy?"

"Yep, it certainly is me," Freeman answered in delight. "I've come to make an appointment."

The sarcasm of Freeman's statement was not lost to the governor as he glanced at his secretary's stand-in. He laughed heartily, waving the assistant from the room. "Close the door, Arthur. This man I definitely want to see." As the bewildered clerk backed out, Chamberlain added, "And if he shows up again without an appointment, show him right in."

197

Still chuckling, the governor strode to the cabinet Freeman had pointed at, pressed on a book titled *Homer's Dialogues* and stepped back as the cover sprang open. "As I recall, you have a taste for Kentucky bourbon."

"Governor, I don't know if I have any taste left at all. Not after drinking that combination of kerosene, chewing tobacco and pure grain alcohol the saloons in eastern Oregon try to pass off as whiskey." He gratefully received the tumbler of amber liquid that was handed to him. He took a tentative sip, then leaned his head back against the chair. "Aah," he sighed happily. "They still do make good whiskey. I was beginning to have my doubts." Setting the drink aside, he exhaled his satisfaction noisily. "I understand you are working on a speech?"

The governor nodded at the top of his desk, which was strewn with open books and scribbled notes. "One I have to give tomorrow morning to the Oregon Daughters of the American Revolution. It's a short talk, but I'm having trouble with the research," he said glumly. "They've specifically asked me to present to them the origin and precise meaning of the name Oregon. So far I've found out it was originally spelled Ouragan." He spelled it for Freeman. "But as to the precise meaning, there are several choices—depending on which book you read. Unfortunately, the word has no recognizable root in the English language and seems to come from the Indians of the Great Lakes region. At least that's what Thwaites claims in his collection called *The Jesuit Relations*. Chamberlain picked up an open book and held it in the air. "He claims Ouragan is a bark dish in which early Great Lakes Indians ate from. McDermott," he picked up another book, "in his glossary of *Mississippi Valley French*, substantiates that. He says it's a vessel or dish of birch bark." He tapped another book. "And so does this vocabulary book by Chambers, who claims it was originally used by the Algonquins."

The governor became reflective and in a voice tinged with humor, said, "Now, how can I compare a greasy, unwashed Indian kitchen utensil with this great state of ours?"

He promptly answered his own question. "I can't. That's why I have decided to choose what Major Robert Rogers wrote in his *Concise Account of North America*. His version is that Ouragan is a legendary river of the west, a great flowing waterway that ran from the Great Lakes to the Pacific Ocean. In essence, from the heartland of this great country of ours to it farthest western limits." He grinned wickedly at Freeman. "I like that version much better." The governor's grin widened. "Being governor is a tough job, Roy, and calls for a lot of hard decisions."

Roy Freeman shook his head, then jerked it toward the door. "And that excuse of a man outside your door said what you were doing was so important you weren't to be disturbed."

Chamberlain's eyes narrowed and he suddenly became serious. "We have not seen each other for over three months, Roy, and as it is not your policy to issue progress reports, I gather some important news has brought you here on this rainy, dismal March day."

He glanced at Freeman's glass. "A refill before you start?"

"No, thank you," Freeman replied. "One is my limit." He bent forward, his face serious and intent. "For months I have been sleeping, eating and living the life of a hired professional sheepkiller. Months before our last meeting here, in fact."

Ignoring the shocked look on the governor's face he went on with his story. "To be accepted as one of them I had to prove myself, which I did. After that, I got to know all of the major players. The lawmen who side with the cattlemen and look the other way when there is a killing, the merchants who supply them with ammunition and poisons, the judges who select the juries, and most of the members of all four sheepshooter organizations." Freeman's voice tightened. "What I haven't had was someone who would be willing to testify against them. And with no witness to give sworn testimony, no right-minded judge in this state—let alone any other—would bring these men to trial. Or even bother to swear in a grand jury."

The tone of Freeman's voice, and the intensity of his narration, brought Chamberlain to the edge of his seat. He stopped breathing when the Pinkerton man said, "I have now found a man who might be willing to do so."

For a long moment they stared at each other. Both trying to read the other's thoughts.

In a hoarse voice that cracked with emotion, Chamberlain asked, "Would you care to tell me who it is?"

Freeman rose to his feet, his restlessness back. He paced the room in long strides, lost in thought. Then he stopped, took a deep breath and answered. "No disrespect intended, Governor, but I'd rather not. If word ever got out who he was, and that he has been in communication with me, neither one of our lives would be worth a plugged nickel."

Freeman swung to face Chamberlain. "I will tell you this, though. He is feeding me invaluable information. For instance, I now know why it has been so hard to get a fix on the merchants who have been supplying the sheepshooters with ammunition. The mercantile stores doing this don't list the cartons of shells they sell on their books, nor do they issue bills of sale. All transactions are done late at night, after store hours. The only mistake made so far was by the Prineville firm that stamped their name on cartridge boxes sold, by mistake, to the sheepkillers."

"Roy," the governor said flatly, "I know you can't rush what you're doing, but I'm starting to take a lot of heat." He bent over an end table that held an assortment of papers and magazines and shuffled through them until he found the copy of *The Oregonian* he had been looking for. It was folded open to an editorial headed, "The Governor's Duty," which he held up. "This ran last week," he said jabbing the page with an index finger. "Let me read you a few sentences. 'If the State of Oregon had a governor with a more sober regard for his duties than merely to look pleasant and draw down his emoluments we should have public order in central Oregon'." The governor stopped and snorted through his nose. "Emoluments!" he exclaimed. "Why don't they just come out and say all I care about are the monetary benefits that go with this office!" He slapped the paper against an open palm and uttered an oath. "And it gets worse. Listen to this. 'Whole communities are terrorized, the arm of the law paralyzed, and anarchy virtually reigns. It is obvious, too, that the criminal sheepshooters will cease only when they kill off one another or until the present Governor of Oregon can be made to realize the lives of its citizens are imperiled, their property in jeopardy and their right to the law's protection denied. The governor can be assured the electorate will not forget his lack of action at the next election'." The governor threw the paper down angrily. "There's more, but that's the gist of it."

Freeman braced himself for the words he knew were to follow. He wasn't disappointed.

"Roy, I don't know how much longer I can keep your appointment a secret. By law I have to notify the House that I have appropriated money to retain your services. If *The Oregonian*," he spat out the word, "keeps hounding me, I will have to let my constituents know that I have not been sitting idly by."

Freeman wiped his mouth nervously with the fingers of one hand. "Of course, Governor, you know that the minute you do, it will make the job I have set out to do impossible."

Chamberlain waved a hand in the air resignedly. "I know that only too well. That's why I have said, or done, nothing to reveal our connection." For a moment he became lost in thought. Then he gripped Freeman's arm. "Tell me honestly. How much more time do you need?"

The Pinkerton man shrugged. "A year, anyway. If we're going to build a solid case, maybe longer."

The governor gazed out of his window at the dark layer of clouds that hung in the sky, and watched the heavy rain that made pedestrians scurry for cover. He swiveled to the man whose life was in his hands, and said urgently, "Six months, Roy. That's all the time I can give you. If there's any chance at all that I can stall longer, I'll do my best. But don't count on it."

CHAPTER 29

On the same morning the governor and Roy Freeman were meeting, the informer, whom the Pinkerton man said might turn state's evidence, and whose name he would not disclose, was leaving the hotel where he had taken his noonday meal. He stopped to pull a toothpick from his vest pocket, then stood, surveying the dusty street and few wooden buildings that comprised the remote desert town of Silver Lake.

He was pleased with himself, for he had just concluded a successful meeting that would put a great deal of money in his pocket. From both ends.

The thought of this recent transaction brought a bemused smile to his face. He tongued the toothpick to the corner of his mouth and stepped off the wooden sidewalk to cross the empty street and enter the mercantile store he owned and ran.

As the door closed behind him, his clerk greeted him respectfully. "Have a good lunch, Mr. Conn?"

"Certainly did, Frank. That shipment come in on the noon stage?"

"It did, sir. Bill of lading is right here." Frank Payne, who worked for J. C. "Creed" Conn, held out a sheet of pink paper. "And it all checks out. Four cases of 30-30 shells and a case each of . 32, . 44 and . 45 sidearm ammunition. That should be more than enough to see us through the year. "

Creed Conn smiled. What the clerk didn't know was that another ten cases of rifle and pistol ammunition had been left by the same stage at the Hutton ranch, just three miles north of town. And there would be no bill of lading for that delivery. He took the frayed toothpick from his mouth and dropped it on the floor. "The ranchers hereabout seem to be pretty low on ammunition, this being a bad year for coyotes and cougars. Take a half-dozen boxes out of each case for the shelves, then put the rest by the back door. "

"Yes, sir," Conn's employee replied, seeing nothing unusual in this request.

After the clerk had done this, Conn said, "Go grab a bite, Frank. I'll watch the store."

Gratefully, his assistant dipped his head in acknowledgement, removed his working apron and left.

As Conn walked by the counter to his small office in the back, he picked up the delivery receipt, wadded it into a ball and dropped it into the wastebasket by his desk. He took a key from his vest pocket and unlocked the battered rolltop. As he sat down he slid the cover up and reached for an ink stained, cloth-covered accounting book. He opened it, reached for a pen, and scribbled the date on one ledger column. Following the date, he added the notation, "Four cases canned tomatoes and four cases tinned peaches received by freight". Then he relocked the desk, replaced the key in his pocket and leaned back in his spring chair, his hands behind his head. "That's the front end of it," he chuckled to himself. When his clerk got back, he would make arrangements to prepare his four freight wagons for the profit he was going to take in a few days from the other end.

Just before closing time, Creed Conn walked to the counter and chose himself a cigar. "Want a stogie, Frank?"

"No thanks, Mr. Conn. The wife says it stinks up the house."

Conn laughed uproariously. "One of the few advantages of being a bachelor, Frank. You go on home to supper. I''ll stay a few minutes to check on past due accounts. Don't bother to lock up. I'll take care of it."

With a mumbled, "Goodnight," his assistant took off his working apron, shrugged on his suit coat and left.

Creed Conn locked the door after him and waited until Payne had disappeared from sight. Then he left by the back door and locked it behind him, leaving the key under a rock by the doorstep. By morning the four cases of ammunition would be picked up by a local rancher who lived just a few miles east of town. He would tell Frank Payne that he had moved them to the storage shed behind the store, a place for which he had the only key.

Farther north, by the John Day River near Twickenham, in a soddy and log cabin, thirteen settlers had gathered to discuss a mutual problem. They were crammed together in one room that served as a kitchen and living area. It was also where two of the owners' four children had their beds. The younger two slept with their parents in an adjoining lean-to bedroom.

The meeting had been scheduled here two weeks earlier, which gave the farmer enough time to arrange for his wife and children to visit her parents at Biggs, a day's drive by wagon. Willard "Bill" Hayes, owner of the modest shelter, was moving among his guests, pouring coffee from a gallon-sized enamel pot. As was the custom when more than a few people gathered for a visit, and knowing the host would not have enough cups to go around, each of them had brought his own.

It was late evening, the only time they could meet as they all rose before dawn and ate, then slept, when the sun went down. Tonight was an exception, for they were meeting to discuss what to do about the incursion of both cattle and sheep on their property. These were hardworking, God-fearing men trying to find a peaceable solution to their common problem. They had put up signboards and posters, printed on wood and bleached flour sacks, that advised both sheep and cattle men not to run or range their stock on land they had marked, and in some cases fenced. Notices that had been ignored, torn down or shot full of holes.

There was a feeling of quiet desperation among them, a desperation that had finally driven them to act, for everything they owned and hoped to be was invested in the land they worked. Their very survival was at stake.

The meeting got off to a slow start, each man hesitating to be the first to speak. Recognizing this, Bill Hayes stood on a kitchen chair to get their attention. His voice was strained with emotion. "It's my place, so I guess it's up to me to start the ball rolling. We've all talked at one time or another, but not all together like this. Like all of you here, I felt if I worked hard and left everyone else alone, things would work out fine in the end. But," he rubbed the back of his neck with a gnarled, work-hardened hand, "they haven't."

204

Even though the fire in the open fireplace had died, it was warm and stuffy in the crowded room. Hayes pulled a worn bandanna from his back pocket and mopped his face. "I've put up notices, but this hasn't worked. And just last week, my fence was cut and the posts pulled out and burned. I know the same has happened to all of you, too." His voice cracked. "Some of us have even joined together to patrol our land, but when we're one place, the cattle and sheep men are someplace else. Besides, we're working folks, and when we ride at night, it's hard to put in a day's work the next."

"That's for sure," a voice below him declared. "I work my tuckess off all day, and am too durned pooped to stay up 'till the wee hours."

"Me, too. "Another called out. "And none of us has a spare nickel to rub together, so we can't hire it done for us."

"What's the answer, then?" a thin and work-stooped figure by the door said angrily. "We got to do somethin' soon, else we better pack up and git out, with our tail 'tween our legs."

"There's only one thing you can do, but you're strangers to it," a voice boomed out. All eyes turned to a giant man standing by the fireplace. He elbowed his way to where Hayes stood. "Mind if I take your chair, Bill?" he asked, looking up. Without a word, Hayes got down. He had invited this man here, and knew him, but the coverall-dressed figure was a stranger to the rest of them.

In an easy motion, the one who had spoken out stepped onto the crude, but sturdy, hand-made pine chair. His commanding presence held everyone's attention.

"My name is Phelps, Frank Phelps." His voice rang out loud and clear. "As you can see from the way I'm dressed, and the red at the back of my neck, I'm a sod-buster like you. I came from Missouri and have a quarter of a section of good, black soil by the marshlands below Steen's Mountain in Harney County." He glanced down at Hayes. "I'm a friend of Bill's. He asked me to join you here tonight." Phelps paused, to assess his audience. Satisfied at what he saw, he continued. "I'm not one for speechifying, so I'll make this short and to the point." He unbuttoned the pocket of his bib and pulled out two pieces of paper. "You aren't the only ones whose land is being trampled by cattle and sheep." Opening the folded papers he held

205

them above his head. "There are 87 names written on these two sheets. Homesteaders like you, from Lake, Harney and southern Crook counties. My name's there, too. Each of us has sworn to take whatever action is necessary to keep uninvited cattle and sheep off our property."

"How do you go about doing that?" a voice rang out.

Phelps eyes swung around the room until he found the man who had asked the question. His mouth set, then he answered, "We shoot them, club them, cut their throats, poison them or kill them any way we can." Phelps took in a great intake of air. "I know that shocks you, we feel the same way. But, believe me, we have tried everything you have without success, and this way works." He emphasized the last four words. "A lot of times, sheep and cattle men might suspect we have killed their stock, but it's hard to tell a man-poisoned animal from one that eats larkspur, death camas or water hemlock. Who's to suspect that sheep, the only animal that is too dumb to protect its own young, won't wander away where the coyotes and lions will get them, or even, when drinking from a stream, might just follow their leader too far out and be washed downriver to drown. Accusing is one thing, proving something else. And," Phelps continued, "more often than not, if we have to resort to killing sheep or cattle, one side is more likely to blame the other if it isn't done on our land."

"But," a settler to Phelps' right stammered, "were they to find out we was responsible we'd be burned out and our livestock would be slaughtered. There's not a one of us can stand up against any of the big outfits around here."

"My friend," Phelps said, with a grim smile, "you just said the magic word."

"Which is?" the man who had spoken up snapped back, bothered by the violence this stranger had suggested.

"Which is the word 'us'. There's not a one of you can stand alone." Phelps again held up the two sheets of paper. "But 87 people can. Believe me when I tell you it has worked for everyone whose signature appears on this list." He bit at his upper lip, then went on. "I have to admit, the first time we fought back, one of the men whose name appears on one of these sheets had his home and barn burned to the ground and his fences were knocked over. We pulled together as a group and rebuilt and resupplied his house and barn from what little we had. Then we restrung his fences. After that we set fire to four ranchers' homes and killed all their animals. At each place we left a warning that the 87 Society would burn six ranchers out for every settler who was attacked, and that we would kill 100 of their animals for each fence that was cut or each trespass made."

"You mean that actually worked?" one homesteader asked in amazement.

"It did, and it still does," Phelps responded. "Not one of our homes or barns has been touched since. Nor have there been any reprisals against us personally." He paused. "I wish I could say there have been no more cattle or sheep on our land. I can't do that, but I can tell you it happens so rarely, and there is so little damage done, we no longer consider it a problem." Having said his piece, Phelps abruptly stepped down.

There was a period of silence, then Hayes took the chair again. "Well? Any comment?" he asked.

A hand shot in the air. It belonged to a fruit farmer trying to establish a cherry orchard by the John Day River, just west of Spray. At Hayes' nod of recognition, he shouted out, "I'm for it. I say we have nothing to lose at this stage of the game, so why not give it a try."

A chorus of voices added their agreement until one cried out, "Vote. Let's put it to a vote!"

A poll was taken, and it was unanimously agreed to join the 87 ranchers Frank Phelps represented.

Willard Hayes asked for quiet, then addressed Phelps. "Frank, I have two questions. The first is, if we were to join you, and one of us was attacked, would your group back us up?"

"To a man, and as soon as we could get here," Phelps responded.

"I guess the next question would be, are your members willing to have the thirteen of us join you, and maybe make it the 100 Society?"

"I'm here, not only at your request, Bill, but also on behalf of all the people that are in the 87 Society. But," Phelps' deep voice filled the room, "I have a suggestion to make. Instead of the 100 Society, let's call it the 101 Society. One hundred of us for one cause."

A chorus of approving yells greeted this suggestion.

CHAPTER 30

It was early spring, and a thin layer of snow covered the desolate country that surrounded Christmas Lake, a giant body of water twenty miles northeast of the small cattle town of Silver Lake.

Bare sagebrush, ridges of black lava and stunted juniper dotted the mantle of white that spread to the dark, rimrocked cliffs on the horizon beyond. Although it was mid-afternoon, a low cloud cover spread a mantle of grey over the frozen, crusted snow.

From a slight rise in the land that surrounded them, five men on horseback watched a lone sheepherder and his two dogs push 3,000 sheep into a temporary corral at one end of a sheltered ravine, cut millions of years earlier by a finger of slow moving ice.

To one side of the open end of the canyon, the Basque herder had pitched his canvas shelter. Once the sheep were safely inside, he would eat the simple meal he had prepared earlier, and, with the help of his dogs, keep the sheep safely contained for the night.

The woolies bore a mark that identified them as belonging to the Benham brothers, prominent Lake County sheepmen.

One of the riders sneered as he spoke, breaking their silent watch. "That herder is plumb going to have a tizzy as soon as we show up."

"Ain't no doubt about that. Before we're done, he'll be up to his knees in sheepberries," one of his companions exaggerated, referring to the excrement that would be left by dead and dying animals.

"Healthy looking Rambouillets, too," another observed. "They're so loaded down with wool, they waddle like a bunch of ducks."

A fourth rider added, with a biting laugh, "Look at all the trouble we'll be saving the shearers come Spring." After he spoke, and from the sidelong glances the other four gave him, he suddenly realized what he had said. They would be depriving ordinary working men, like themselves, from earning a living to support their families. He mumbled apologetically, "Better their jobs than ours, I guess."

The cowhand who had spoken first said, "He's got them corralled" as he stood in his saddle and noisily passed a great expulsion of intestinal gas. With a satisfied smile he sat down. "Durn, I'm getting tired of beans. Suppose that sheep feller has something else in mind for supper?"

One of his companions answered. "We'll never know. By the time 12,000 hooves trample whatever he's cooking, it'll be under a foot of desert dust."

"Enough of this palaver," the one who had passed wind and was in charge of the group said. "Put your masks on. It's time to get to work. And remember," he cautioned, "to make this whole thing look legitimate, we have to run them to the boss's land, a half-mile away."

The sheep herder had cocked his head and was listening intently to the sounds of the bells on the bellwether sheep. This was his way of counting. Each flock was led by a ram whose bell issued a different tone. Unlike the Irish, whose bells all sounded the same, the Basques, born sheepmen, had perfected this method of keeping track of their animals.

The herder paused, cupped a hand to his ear and looked at the sky. It didn't look or feel as if a storm was brewing, but he thought he had caught the sound of thunder. He stood, still straining to hear over the bleating and blatting of nervous sheep, then a chill ran down his spine as he made out a series of high-pitched cries and the drum of horses feet. Before he could run more than a few yards, a horseman slid to a stop by his side and he looked up into the muzzle of a rifle held by a hooded figure. The rider dismounted and roughly shoved him toward his crude tarp shelter. A muffled voice came from a slit in the burlap where the mouth would be. "Take off your shoes."

When it became apparent the Basque didn't understand English, he was shoved to the ground and held pinioned by the barrel of the rifle. He moaned in fear, then closed his eyes tightly as the dark figure above him withdrew a sheath knife. He muttered a prayer, knowing he was about to die.

With no wasted motion, the rider reached down with his blade and swiftly cut the laces on the herder's ankle-length work boots, pulled them off sockless feet, and threw them backwards into the brush.

The Basque's eyes flew open as he was roughly jerked to his feet and given a push. "Git!" the cowman said, firing at his feet. This action the herder instinctively understood. He ran for his life, ignoring the sharp rocks and icy snow that were cutting into his bare feet.

After they had pushed the sheep across the boundary of their own land, the cowmen began firing into the milling herd. The sheep panicked and stampeded toward the rimrock cliffs a quarter of a mile away. They were followed by three cursing and yelling riders. The other two dismounted and methodically began killing the small groups of Rambouillets that had not bolted and remained behind.

A new moon obscured by clouds allowed four hundred sheep to escape. Most of which would eventually be stalked and killed by coyotes or mountain lions. The rest would eventually freeze to death.

Once the riders had accomplished what they had set out to do, they rode away.

The half-frozen herder limped through the night until he reached the town of Silver Lake. The sheriff was summoned from Lakeview, a hundred miles away, but, when he arrived three days later he could find no one who was willing to give him any information. After a few days of fruitless investigation, the sheriff returned to Lakeview. The day after the peace officer's departure, a letter was mailed to a box number in Prineville, describing in detail what had taken place, who the riders were and what ranch they worked for. It was from a Pinkerton agent to Roy Freeman and carried the news their Silver Lake informant was ready to talk, providing he would be granted immunity. A time and date for a meeting had been set at an abandoned homestead shack a half-mile from the stage route, three miles north of Silver Lake.

Creed Conn was up early to check on his line of freighters that stretched from one end of Silver Lake to the other. There were four in all, with a ten mule team hooked to each wagon. It was the morning after the slaughter of sheep at Christmas Lake and he would soon be on his way to collect the second half of the bargain he had made with the Silver Lake Sheepshooters.

Conn reached out to pat the neck of the lead mule of the first wagon in line, checking on her harness as he did. Before he left for the next freighter, he reached into his left coat pocket and pulled out a green apple, which the jenny greedily snatched from his open palm.

"Don't be in such an all-fired hurry, Nellie. You like to have taken a couple of fingers off." He was openly pleased at how eager the lead mule had been to be hitched up. It was as if she couldn't wait to start the day's work. And because she was bound to set a lively pace, the others would be obliged to do the same.

As he worked from wagon to wagon, Conn greeted all of the drivers and shearers who stood by each. After assuring himself that everything was in order, he returned to the front wagon, hoisted himself up and settled on the hard, plank seat. Turning to his head teamster, he waved a hand forward. "Let's go, Miles."

One of the merchants who saw the freighters lumber out of town, turned to his customer and snorted. "Didn't take him long to get his wagons together to go pick over the bones." The customer, a small rancher who ran a few head of cattle east of town, blanched and looked around nervously before he replied. "Horace, was I you, I'd be careful who I said that to."

Another snort greeted this warning. "There ain't a soul in town that don't know what's going on, so I see no reason not to say what's on my mind."

"Just so you don't say it to any strangers, or when the law's around."

The merchant tilted his head down and looked over a pair of bent and scratched wire-rimmed spectacles at the man who had given him this advice. "Tom," he said, his voice much more serious, "the day I do that is the day I'd best have my tombstone chiseled and ready."

211

After the wagons arrived at the scene of carnage, Creed Conn stood up to assess the situation. Fat, fleece-laden bodies stretched over the terrain as far as the eye could see, and each body was outlined in blood-crusted snow.

Conn jumped down and looked up at his driver. "Miles, take three wagons below the rimrock cliffs. I'll put the other to work here."

Miles Koonts shook his head and gave a low, descending whistle. "Mr. Conn, I don't know how many bodies there are below the cliff, but there appears to be at least a full day's work here."

"I know, Miles," Creed Conn replied, grinning happily. "Best we get to it."

By the end of the third day, as the heavily loaded wagons made their last trip back to Silver Lake, Conn mentally calculated what this clean, prime fleece would bring. At the current market price of 17 to 18 cents a pound, less cost of cartage and labor, his take should amount to . . . Conn stifled a gasp. Over $3,000! Not bad for a few days of labor, he thought.

While Creed Conn's shearers had been clipping the frozen bodies at Christmas Lake, over a hundred miles north, near the town of Mitchell, the carcasses of twelve range cows that had broken through a settler's wooden fence line were found by their owner. They had been poisoned. A week later, forty miles northwest of Mitchell, a hay grower had his wire fence cut to allow a band of sheep to enter his property. The same 500 sheep were found a week later, drowned in the middle fork of the John Day River.

Along Mill Creek, twenty miles east of Prineville, 165 head of sheep pushed onto land where a homesteader was raising domestic swine. They knocked over his hog pens, trampled several sacks of seed potatoes and tore down the sides of a well maintained irrigation ditch. Four members of the 101 Society joined together to run them onto public land, inside the cattlemen's death line, and dispatched them with rifle fire. The following Thursday, The *Prineville Review* reported, "The sheepkillers have struck again at the very outskirts of our peaceful community by brazenly shooting a flock of innocent and defenseless animals."

The plan presented by Frank Phelps was working. Even the 101'ers weren't sure whether their members, or sheepmen, or cattlemen were responsible for the stock killings and destruction of property that was taking place.

Emboldened by their success at Christmas Lake and other raids that had spread into adjoining Grant County near Baker City, the sheepkillers openly began trespassing on private land that belonged to woolgrowers.

In May, a band of six cattlemen, their faces blackened with charcoal and kerchiefs pulled over the lower part of their faces, rode into Fred Smith's front yard at Grindstone Creek, near Paulina. They forced Smith out of his home at gunpoint and trussed him, blindfolded, to an apple tree. Then they brutally killed 300 sheep he had wintered in shelters that had been built near his house. Finally, tiring of their efforts, and their ammunition low, they scattered the remaining 200 sheep in the nearby hills. At the same time, Smith's lambing sheds were burned to the ground.

Violence began to feed on itself. No longer was it directed at migratory sheep, or those wool growers who had violated the death lines established by the cattlemen's associations. It was now out of control as neighbor was pitted against neighbor, and, as the story of the disappearance of Shorty Davis spread, in many exaggerated versions, no one dared ride out alone. Even on their own land. It became so bad that cattlemen turned on each other for no better reason than to avenge a personal grudge or a petty disagreement. Headlines in *The Portland Oregonian* screamed, "Terror sweeps eastern Oregon like a wind-blown prairie fire!", and Governor Chamberlain's office was besieged by civic groups demanding that something be done to bring law and order to the area.

CHAPTER 31

Roy Freeman had not been to town for over two weeks and was anxious to collect his agent's reports. He told the Crooked River rancher for whom he worked that he needed to ride into Prineville to have his saddle stitched and repaired, and asked for Saturday off.

"Sure thing, Roy," his employer had replied. "But why don't you go in on Friday, spend a couple of nights flushing the rust out of your system and ride on back Sunday. With all the extra hours you've been putting in night-owling, you've earned a break." He winked at Freeman knowingly and pressed a $20 gold eagle into his palm. "Here's a little something extra for the blood-letting we did last Friday night at Little Summit Prairie." Then his tone changed. "Just be careful who you talk to and what you say," he cautioned.

When Freeman reached Comb's Flats, he stopped at the ridge that looked down on the valley in which Prineville was nestled. A hub of five roads from all directions of the compass led to and from this growing community of 1,300 people. The Pinkerton man gave an inward sigh. He had become fond of the area and its people, and although the killing he was involved in bothered him, he accepted it as part of doing his job. And, if his job was successful, everyone who lived in this valley, and all of the land east of the Cascade Mountains, would be able to live together and raise their families in peace.

As he rode up Main Street, Freeman stopped in front of Burmeisters Saloon and tied his horse to the hitching rail. He would walk to the Prineville Hotel, just up the street, pick up any mail that might be waiting for him, and return to the saloon to read it. There would be few, if any, customers in Burmeisters this time of day, and he knew the taciturn bartender would respect his privacy. He also knew that picking up his mail, then having a drink, would be the natural thing to do. So far he hadn't drawn attention to himself and he intended to keep it that way.

The hotel lobby was deserted when he entered, and the young girl whose pleasant manner he always enjoyed was at the front desk. In many ways she reminded him of his own daughter in Denver. He was looking forward to the time when this job would be finished and he could be with his family again. Freeman struggled to think of the girl's name as he walked up to her, and was relieved when it came to him as she looked up from a copy of the newspaper she had been reading. "Afternoon, Louise," he said. "Anything of note in the paper?"

Her innocent smile brightened. "Good afternoon, Mr. Freeman." Then, in answer to his question, "Actually, I was looking at the advertisement for Wurzweiler and Thompson. They're having a spring millinery sale." A flush of red appeared on both cheeks. "Just dreaming about what I would buy if I had the money. Which I don't."

Freeman glanced down at the ad, which took up most of the front page of The *Ochoco Review.* They were no longer using the slogan, 'The Cattleman's Friend' he noted, as they had expanded into women's wear and household furnishings. Even packaged homes. But they're still the cattleman's friend, Freeman thought, remembering the wagon load of ammunition that had just been delivered by them, in the dead of night, to the ranch where he worked. The cynical thought also passed through his mind that, once it became more profitable for them to cater to the settlers and townspeople, they might no longer remain the cattleman's friend. The dropping of their slogan was certainly a step in that direction.

His attention turned back to the clerk. "Dreams are what life is made of, Louise. One of these days I imagine you'll be able to buy anything you like at that store."

"Do you really think so, Mr. Freeman?" she asked earnestly.

"Yep. As sure as you're born. You just keep looking as pert and pretty as you always do, and one of these days, some rich, handsome young man will sweep you off your feet, carry you away and let you buy anything your

215

heart desires. At least that's what I'd do if I were rich, handsome, and," he chuckled, "thirty years younger."

The young girl blushed violently, then gathered her composure and laughed pleasantly. "I guess then you just came in for your mail and not to propose?"

"You guessed right, Louise," he joked back, "seeing as how I lose out on all counts."

She turned to the rack of open boxes behind her and pulled four envelopes from one of the larger ones. Placing them on the counter, she commented, "You do get a lot of mail, Mr. Freeman."

"I'm from a large family," he replied easily, "and we like to keep in touch." Jerking his head toward the lobby, he asked, "Mind if I use your writing desk a little later? I may want to answer one or two of these."

"Not at all," she replied. "There should be paper and envelopes in the middle drawer. Let me know if you need more."

He started to turn away, then came back. "Old age, I guess. I forgot to ask for a room. I'll be here at least two nights, maybe longer."

Freeman studied the envelopes as he walked back to the saloon. None had return names or addresses on the outside, but one envelope was of quality bond. He looked at its postmark. It was from Salem. The other envelopes bore the cancellations of Lamonta, Mitchell and Silver Lake, towns close to where his detectives were working.

As he pushed open the half-doors of Burmeisters, a sour smell of stale tobacco and spilled beer assailed his nostrils. He stepped inside and put his back to the wall, pausing just long enough to let his eyes adjust to the dim light. He had learned as a young detective not to walk into a dark saloon without giving his eyes a chance to adjust and see who was there. In this case, with the exception of the lone bartender who was busy washing glasses, he was alone. He walked to the counter. "A large beer, Jeb," he said to the sideburned barman. "I'll take it at the corner table." He walked across the room, sat down and placed the envelopes on a pile in front of him.

"Good news, I hope," the aproned saloonkeeper said as he gave the table a quick swipe with a soiled, damp cloth before setting down a foaming mug of beer.

Freeman grunted a reply. "More likely one of my brothers wanting a loan." He sighed heavily, as if this were often the case.

"I know what you mean," the bartender replied. "Only with me, it's my brother-in-law. Wave if you need another."

Once alone, Freeman picked up the letter from Lamonta and forced the flap open with his thumb. It told of a large movement of sheep by the Baldwin Sheep and Land Company to a spur of the Blue Mountains that would be close to the cattlemen's death line. He put it aside. The letter from Mitchell told of a planned sheepkillers raid that was to take place in less than two weeks, ten miles east of Dayville. Freeman exhaled a gust of air from his lungs through his nose when he read the letter's second paragraph. His agent reported that a group of Izee shooters would be meeting with several cattlemen from Baker City to discuss the formation of a sheep-shooters association in Grant County. That would be bad news if it came about, and would require notifying Denver that he needed another Pinkerton agent to infiltrate this new organization.

He next reached for the third letter, the one from Silver Lake, and scanned it quickly, as was his habit. Then he read it again, this time more slowly. He leaned back in his chair. His lips were closed, but they took on a satisfied look. It contained good news. News he had been waiting and hoping for.

Roy Freeman had saved the letter from Salem for last. He took a deep drink from his mug and wiped the foam from his lips with a bent index finger as he held the envelope up for examination. He knew who it was from, and momentarily considered burning it, unopened, when he burned the other letters he had received. But he knew that would do no good, just as he knew the contents would probably not be good news. With a resigned shrug, he worked a finger under the flap and ripped it open. A quick glance told him he had been right. It was not good news.

The message was handwritten on a plain sheet of paper. It read:

"Roy:

I'm afraid I have bad news. The latest sheepkillers raid at Christmas Lake has thrown the whole capitol in an uproar.

A committee from the legislature visited me this morning and flatly stated I must act immediately or they would convene a special session of Congress to take the matter out of my hands. This means I must not only call for an emergency session of both houses to get their approval of the discretionary funds I have allocated to retain your services, but I must also disclose that something is currently being done to put a stop to all this madness.

I know I promised you six months, and I realize what position this puts you and your men in, but I have no other choice.

The only thing we have in our favor is the speed at which our legislative branches operate. If it is at all possible to expeditiously complete your work, I humbly urge you to do so.

I remain, most respectfully,"

There was no signature, only the scrawled initials, "GC".

Leaving his beer unfinished, Freeman left a quarter on the table and hurried to the hotel. He went directly to the writing desk and pulled a sheet of hotel stationery from its drawer. For five minutes he scribbled furiously, pausing only to organize his thoughts, or to dip the point of the pen in the desk inkwell. When he had finished, he addressed an envelope to a post office box in Salem and inserted his two written pages. Stiffly, he rose, licked and closed the envelope, and walked to the reception desk. Reaching in his pocket he pulled out two pennies and placed them on the counter. "I'll need a stamp, Louise. And would you please see to it that this letter goes in the next mail pouch to the valley."

As he stepped outside, Freeman lit a cigar and appeared to be casually observing the bustling activity going on in the street. In reality, he was mentally reviewing the letter he had just written the governor. He had pleaded for more time. He told the governor he had just received word from his agent in Silver Lake and the informer he had mentioned at their last meeting was now willing to turn state's evidence and that a meeting had been set for them to meet, two days from the date of his letter.

Tight-lipped and concerned, Freeman studied the ash of his cigar. He hoped his message would arrive in time for the governor to stall a while longer, but the governor's letter to him had been written ten days ago and it might be too late for him and his men to continue working undercover.

Freeman had reason for concern, in fact he would have been apoplectic had he known of the article that appeared on the front page of *The Portland Oregonian* the day after the governor had written to him. It trumpeted in glaring headlines:

DETECTIVES TO SOLVE THE RANGE MYSTERIES
Governor Chamberlain Has a Plan

"The only way I can see to remedy the situation is for the Legislature to approve placing money at my disposal so that I can employ Secret Service men to go to the neighborhood of the trouble and stay there until the guilty persons can be located, and evidence enough secured to convict them. To send out militia would do no good. The men who do the shooting may be in Crook County today and in Lake or Harney or Wasco tomorrow or the next day. They would commit no offense while officers of the law were around. They travel long distances in a wild, thinly-settled country, and commit their crimes where there is no one near except a defenseless sheepherder. They are masked and cannot be identified. The only way I can see to bring them to justice is to send Secret Service men to live among them, learn their ways and follow their movement until they have evidence that will convict them."

The newspaper had added the notation: *The above is a release from Governor Chamberlain's office directly to this newspaper.*

Below this was an italicized paragraph marked, *Editorial Comment—*

Our own sources tell us the governor has, for some weeks now, obtained the sum of $10,000 through a little-known emergency powers act enabled in 1866, and the approvals needed from both houses of the legislature are a mere formality.

We have also heard the governor has already employed the Pink-erton Detective Agency, and their agents are currently in place and receiving beneficial information. One well-informed source is be-lieved to be in the Silver Lake area.

CHAPTER 32

"Pa! Pa!" the boy's voice was shrill and tinged with fear. "There are some cattle in our pasture and they're tramplin' the new alfalfa."

The farmer looked up from his anvil, where he had been working a broken tire iron. The hot scent of burning charcoal filled the air and acrid smoke hung in the lean-to shed that served as a blacksmith shop. His sleeves were rolled up and beads of sweat ran in rivulets down his face and neck to soak the denim shirt that hung on a muscular frame. He silently picked up a pair of smithy's tongs, grabbed the newly-formed steel and thrust the white hot rim into a barrel of oil-slick water. His face screwed into a squint as he stared at the excited face of his son who stood before him, nervously shifting from one foot to another.

"How many, Tad?" he asked in a quiet voice.

"Twenty or more, pa. And there are two riders with them."

Reaching for a stained rag, the farmer slowly and deliberately wiped his hands. "Fetch me the rifle while I shut down the forge. Then you go wait in the house with your ma."

"But pa ..."

"No 'buts' about it, young man. Your mother is not to be left alone."

Less than five minutes later, he was striding through a field of thriving, ankle deep green alfalfa. It's fresh scent filled the air, but went unnoticed by the settler as he fed a shell into the chamber of his Winchester carbine and lowered the hammer to its safety position. A copper taste filled his mouth when he saw the cattle, grazing contentedly in the middle of his field. Two riders sat in their saddles, watching his progress across the cultivated pasture. One sat with an arm on his saddle horn. The other casually formed a smoke, which he put in the corner of his mouth, then lit. Smoke rose from a flared match which was held to the tobacco then waved out and dropped to the ground.

Shaking with an inner fury, the farmer stopped twenty yards in front of them. With a great effort, he tried to control his voice so as not to give way to the anger that was burning inside him. He had noted the brands on the cattle. They carried the CW mark of Clem Woodard, whose ranch was just south of the town of Spray, twenty miles away. Woodard had the reputation of ignoring his neighbor's rights, and used their grass and watering holes at his pleasure. He was respected by no one, but this didn't bother him in the least for he mentally justified everything he did—right or wrong. In Clem Woodard's own mind, whatever Clem Woodard did had to be right.

"I guess you fellas know you are trespassing on my property," the settler said, his thumb feeling for the hammer of his rifle.

"Well, sodbuster," the rider to his right replied laconically. "That's a matter of opinion." He jerked his head in the direction they had ridden from. "We didn't see no fences, and you know the rules. Unless a place is fenced in, the law says cattle can graze wherever they please." He grinned at his companion, then straightened and looked down at the coverall clad farmer. He pulled a plug of tobacco from his shirt pocket, twisted off a piece with clamped teeth, chewed it into a wet ball then spat a stream of brown-stained juice near the feet of the man below him. "Woodard said to graze through this valley and that's what we're doing. If you have a complaint, I suggest you take it up with him." Picking up his reins, he was about to urge his horse forward when the farmer cocked the hammer, then fired a shot into the ground in front of the surprised rider, who struggled to gain control of his frightened horse.

"The two of you listen, and you listen real good," the settler said, his voice filled with menace. "I know all about your boss and how he operates. He may impress himself, and he may impress you, but he doesn't impress me or most of the people who know him." In spite of his efforts to control his emotions, the farmer's voice pitched higher as adrenaline surged through his body. "As for the law about fences, that's something you cattlemen dreamed up so you could find an excuse to graze wherever you want without considering the rights of others. Fence or no fence, you have invaded my property. You either move those cows off now, or I'll shoot each and every one where they stand." Trembling with rage, he added, "You tell that no-good you work for what I said, and if he has a complaint, he can talk to me."

As the farmer spoke, one of the riders kneed his horse one step to the left. Then he nudged it again. The two cowboys exchanged a look which alerted the farmer, who quickly jacked another shell into the chamber. As he did, the puncher who had moved reached for his pistol. It was half out of its holster when a .30 caliber slug caught him in the chest and threw him backwards and out of the saddle. The farmer swung his rifle to the left and fired at the other rider. His bullet entered the eye of the CW hand a split second after the cowpoke drew and fired his own .45.

The settler, stunned by the suddenness of what had happened, slumped to the ground. His reactions had been instinctive, and he had given no thought to the consequences of what might follow. He had acted without thinking, just like he had at Gettysburg when, out of ammunition on the steep slopes of Little Round Top, he led a bayonet charge against a superior force of Confederate soldiers and drove them, in full retreat, from the top of the hill he had been told to hold at all costs. Had he not done so, General George Meade's army would have been outflanked and defeated.

When he rose to examine the bodies, pain pierced his side. Looking down, he saw a growing dark stain form on his shirt. He pulled it up to examine a puffy wound that was bleeding profusely. Reaching into his back pocket he took out a folded red kerchief and held it over a bullet crease four fingers wide. Then he did an unusual thing. He threw back his head and laughed. It was a laughter of release. Finding the wound erased any feelings of guilt from his mind. Both men had tried to kill him, but his responsive action had saved his life.

As the wounded Civil War veteran walked back to the rough-hewn cabin he had built with his own hands, he ignored the cattle who grazed peacefully, unconcerned with the violence they had just witnessed. His mind was already fast at work to solve the problem of the two dead punchers.

Fifty yards away from the house, his wife came running toward him, holding up full skirts, her long, auburn hair bouncing from her back and shoulders. Beside her was their son, Tad. Dropping his rifle, but still clutching the bandage to his wound, he caught her in one arm and held her. As she hugged him tight, he gave a sharp cry. She stepped back, then seeing the pain on his face, glanced down at the bloody rag he was holding to his side. She gasped and put the back of one hand to her mouth.

"It's nothing, Elizabeth. Nothing at all. Just a scratch. A little ointment and a fresh bandage and I'll be as good as new." He turned to his son. "Tad, there'll be no more plowing today. Saddle old Dan. I would like you to take a message to Mr. Hayes."

At dusk, Willard "Bill" Hayes and five other members of the 101 Society arrived, as had been requested in the note Tad Scanlon delivered for his father, Jim. Silently, they dismounted and walked their horses to a nearby pole corral before entering the small cabin. The elder Scanlon turned to his son after greeting his guests. "Tad, stay outside and watch the horses, if you would, please. And let us know immediately if you see or hear anyone else riding in." As his boy left, Jim Scanlon turned to the others. "He doesn't know about the 101, but Liz does." He looked over at his wife, who was busy preparing coffee and the two apple pies she had baked for the meeting.

Bill Hayes and the others doffed their hats as they greeted her, then Hayes put both hands on Scanlon's shoulders. "Well, Jim, as you can see, I got your note. We all know what happened, but maybe you could fill in the details for us."

Scanlon recounted what had taken place, from the time his son had alerted him to the cattle until he had shot Woodard's men. He then added, "After I sent Tad with the note, Liz and I pushed the cattle up the ridge to that high, rocky draw south of here." He glanced at his wife proudly. "Then we stretched a rope across the open end so they couldn't get out. I checked an hour ago and they're still there." Scanlon leaned forward intensely. "With the help of the six of you, here's what I have in mind." Ten minutes later he had finished outlining his plan.

Bill Hayes glanced at the others who had accompanied him. Each nodded their approval. For the first time since they arrived, a grin spread over Hayes' face. He turned to the pudgy-faced Scanlon, whose pale complexion was highlighted by a permanent flush of red on both cheeks. "You know, Jimmie, I like it. It just might work, too." His grin widened. "I never suspected you had such a devious streak. Junior Rhodes is probably the closest thing to a friend Woodard has—at least when he wants something from him. And they're birds of a feather. It would do my heart good to see them at each other's throats." He turned around to speak to Scanlon's wife. "Liz, I think it's about time we sampled that pie and coffee you've been fussing over."

Two days after the incident on Scanlon's land, one of Woodard's line riders rode an exhausted and lathered horse up the lane that led to Clem Woodard's ranch house. He slid to a stop, jumped from the saddle and ran up the porch steps to pound noisily on the etched glass and wood front door. Woodard himself answered, a questioning look covered his face, creating lines on a high forehead that was accentuated by a prominent widow's peak that speared toward small pig-like eyes and a petulant mouth. Black eyes, the heritage of Indian blood, flashed in annoyance as they swept over the dusty, sweat-stained rider that stood before him. "This had better be good," he snarled. "You're supposed to be keeping an eye on my stock. Not only that," his voice was tinged with impatient anger, "I'm about to sit down to dinner."

"Sorry, Mr. Woodard," the rider replied, his words tumbling out as he struggled to catch his breath. "I got bad news. Real bad news."

Woodard's face darkened as the hand gasped out his story. "Charlie and Bob are dead. Both shot. I found their bodies. And that's not all. The two dozen yearlings they were tending were spread out around them."

"Spread out," Woodard sputtered, "what do you mean spread out? Were they starting to wander off?" His question showed no interest in the two men who had lost their lives working for him. He was interested only in the cattle.

"The cattle was dead, Mr. Woodard. Shot dead like Charlie and Bob."

Woodard began firing questions. "Who shot them? When did it happen? Where did you find them?" The questions came so rapidly, the uneducated ranch hand had to pause and think each one through. His silence infuriated Woodard, who grabbed him by the shirt front and pulled him to his toes. "Dammit," he cursed, "when I ask a question, I want an answer."

"I guess it must have happened a day or so ago, Mr. Woodard," the frightened puncher stuttered. "I don't know who shot them, but they was on Junior Rhodes' land, near Squaw Creek."

"Rhodes' land, you say?" Woodard hissed the name as white froth gathered at the corners of his mouth. His eyes glazed over and he roughly shoved the small man he had been holding away. "Get the crew," he ordered. "Every man you can find. We're going to pay a little visit to some of Mr. Junior Rhodes' cattle. If he thinks he can treat me the same way he does everyone else, he's dead wrong." When it occurred to him what he had just said, he repeated bitterly, "And when I say *dead* wrong, that's exactly what I mean. We'll take four of his steers for every one of ours he killed."

CHAPTER 33

Junior Rhodes and Clem Woodard were cut from the same bolt of cloth. Both had been born dirt poor and both were raised by domineering fathers who rose to positions of power by bullying anyone who got in their way. Those their fathers couldn't intimidate by threats or actual violence, whether they be cattlemen, sheep owners, settlers or merchants they bought their supplies from, they proceeded to ignore as if they didn't exist.

It was a lucky thing for Junior and Clem that they inherited their wealth, for they never would have been able to earn it on their own.

Rhodes, a small, pompous and egotistical man wore a gaudy gold and diamond ring that he flashed at every opportunity. He thought it impressed people, but it only brought snickers from those who knew he was putting on airs. Normally, he drove a buggy with two matching white horses and held his discussions with others while remaining on the buggy seat. That way, they had to look up at him. When he appeared on his own range land, his riders had learned to get down from their horses to accord him the respect he demanded. Those who didn't do this, or refused to do so, were summarily dismissed. Rhodes' face was usually lit by an insincere smile in an attempt to maintain an air of fellowship. But his cold, calculating eyes, set in a drinker's bloated face, gave away the nature of the man. A prominent gap, where a front tooth should have been, added its affect, making his smile all the more incongruous. Without the distraction of the missing tooth, he looked, as Reub Hassler once observed, "Like a puffed-up sage hen."

When alone, Rhodes usually walked in a slouch, with his hands thrust deep in his pockets, his shoulders hunched forward. But when he was with people, he made a concentrated effort to stand ram-rod straight, as General George Crook had when Rhodes first met the military man after whom

Crook County was named. Egotism oozed from Rhodes like the ever present sweat on his brow.

The residents of the area, whose families had settled in the Ochocos for two or more generations, and knew of his origins and the "poor white trash family" he came from, laughed at him behind his back. Just as they did with Clem Woodard.

Of the two, Rhodes was the more shrewd. He used Woodard by playing on his vanity and complimenting him on the success he had made out of his life—even goading him when it was in Rhodes' interest. On a few occasions, the two had formed an uneasy alliance on land that provided enough grazing for them both. It was on one of these pieces of property, near Twickenham on the John Day River, that Rhodes got word a hundred head of cattle had disappeared. He fumed and stormed, then ordered his foreman to find the missing stock. "If a sheepman is involved, track him down, kill his sheep and burn his buildings. Then hang him. I want my cattle back," he raged.

That very afternoon, the foreman returned to report the missing steers had been located, and that they were on Woodard's half of the property he shared with Rhodes. As the foreman stood, fiddling with his hat and staring at the floor, Junior Rhodes said, "Guess they must have wandered off. I gather you moved them back to our graze where they should be." His eyes flashed. "And I hope you fired whoever is responsible for letting them get away!"

The foreman reached an arm up and wiped some beads of sweat from his forehead with his shirtsleeve. His shuffling irritated Rhodes, who impatiently snapped, "Well, you did, didn't you?"

"Junior," the foreman started to speak, but was immediately cut off.

"It's Mister Rhodes to those who work for me. And don't you ever forget that!"

The foreman, who had worked for the Rhodes family for twenty years and was fifteen years older than Junior Rhodes, grimaced with the insult and replied, "I didn't bring 'em back because we got a problem, Mr. Rhodes." He sourly emphasized the word 'Mr'.

"Why do 'we' have a problem?" Rhodes shouted. "You certainly took enough men with you to do the job. And I can see no reason to leave them there to irritate Woodard by eating his grass."

"I guess it's going to be you who is irritated, Mr. Rhodes," again the foreman put stress on the word 'Mr'. "I know the cattle we found were yours because I raised most of them from yearlings. Know them as well as their mothers, I expect. The only thing is, they all have had new brands burned in with a running iron. Not a very good job, either. Our," the foreman stopped and corrected himself, "your brand has been changed from a Half-Circle to a CW."

Rhodes bottom jaw dropped in surprise and shock. He stood dumbstruck. Finally, he found his voice and hoarsely rasped, "You, you mean you found my cattle on Clem Woodard's section of land, with my brand changed to a CW?" A madness lit his eyes as he said this.

"Yessir, that's it, and because the burns were fresh I didn't bring 'em back. I thought you may have sold those cattle, and I didn't want to stir up trouble between the two of you."

Rhodes stormed around the room, kicking the furniture. "You idiot! Why do you think I sent you to look for those cattle? You must have been behind the barn door when the brains were passed out. If I had sold them, I wouldn't have had you go look for them, now would I?"

The foreman's face was beet red. Few men had the nerve to talk to him like that. He gritted his teeth, clenched his fists and kept silent. If he hadn't a sick wife and needed the job, he would have thrashed Rhodes within an inch of his life.

"Why is it I have to do everything myself," Rhodes screamed. "Saddle my horse. Get the men together and break out the rifles and extra ammunition. We'll leave in ten minutes."

"But Mr. Rhodes, we ain't et since last night. Before we go, could we grab a bite?"

"Eat?" Rhodes' voice rose to a shriek as spittle flew from his mouth. "You want to stop and eat when a hundred of my steers have been stolen, right from under your nose? You'll eat when you get the job done, and not before. Now. Get out of here and do as you're told."

Rhodes stormed into his office, brimming with fury, and grabbed an ornate cartridge belt that held two matching .44 pearl handled Colt pistols. He strapped them on, tucking in an overhanging belly, and bent to tie the laces that would hold the holsters firmly to his legs, muttering to himself as he did. "So Mr. fancy Clem Woodard thinks he can pull a fast one on me, does he? He'll find out different. There's only one top dog in this part of the country and that's Junior Rhodes."

Before he left, Rhodes yelled through the kitchen door to his house-keeper. "Martha, fix me a sack of something to eat as I'll be gone the rest of the day. And I want it right now."

Five minutes later, grub sack in hand, he burst through the front door to find a semi-circle of riders waiting around his porch veranda. The foreman was standing, holding Rhodes' horse. Junior Rhodes stepped into the stirrup, then swung onto the hand-tooled, highly polished leather saddle that carried his initials in silver. Pulling his back straight, he adjusted a new, black Stetson low over his eyes. Like a cavalry officer leading a charge, he raised an arm, thrust it forward and led his band of cowhands north toward the John Day.

Two hours later, they found the cattle grazing peacefully on pasture that had been allocated as Woodard's share. Rhodes jumped from his horse and carefully examined three of the reworked brands, running his fingers over the freshly scabbed wounds. Pointing to four men, he said, "You take these back to where they belong. The rest of us have a job to do."

They continued riding north until they found a large herd of yearlings and cows with new calves, milling in a verdant valley fed by tributary streams of the North Fork of the John Day River. Rhodes' eyes took on an evil look as he gazed down at the animals from a bluff above them. His men gathered around, glancing at one another uneasily, concerned about what orders they were going to receive.

Rhodes swiveled left, then right, appraising each one. Then he called out his foreman's name. "Jasper, circle those cattle and shoot every damn one. When you're finished, we'll head for home."

The riders, aghast at these orders, looked to their foreman, waiting for his protest. Cattle were their livelihood, and killing or maiming animals that kept them clothed and fed went against their grain. The foreman started to protest, but was cut off by Rhodes. "I don't want any arguments," he fumed. "If anyone here doesn't want to do as I say, he can leave now without his wages, and I'd better not see him again in this part of the country, or anywhere else."

One rider muttered a one-word obscenity, spun his horse and left. The others nervously glanced at each other, not knowing whether they should leave or stay. Their decision was made for them by the foreman, who, in a resigned voice said, "You heard Mr. Rhodes. Let's get the job done." He paused momentarily, then added, "Kill them mercifully. Don't leave any alive to suffer."

As the riders left to do as they were told, Rhodes dismounted, untied the sack that contained his meal and stretched out under the branches of a pine tree. There, in the shade, he ate his lunch and watched the bloody slaughter of helpless animals in the meadow below.

Unbeknownst to Rhodes, or his riders, a lone cowhand on a hill overlooking the herd to the east had been taking a nap. He was awakened by the sound of gunfire. He should have been watching the herd, but as the sheltered valley kept them confined, and as he knew they would graze on the abundant grass for hours, he had taken the opportunity to catch a few winks of sleep. Now wide awake, he knew there was nothing he could do but watch helplessly until the Half-Circle riders completed their job and rode away. Only then did he mount his pony and race to tell Clem Woodard what had happened and whose riders did the killing.

Six months after Junior Rhodes had struck his first blow against Clem Woodard, Bill Hayes made a special trip to see Jim Scanlon. Hayes found Scanlon piling rocks on a horse drawn sled in a field he was clearing. He rode to where Scanlon was working, stopped to watch as the shirtless settler heaved a heavy boulder onto the sled, then straightened up, holding both hands to his back to ease the ache. Neither said a word for several seconds.

231

They just stared at each other. Finally Hayes spoke. "It's a hard job, clearing a field. I expect you're going to plant more alfalfa."

Scanlon placed one had over his eyes to shade them against the sun and looked up. "Yep. Another ten acres when I get the rocks out."

Hayes leaned comfortably against his saddle horn. His eyes twinkled and the beginning of a grin spread over his face. "I don't suppose you're too worried about Woodard's cattle traipsing over it now." It was said as a statement, not a question.

"Nope, nor Rhodes' animals either. From what I hear, neither of them has enough stock left to worry about."

Hayes scratched his chin thoughtfully, then said, "You know, it's a downright shame the 101 Society can't take credit for what happened."

Scanlon bent to hoist another large rock onto the wooden slip. With a grunt he dumped it on top of the others before he replied. "I guess it isn't credit we're after, is it Bill? It's raising our crops and families the way we want, with our own set of values and being left alone to do it." He mopped his brow with the work shirt he had left on one runner. "It's a warm day and these rocks aren't going anywhere. How about a cool glass of buttermilk?"

Hayes' grin widened from ear to ear. "Jimmie, that's the best offer I've had all day."

CHAPTER 34

Impatiently, Roy Freeman glanced at the gold Hamilton pocket watch he pulled from a vest pocket. He had shed the dress of a working cowhand and was attired in the same dark wool suit and velvet vest that he wore when he met with the governor, Mrs. Williams and representatives of the executive and legislative branches in January.

He dug into his inside coat pocket and pulled out the letter he had received from his Silver Lake agent, rereading it to assure himself that he was in the designated place for the 9:00 a.m. meeting that had been scheduled with Creed Conn, the informant who had agreed to testify against the sheepshooters. He had, in fact, arrived an hour early, backtracking to be sure he wasn't being followed. As he snapped shut the watch cover, a tingle ran down the nerve at the back of his neck. Something definitely was wrong. The delicate hands of the timepiece had told him it was well past noon.

Had the man who was to meet with him gotten cold feet and changed his mind, or was there some confusion as to the time and place of the meeting? Perhaps it had been changed, and he had missed the letter telling him so. He would wait another hour, then ride to Silver Lake and find out.

While he waited, Freeman mentally reviewed what he knew about the man he was waiting for. Seven months ago, Lafe Conn, district attorney for Lake County, had contacted the state's attorney general to inform him of a case he had been preparing against the sheepkillers. He had told the state's legal officer that he had gotten help from an informant within the Sheepkillers Association. The attorney general notified the governor who passed this information along to the Pinkertons. Further contact with Lafe Conn by Roy Freeman, disclosed the fact that Lafe's information was coming from his brother, Creed, a merchant in Silver Lake. Freeman promised Lafe

Conn that he would never disclose this fact without permission. Not even to the governor. And he hadn't.

It was only after the burning of Creed Conn's freight wagons—the ones he used to gather wool from the Christmas Lake massacre—and the later poisoning of Creed's favorite horse, that the brothers felt the sheepkillers suspected Creed was revealing information on their activities and had done these things as a warning to keep silent. At Lafe Conn's urging, and the assurance Lafe had received from the Pinkertons that no charges would be filed against his brother, Creed contacted Freeman's agent at Silver Lake. The agent then wrote to set up the appointment Freeman had kept.

The Pinkerton detective glanced one last time at his pocket watch. It was now 1:18 p.m. With an inward sigh, Freeman realized there was no reason to wait any longer.

At 7:30 a.m. on the Friday morning he was to meet with Roy Freeman, Creed Conn finished his breakfast at the Silver Lake Hotel. He then went to the livery stable and saddled his horse. As it would take less than an hour to ride to the spot where the meeting was to be held, Conn stopped at his place of business. He asked his clerk Frank Payne, who had opened at 7:45, if he would mind tending the store by himself until early afternoon as there was some business he needed to take care of.

At 8:15, a mile west of town, Conn greeted Mrs. R.H. Mosely and her two small boys as she was driving into town for supplies. An unexpected light spring snow had just began to fall and she remembered he was wearing neither a raincoat or an oilcloth slicker, but was dressed in his usual black wool suit and white shirt with black string tie. Around his waist was a single holstered gun, which she thought odd as she had never seen him wear one before.

When Creed Conn did not appear at the store that afternoon, Frank Payne assumed the business he was attending to took longer than his employer had thought. When Conn did not appear at the store the next morning, Saturday, the busiest day of the week, the clerk hung a "Closed for ten minutes" sign on the door and crossed the street to the hotel. He and the desk clerk, who let him in Conn's room, found the bed had not been slept in. Word soon spread and a search party was organized. Roy Freeman, who had been making his own discreet inquiries around town, and had been passing himself off as a barbwire salesman, joined them.

The search, composed of five parties of ten men each, went on for four weeks. Creeks, swollen by melted snow, were followed by men afoot and on horseback. Then they were dredged from boats. After a month, rumors began to abound. One was that Conn had been murdered and his body buried; another, that his knowledge of the sheepkillings, and possible involvement in their activities, had caused him to flee. Yet another, started by a group of influential cattlemen, was that he had been depressed over recent business losses and had committed suicide.

A witness turned up who said on the day Creed Conn disappeared he heard a single pistol shot near Silver Creek Bridge, a quarter of a mile from where Conn was known to have greeted Mrs. Mosely on her way to town. The witness dismissed it at the time as being some boys out shooting sage rats.

During the four weeks the search was taking place, Roy Freeman had been in constant touch with Governor Chamberlain. Realizing there was no advantage in working undercover now that it was known the governor had called in the Pinkertons for help, Freeman abandoned his disguise and let it be known who he was. His operatives, however, remained undercover and continued to supply him with information on the activities of the sheep-killers. The only lead Freeman had on the disappearance of Conn was from his Silver Lake agent, who was working at a nearby ranch in Christmas Valley. At a secret meeting one night, in a two-hole outhouse behind one of the town's saloons, this agent whispered to him that he heard the Camp Creek/Silver Lake Sheepshooters had hired an itinerant cowhand by the name of Louis Videtta to do the killing. The agent was able to give Freeman a good description of Videtta; his most prominent features being that he was missing three fingers on his left hand and there was a scar and indentation on his left jaw where he had once been kicked by a horse he was breaking.

Two months after Creed Conn rode out of Silver Lake, Fred "Kid" Austin, a vaquero who worked for the ZX Cattle Company, galloped into town bearing the news he had found Conn's body lying in an open field less than two miles away. It was only fifty yards from the road that led to the abandoned settler's cabin where Roy Freeman had been waiting to meet him.

The group who rode back to the body with Austin found Conn lying on an outcropping of rock, face up, his arms outstretched, a revolver by his side. Two bullet holes were found in his chest and there were two empty cartridges in Conn's gun. When they moved the body, they discovered a flattened lead bullet under it.

"Kid" Austin claimed he was out hunting along Bridge Creek and stumbled across the body a short distance beyond the plank bridge that spanned the creek. The man he worked for, J.M. Welch, owner of the ZX, verified Austin's story that he had left the ranch for the specific purpose of hunting jackrabbits.

Conn's body was taken back to town for further examination. The coroner concluded the first bullet that entered Conn's chest pierced the upper part of the heart and probably killed him instantly. It was found lodged in Conn's spine. The second bullet hole, two inches above the first, passed through his body without hitting any vital organs. The coroner concluded the first shot, the one that shattered the heart, probably entered from at least two to three feet away as there were no powder flash burns on either skin or clothing. There were visible powder burns around the clothing and skin of the second shot.

A coroner's jury was called to determine the cause of death. The jury was composed of stockmen from around Silver Lake and the committee chairman was a well-known member of the Camp Creek/Silver Lake Sheepshooters Association.

The jury met, but before they could bring in their verdict, four detectives arrested Louis Videtta as he was leaving a saloon at Front and Washington Streets in Portland. Two days later, arraignment proceedings against Videtta were dropped and Videtta had to be released when the Portland Police Department received notification the coroner's jury in Silver Lake had unanimously found Creed Conn "suffered death as a result of suicide." The jury reached this verdict less than fifteen minutes after the chairman had been notified by telegram of Videtta's arrest.

Roy Freeman was in a rage. He heard the decision of the coroner's inquest just as he was sitting down to a meal of roast beef and mashed potatoes in Silver Lake's only hotel. He threw his napkin on the table in disgust and stalked out of the room. At the front desk he asked for writing paper and a stamped envelope. Then he strode to his room on the second floor, slammed the door and seated himself at a small desk that looked down on Main Street and the flat desert land beyond. Unscrewing the top of the pocket pen he had left on the desk's stained ink blotter, he began to write.

"Dear Governor Chamberlain:

By now you have received word that the death of Creed Conn has been ruled a suicide by a jury composed of cattlemen, their employees and the secretary of one of the largest cattle companies in the county.

This travesty of justice is an insult to the intelligence of every law-abiding person in the State of Oregon. I am sure you have already been visited by those people representing the cattle interests in the capital who want to assure you this was a just verdict. Let me assure you it was not. Here are the facts as I know them.

First, Creed Conn's body was found in a field that had been searched, after he was found to be missing, by at least ten riders. It is more than suspicious that one of these same riders, six weeks later, found the body while allegedly hunting rabbits.

Second, Conn had been shot twice. The first time in the heart, which left no powder burns on skin or clothing. However, there were powder burns around the second bullet hole in his chest. The

237

coroner personally told me there was absolutely no doubt in his mind that the first shot had killed him instantly.

Third, the coroner's jury ruled Conn had shot himself twice, yet those who removed his corpse testified under oath there was a flattened bullet embedded in the rock under his body.

Fourth, I examined Conn's remains myself. Decomposition had started. Enough so to have attracted buzzards, magpies, coyotes or other scavengers. Yet there was no evidence of this.

Fifth, I talked to his clerk, Frank Payne, who swore Conn was carrying a string-wrapped parcel when he left. This was not with the body. Nor was his horse, which is yet to be found.

These five points, as well as the composition of the jury, lead me to the following conclusion: Creed Conn was on his way to meet me at the appointed time, and was bringing with him tangible evidence that could be used in a court of law. He was stopped on the road, shot and killed. His body was then hidden, possibly in someone's cold cellar, while those who killed him tried to spread rumors he had either committed suicide in some remote spot or left the country. Had the furor over his disappearance subsided, his body would have been disposed of. As it didn't and as they knew our agents were searching for evidence, they moved the body, laid it on the ground, held Conn's pistol to his chest and fired into him once (which left tell-tale powder burns), then again, in the air, to show two bullets had been expended from his gun in an effort to mislead us into thinking he had shot himself twice.

Two things foiled this plan, the bullet found under his prone body and an honest coroner.

Because of the publicity the press has given to our activities (the Pinkerton Agency), I have decided, for their personal safety, to withdraw all agents who are working within the four sheepkiller organizations. There is nothing more that we can accomplish. Now

*that Creed Conn is dead, I know of no other person who is willing
to testify against the sheepkilllers.*

*We have one option left, but it must be taken immediately and
without delay. That is to hold a closed hearing and let our agents
and myself testify. We have the names of the sheepkillers, their
supporters and their suppliers. With the evidence that we have
gathered we might be able to convince the county judge to convene
a grand jury composed of honest citizens. If this jury finds just
cause, then we can proceed to a public trial.*

*It will take ten days to contact my agents and have them join me in
Prineville. From there we will proceed at once to meet you in Salem,
should you so desire. In the interim, I will be at the Poindexter
Hotel."*

Although Freeman was not in a humble mood, he still signed the letter,

*"Your humble and obedient servant,
Roy Freeman"*

True to his word, Freeman and his four agents met in Prineville ten days
later. They were lined up at the hotel's bar having a drink when a pale and
well-dressed younger man approached. He obviously felt out of place in
this noisy, rough environment. Clearing his voice to attract their attention
he asked, "Mr. Roy Freeman?" One of the agents jerked his head at their
chief, who placed both elbows on the bar, leaned back to further study the
stranger, then replied softly, "I guess that's me."

An envelope was thrust toward him. Freeman hesitated, then took it, his
eyes never leaving the face of the cleanly shaven newcomer. His nostrils
flared as he caught the slight scent of an expensive after-shave lotion.

"From the governor," the man leaned forward and whispered softly.
"He asked that you receive this personally. I am to get your response, after
which I will take the next stage back to Salem." ·

Freeman eyed the letter, then the dandy standing before him. "I gather you're on the governor's staff?" he asked.

"Yes sir, I have that honor."

"Well then, young fella, why don't you join us in a drink while I see what the governor has to say."

When the young bureaucrat blanched, Freeman glanced at his companions, then turned to the embarrassed figure standing before him, "On second thought, they're probably out of sarsaparilla. Why don't you just wait in the lobby." A relieved look came over the young man's face and he hurried away.

"Damn, how I hate mealy-mouthed politicians." Freeman bit out the words then nodded toward an unoccupied corner of the saloon. "Let's grab that empty table and see what this is all about." As they seated themselves, Freeman tore open the envelope. He snorted as he looked at his men who were leaning forward to hear what the governor had to say that was so important it needed to be hand delivered. "Official stationery, embossed and everything. He must have been feeling pretty official when he wrote this." He read the letter aloud.

"Dear Roy:

I have discussed your suggestion about holding a grand jury hearing with the State Attorney General and he is in full agreement.

There is no doubt in our minds that Creed Conn was brutally murdered, and we believe your accounting of his death gives the true facts.

We were considering holding a hearing in Lake County until we received word that Lafe Conn, who had assured us he would do all in his power to bring the sheepkillers and murderers of his brother to justice, had been defeated for office. He lost to one of the men on the coroner's jury who held that Creed Conn had committed suicide.

Consequently, we have been in contact with the district attorney of Crook County, who has offered his full support and strongly feels he will be able to convene a fair and impartial group of residents in that area."

Without comment, Freeman put the first page down, reached for the second and continued reading.

"The reason I have sent a messenger from my staff is one of confidentiality. This matter has become so sensitive I no longer can trust the mail or even certain employees in the governor's office. I need to know as soon as possible whether you have gathered your men and if you still feel we have enough of a case that we should continue. If the word I receive is "yes", it will not be necessary for us to meet. However, you will need to contact the Crook County District Attorney at your earliest convenience. Rest assured that I will do everything in my power to support you. I also give you my solemn oath that politics will no longer be a factor in my thinking—even if it means I will not be re-elected to a second term in office. The fate of law and order east of the Cascade Mountains now rests in your hands. May God be with you.

Most respectfully submitted,
George E. Chamberlain
Governor, the State of Oregon"

Freeman glanced at the sober faces that surrounded him. In a quiet voice he said, "It's not often I have to eat my words, but I take back what I said about mealy-mouthed politicians." As he burned the letter in a cut-down tomato can that served as an ashtray, he nodded to one of his men. "Harley, go tell that young fella that my message is "yes." I imagine he'll want to go to bed early if he plans on taking the four o'clock stage to Salem tomorrow morning."

CHAPTER 35

Rachel Williams and Tom Pickett were sitting together, holding hands in front of a roaring fire. They had been chatting animatedly about their future plans, which included being married in spring. They had agreed Rachel would lease her ranch and move in with Tom. She was outlining the additions and changes she planned to make in the ranch house once they had returned from a honeymoon trip to San Francisco.

When she finished, she added, "Of course I won't do anything unless it meets with your approval."

After a short pause, she gazed around at Tom's spartan, but utilitarian, furnishings. "I think we should start here first, don't you? It's where we'll be entertaining, and. . ." She was interrupted by a loud knock on the closed oak doors that gave privacy to the living room.

Tom looked at Rachel, frowned questioningly, shrugged his shoulders, then called out, "Come in".

Reub Hassler entered, dusting a light covering of snow from his clothes with his hat. He stood apologetically, a worried look on his face, not wanting to intrude but knowing they had to hear the news he brought. Reub had been posted in town to keep them informed on the grand jury's investigation, which was entering its fourth month. Hiner, who had been lying down by the fire, stretched and walked to Reub, who leaned down and rubbed the dog's ears.

Rachel and Tom both rose to their feet. "What is it, Reuben?" Rachel asked questioningly. Then as the realization hit them both that this was Wednesday, and Reub usually reported back each Saturday, they spoke in unison. "The hearing's over?"

Reub nodded vigorously. "Yep. They voted to make the sheepkillers in Crook County stand trial. I was told they cited names and everything. Today the district attorney was going to issue injunctions."

Rachel and Tom looked at each other blankly, then back at Reub. Tom held up a hand. "Whoa, Reub. What do you mean 'was' going to issue injunctions?"

"Just that." Nervously fingering his hat brim, Reub went on. "Late yesterday afternoon the county clerk put all the trial records in the hall, intending for them to go in the safe the next morning." He paused. "At least that's what she claimed. This morning they were gone."

"Gone?" Tom croaked hoarsely.

"Gone." Reub replied. "During the night someone took them. Fact is, some say, they're gone because the clerk is a relative of one of the men about to be indicted."

Tom, lips set tight, nodded in agreement.

Rachel reached for Tom's arm. "What does this mean?" she asked hollowly, still stunned by the news she had just heard.

He replied uneasily. "This means that although the individual members of the sheepkillers have been exposed. . ." He stopped before finishing, looked at Reub and asked, "I gather names of the sheepkillers in all four of their associations were mentioned?" After Reub's affirmative nod, he continued. "Without evidence they can't be brought to trial, nor can their names be published—either in any legal proceedings or mentioned in newspapers—as grand jury proceedings are sworn to secrecy and what goes on behind closed doors can not be made public. This can be done only in a trial by jury."

"Does that mean that the sheepkillers have won, then?" Rachel asked anxiously.

"No, it just means they can't be brought to trial."

"But can't the grand jury convene again?"

Before answering, Tom inhaled deeply and expelled the air in his lungs in one continuous breath. "They could, but I doubt if they will. First of all, the county doesn't have the money to hold another session, and second, the Pinkerton men gave their testimony weeks ago and by now have spread to the four winds. Third, it would be almost impossible to find another jury willing to spend three months, or maybe longer, away from their jobs and families."

Rachel looked confused. "I still don't understand."

Tom took her hand and held it. "It means we won a Pyrrhic victory. Now that the sheepkillers have been exposed, they have no other option than to disband. The victory we have won, though, was won at excessive cost as those who have killed and destroyed the property of others will go unpunished."

"But that's not fair!"

Tom patted her hand gently. "Nobody ever said that life was fair. It's just the way it is. We have to play out the hands we're dealt, win, lose or draw. This time it was draw."

EPILOGUE

On March 15, 1906, twelve months after the records of the grand jury hearings were taken from the halls of the Crook County courthouse in Prineville, Oregon, President Theodore Roosevelt, encouraged by the efforts of Governor George Chamberlain who was re-elected to a second term, signed a proclamation establishing the Blue Mountain Forest Reserve. Responsibility for its implementation was given to the United States Department of Agriculture. This announcement eliminated free grazing rights on all federal land in central and eastern Oregon.

Later, the Reserve was put under the administration of the U.S. Forest Service and allocations for grazing allotments were established and controlled by forest service officers headquartered in Prineville. The purpose of these allotments was twofold: To separate grazing lands for exclusive use of either sheep or cattle by the issuance of permits, and to save the land from being overgrazed by restricting the number of animals per acre.

Roosevelt's action ended, once and for all, the conflict between Oregon sheep and cattle interests that had raged from 1896 to 1906—a decade of violence.

What Tom Pickett thought was a draw in fact turned out to be a resounding victory, and what Rachel had worked so long and hard for finally came to pass.

Again, my thanks to Glenn and Irene Helms, the staff of the Bowman Museum and the Crook County Historical Society, the Oregon Historical Society, the rare manuscripts division of the University of Oregon Library and all those individuals who contributed to this novel with material from their own personal records. Their help in pulling together the missing pieces of this story was invaluable.

The author